ρ

WITHDRAWN

Guide to the

Battle of Shiloh

Edited by

Jay Luvaas
Stephen Bowman
Leonard Fullenkamp

University Press of Kansas

Published by the University Press of Kansas (Lawrence, Kansas 66049), which was
organized by the Kansas Board of Regents and is operated and funded by Emporia
State University, Fort Hays State University, Kansas State University, Pittsburg State
University, the University of Kansas, and Wichita State University

Library of Congress Cataloging-in-Publication Data

Guide to the Battle of Shiloh / edited by
  Jay Luvaas, Leonard Fullenkamp, Stephen Bowman.
      p.   cm. — (The U.S. Army War College guides to Civil War
  battles)
    Includes bibliographical references and index.
    ISBN 0-7006-0783-8
    1. Shiloh, Battle of, 1862. 2. Shiloh National Military Park
  (Tenn.)—Guidebooks. I. Luvaas, Jay. II. Fullenkamp, Leonard.
  III. Bowman, Stephen. IV. Army War College (U.S.) V. Series.
  E473.54.U44   1996
  973.7'31—dc20   96-24199

British Library Cataloguing in Publication Data is available.

Printed in the United States of America

10 9 8 7 6 5 4 3 2 1

The paper used in this publication meets the minimum requirements of the
American National Standard for Permanence of Paper for Printed Library
Materials Z39.48–1984.

CONTENTS

PREFACE

This book has been a number of years in the making. We were well along, with perhaps one-third of the stops completed in about 1988, when Brig. Gen. Hal Nelson was named Chief of the U.S. Army Center of Military History in Washington. His immediate successors at the Army War College did not share our interest, and it was not until Col. Len Fullenkamp became Director of Military History at the Army War College and Col. Steve Bowman arrived on the scene as Director of the U.S. Army Military History Institute at Carlisle Barracks that the project was revived. Both officers have advanced degrees in history and have taught military history at West Point.

The three of us spent several intensive days on the battlefield in the fall of 1993. An old friend, George Reeves III, Chief of Interpretation and Resource Management at Shiloh National Battlefield Park, devoted an entire day to our project, generously sharing his knowledge of the battle and experience in conducting tours over the battlefield—often with army units. He had changed his approach appreciably since Nelson and I first visited Shiloh, and the new tour makes it much easier to get a feel for how the battle developed. Unexpectedly, George died a few weeks later, and we take this opportunity to acknowledge our great debt to him for his help and cooperation.

When the text to accompany the individual stops was completed, we visited the battlefield again, this time with an unusual collection of men, some of whom have been tramping battlefields together for forty years or more. Many had been to Shiloh (one at least looked old enough to have participated), and we benefited from their reactions and criticisms—all freely given! We thank the self-styled "Army of the Cussewago" for their active involvement and their willingness to offer practical advice. The book is much the better for it.

ACKNOWLEDGMENTS

This fifth volume in the series of U.S. Army War College guides would not have been possible without the enthusiastic support of Maj. Gen. Richard Chilcoat, Commandant of the U.S. Army War College, and his predecessor, Maj. Gen. William Stofft, retired.

Our thanks also are due to the staff of the U.S. Army Military History Institute who assisted us in locating appropriate illustrations to accompany the text at various stops.

We also thank for coming to our rescue, above and beyond the call of duty, Mr. Dan Barnett, who produced the detailed maps accompanying nearly every stop.

Last and certainly not least, this book would not have been possible without the cooperation and support of Mr. Stacy Allen and his colleagues at the Shiloh military park.

Our very special thanks to Christine Hockensmith, who in a number of ways contributed substantively to the preparations of this volume. She coordinated travel arrangements, produced several drafts and the final manuscript, and cheerfully contributed helpful suggestions.

HOW TO USE THIS BOOK

A noted English historian declared some eighty years ago that "the skilled game of identifying positions on a battlefield innocent of guides, where one must make out everything for oneself—best of all if no one has ever done it properly before—is almost the greatest of outdoor intellectual pleasures."

This guide is designed to help you enjoy this experience at Shiloh. The stops are arranged to present the most important phases of the battle as it developed, recognizing that in this particular battle we cannot take a strictly chronological approach to all events as they unfolded. The selections were chosen to enable you to appreciate what it must have been like to the officers and men of both armies as they grappled in thick woods, steep ravines, and exposed fields.

This is not intended to serve as a *history* of the battle—for that you should consult the more standard works on the Civil War or narrative histories of this campaign. Those who visit battlefields with us report that the most productive study begins *after* they have stopped at key points, viewed the terrain, and shared the recollections of participants—the approach you will experience by using this guide.

MAPS AND ILLUSTRATIONS

Maps

Illustrations

INTRODUCTION

Shiloh is one the most difficult battles of the Civil War to comprehend. In some respects it was like an Antietam fought in the woods, a bitter struggle between brigades and regiments, often without guidance or control by higher authority, in which the defending army barely managed to hold on until reinforcements arrived from across the river. Albert Sydney *Johnston* at Shiloh and George B. McClellan at Antietam had about the same impact on the outcome of the battle; one had a plan that was too intricate for raw troops to execute, while the other failed altogether to explain to subordinate commanders whether the opening movement constituted "the main attack upon the enemy's left" or was simply "a diversion in favor of the main attack" elsewhere. The Hornets' Nest at Shiloh held up the advance of the opposing army nearly as well as the Sunken Road at Antietam, and the number of casualties in these battles was comparable.

In one respect, however, there was a significant difference. The partnership between Lee and Jackson had already been cemented in the battles that preceded Antietam, whereas the union of Grant and Sherman was forged at Shiloh.

Grant had been restored to command only recently, and he differed from his superior, Maj. Gen. H. W. Halleck, in command style, ability, and personality. He assumed command of the army encamped at Shiloh and considered—but dismissed—the notion of fortifying the camp. In his *Memoirs* he fully accepts the disposition of forces and makes no excuses for their posture at the time of the Confederate attack.

Generalship is decisive in this battle. The sound leadership of Grant and Sherman was the major factor in the success of the Union forces. On the other side, three of the six most senior generals in the Confederate army participated in the battle. Their lack of combat experience in fighting large formations is apparent, especially in the basic Confederate plan of attack. Albert S. *Johnston's* battle plan reflects the inexperience of both the troops and the senior commanders, for it seems to have been formulated without regard to terrain. The main attack, which he intended to sweep

1

around the Union left and cut off Grant's army from the river and its line of communications, foundered in the Dill Branch ravine.

Nor does *Johnston's* attack formation—corps on line in column—seem appropriate for his plan. (In point of fact, the "corps" was not a recognized or authorized formation in the Confederate army until after Antietam.) *Hardee's* "corps," which was about the size of a division, struggled to maneuver to the right as intended while at the same time engaging the enemy to its front. Not surprisingly, follow-on units became decisively engaged, lost freedom to maneuver, and eventually became intermingled with units in the first line, which blurred and confused command and control. Brigades from *Polk* and *Breckenridge's* commands pushed forward to add to the confusion, and when General *Johnston* was mortally wounded near the Peach Orchard, all efforts to carry out his orders died with him.

Consider how much more effective the Confederate assault might have been had *Hardee* been given the mission of fixing the Union right, and *Bragg*, with brigades on line and corps in column, been assigned the task of making the main attack and maneuvering against the Union left.

We are impressed by the generalship on the Union side. Grant may be faulted for failing to entrench his army in defensive positions, but he was thinking offensively and planning to move forward upon the arrival of Buell's forces. The time would be better invested, he believed, in drilling his green troops than putting them to building breastworks. Besides, as Sherman points out, all were convinced that as soon as Buell's Army of the Ohio arrived, Grant's forces would march to Corinth to attack the Confederates.

Grant visited all of his engaged divisions during the heavy fighting on the first day, assessing the flow of the battle, giving orders, and exercising command by his presence. Obviously he had a "feel" for battle, remaining calm and unshaken even when things appeared at their worst. As the fight developed, Grant moved about the battlefield, visiting subordinate commanders and giving directions that shaped the battle. His order to Prentiss to hold the center at all hazards is testimony that Grant had assessed the situation and identified the critical point on the battlefield.

Despite appearances that seem to portray an army routed, Grant's forces were never unhinged by the Confederate attack, which reached its "culminating point" near the end of the first day. The Grant we see fighting Lee in the Wilderness in 1864 is the same man who commands at Shiloh, when he ordered Sherman at the end of the first day to assume the offensive the next morning. Earlier at Fort Donelson, when the battle had reached a crisis and both sides seemed defeated, Grant had learned that "whoever assumed the offensive was sure to win."

Carl von Clausewitz, the Prussian authority on war, had tried forty years earlier to identify and explain military genius, which he defined as "those gifts of mind and temperament that in combination bear on military activity." First comes courage, a compound of bravery in battle but also the courage to accept responsibility. Next is a "skilled intelligence" enabling a commander to feel his way through uncertainty. The commander also must be able to recognize a truth that evades the ordinary mind or is perceived only after long study and reflection, and he also must possess the qualities of determination and presence of mind. In an environment comprising danger, exertion, uncertainty, and chance, such a man, Clausewitz contended, deserved to be considered a "military genius."*

Clausewitz could not have known it, but he was describing Grant, who was aware that General Buell had reached the banks of the Tennessee opposite Pittsburg Landing, and that his forces would be available when he renewed the attack the following day. Ironically, it was Maj. Gen. Lew Wallace, who played a controversial role at Shiloh, who gives one of the best glimpses of Grant under pressure. Writing after the war of the capture of Fort Donelson, which had occurred less than two months prior to Shiloh, Wallace reflected:

> In every great man's career there is a crisis exactly similar to that which now overtook General Grant, and it cannot be better described than as a crucial test of his nature. A mediocre person would have accepted the news [that one of his divisions had gone astray] as an argument for persistence in his resolution to enter upon a siege. Had General Grant done so, it is very probable his history would have been concluded then and there. His admirers and detractors are alike invited to study him at this precise juncture. It can not be doubted that he saw with painful distinctness the effect of the disaster to his right wing. His face flushed slightly. With a sudden grip he crushed the papers in his hand. But in an instant these signs of disappoint-

---

*Carl von Clausewitz, *On War*, edited and translated by Michael Howard and Peter Paret (Princeton, N.J.: Princeton University Press, 1976), pp. 100–103.

ment or hesitation—as the reader pleases—cleared away. In his ordinary quiet voice he said . . . "Gentlemen, the position on the right must be retaken." With that he turned and galloped off.*

We have not refought the second day's battle in much detail. Union forces, now heavily reinforced, pressed forward all along the line to regain nearly all of the positions lost the day before, and we have included just enough to convey something of the scene to the reader.

Shiloh may appear to be a simple, static battle, with Confederate forces attacking head-on into Union lines that are slowly but inexorably pushed back to Pittsburg Landing. Actually it is a very complex battle, especially when one traces the movements of individual units throughout the day. For example, Munch's Union battery in support of Prentiss's division engaged Confederate forces in the early morning near Spain Field (Stop 11), two miles from Pittsburg Landing. Withdrawing under pressure and fighting as it fell back, the battery made a stand at the Hornets' Nest (near Stop 18) before retiring all the way back to the high ground at the landing overlooking Dill Branch (near Stop 21). Here the battery contributed to the determined defense that stopped the final Confederate drive.

Or take Gage's Confederate battery, supporting Chalmers's brigade throughout the day. This battery moved east, along the Corinth road at first light, traversed the width of the battlefield, and fired in support of the attack on Spain Field (near Stop 11). It then continued east to support the attack on Stuart's Brigade (near Stop 12), cut its way north to support the attack on Lauman's Brigade (near Stop 15), and then on to the Hamburg-Savannah Road (vicinity of Stop 16), where it joined the artillery that compelled Prentiss to surrender in the Hornets' Nest. Wheeling about, it moved to the north and east, ending the day firing in support of Chalmers's brigade as it charged down into Dill Branch, "cutting their way through thickly wooded country over ravines and hills almost impassable to ordinary wagons."**

---

*Major General Lew Wallace, "The Capture of Fort Donelson," in *Battles and Leaders of the Civil War,* 4 vols. (New York: The Century Company, 1884–88), vol. I, p. 422.

**Official Records of the War of the Rebellion* (Washington, D.C.: Government Printing Office, 1884), series I, vol. X, pt. 1, p. 550. Herefter cited as *O.R.*

Perhaps the most remarkable feat of the attacking Confederates is Trabue's Brigade of *Breckenridge's* Corps. Positioned at the head of the Reserve Corps as it progressed up the road from Corinth, this brigade pressed on behind the fighting in Fraley Field (near Stop 2) before supporting the attack against Sherman's units engaged west of Shiloh Church (Stops 5 and 6). The brigade then continued to fight its way to the north and east, pushing Sherman and then McClernand steadily back upon Pittsburg Landing, in the process passing McDowell and Cresent Fields. By midafternoon Trabue is found wheeling to the east and passing south of Cavalry Field to attack toward the Hornets' Nest. Finally, facing south, this brigade closes the ring around the Union strong point as Prentiss is forced to surrender. Then, with hardly a pause, the brigade moves off to the east until, at day's end, it takes up a position on the extreme right of the Confederate line, having traversed a distance of more than four miles, fighting and moving throughout the day. Although Trabue describes his movements in his after-action report, he is so casual that without a map to trace his progress the scope and difficulty of his accomplishments cannot be appreciated.

Organization was something of a problem for the Confederates. Whereas the Union forces were organized by divisions, brigades, and regiments, with cavalry and artillery not attached to specific brigades, two of the four Confederate corps contained brigades but no divisions! While this may have accommodated the senior officers, it is bound to have affected command and control during the battle. Each Confederate brigade had an artillery battery attached and there was no artillery reserve, so massing the guns would have been a problem in command and control even if the terrain had been more open. This makes it all the more remarkable that Brig. Gen. Daniel *Ruggles*, confronting the Hornets' Nest, somehow managed to mass four times the number of batteries assigned to his own division.

The main problem the visitor to the battlefield encounters today is the restricted field of observation compared with that in 1862. Trees then were not so tall, because mature timber was logged to help stoke fires on the riverboats, and the fields were larger, of different shapes, and more numerous. At the time of the battle, for example, it was possible to look from Shiloh Church all the way into Rhea Field, and pictures indicate that there were no trees on the southern heights along Dill Branch near Pittsburg

Landing. Obviously there was greater scope for field artillery over much of the battlefield than one might assume driving around today.

Indeed, even in those areas that remain fields, the view can be deceptive. Initially we had planned to have Stop 15 in the parking lot by the Peach Orchard, which seemed like the logical place to read Hurlbut's narrative of events there. It is a detailed account, and the maps indicated that this precise location would be the most suitable for our purposes. When we tested it in the field, however, nothing that we could see matched Hurlbut's description of the terrain. We tried it again at Mann's Battery, a short distance into the open area, and everything in the *Report* fell neatly into place. We have not had this experience on any other Civil War battlefield.

There were no good maps of the terrain at the time of the battle. Dill Branch is not even indicated on the map used by Gen. A. S. *Johnston*, which means that the Confederate soldiers of *Chalmers* and Jackson would have had no reason to anticipate the "precipitous sides of the ravine" that kept them from reaching Grant's final line.

There has long been a problem reconciling roads and fields as they existed at the time of the battle with more recent maps. Indeed, one of the early maps had prompted Sherman to recall

> fifteen years after the event that many of the roads indicated did not exist at the time . . . of the battle. Then there was but one single road—"the Corinth road,"—which reached the river, affording room for only four or five boats to unload, but as other boats accumulated, other roads were improvised up the hill from the water's edge to the . . . plateau above, and new roads were made by the wagoners hauling out from the boats to the several camps. All these roads as marked on the map were mud roads; not roads at all in a military sense, but simply open ways by which six mules could haul about a ton of freight from the river to the camps. The . . . plateau, excepting the cleared fields, was wooded with oak, maple, and hickory, the latter in some places so thick that there was real difficulty in forcing one's way through on horseback.*

---

*Edwin C. Bearss, *Historical Base Map, Shiloh National Military Park and Cemetery* (Denver: Denver Service Center, National Park Service, U.S. Department of the Interior, 1973), p. 25.

The maps accompanying the text to depict tactical events were drawn largely from the work of Atwell Thompson and D. W. Reed, published in 1900. Thompson, while employed as the Shiloh battlefield park engineer, had prepared a topographical map of the battlefield, and for years this map was accepted as accurate. In 1973, however, the battlefield superintendent asked Edwin C. Bearss of the Park Service to update the historic base map, and in the process of doing so he discovered numerous inaccuracies. Combining historical research with an updated survey of the battlefield, Bearss discovered instances where Thompson had erred in locating streams, roads, and trails, and had failed to depict features such as orchards and cabins. To compound the confusion, Thompson had included trails and roads that had been constructed *after* the battle. We gratefully acknowledge our debt to the meticulous work accomplished by Mr. Bearss.

Since 1973 the Shiloh battlefield park administrators have been trying to restore historic fields to their correct configuration and acreage. At the time of the battle there were few roads in the area, and with the exception of cleared fields, thick woods and dense brush blanketed the plateau above the Tennessee River. To make it easier for the reader to recognize terrain and locate units on the battlefield, we have used a modern military topographical map as the base map for most of the maps used in the text.

The visitor, armed with map and compass, may still get turned around and confused by the directions of attack and lines of defense during the battle. The fields are much smaller now, which severely limits vision, and the roads, even when built to take the visitor around the battlefield, rarely follow the lines of advance or connect the positions of large formations at a given stage in the battle. One can drive along the Confederate lines at Gettysburg, Fredericksburg, and Antietam, or follow the flanking movement and attack by Stonewall Jackson at Chancellorsville, but something comparable is rarely the case at Shiloh.

The map for each stop in the *Guide* is designed to offset this— in the mind if not on the ground—and the overview that introduces readings from the official reports should enable the user to place events at a given position in the proper context. Take heart! Even if momentarily confused, you will have a much clearer vision than did most of the participants during the battle.

Signs abound everywhere on the battlefield. Rectangular tab-

lets mark positions where troops were engaged on April 6; oval
tablets indicate locations for April 7. Large square tablets contain
historical information such as the strength of armies and movements of corps and divisions. Pentagonal tablets mark the front
and center of unit camps. Bear in mind that the person reading a
sign is facing the same way as the troops mentioned on the tablet.

The different colors of the tablet pedestals designate which
army was involved: blue marks units of the Union Army of the
Tennessee, yellow designates General Buell's Army of the Ohio,
and red identifies the Confederate Army of the Mississippi. Union
armies were named after river systems, suggesting the operational
and logistical importance of rivers to an invading force. The Army
of the Mississippi was probably so named because its operational
area was generally in the Mississippi region.

Originally we had hoped to include two pieces to be written by
George Reeves as appendices. Because the Shiloh National Military
Park possesses an unusually fine collection of Civil War ordnance,
we had asked him to describe the features and capability of the
various pieces. He also had agreed to contribute an essay on the
typical Confederate soldier early in 1862 based upon his earlier
writings.

We now offer two alternatives that should interest and be of
some value to the reader. The first is a previously unpublished
lecture delivered at the U.S. Army War College by Maj. Eben Swift,
U.S. Army, in the early years of this century. Swift had a profound
influence upon the evolution of the army school system at Leavenworth and later at the Army War College, where he served as director. He contributed significantly to the evolution of the "Historical
Ride" at Leavenworth, and he subsequently introduced what is now
called the staff ride at the Army War College. His lecture is a first-
rate analysis by one of the more influential minds in the army of
that day, and it should help the modern visitor to place many
phases of the battle in clear perspective. Occasional inaccuracies in
times, troop strengths, distances, and so forth, in no way diminish
the overall value of the lecture as an illustration of how the army
was using critical analysis of Civil War battles and campaigns as a
tool for teaching the profession of arms.

Appendix II offers the reader the opportunity to make his or
her own judgment about the controversial role of Maj. Gen. Lew
Wallace's division on the first day of the battle. Grant subsequently
modified "very materially" what he had written about the incident

n view of a letter he had received from the widow of another general.* If nothing else, the episode demonstrates to the modern soldier what Clausewitz meant by the term "friction."

> Everything in war is very simple, but the simplest thing is difficult. The difficulties accumulate and end by producing a kind of friction that is inconceivable unless one has experienced war. . . . Friction is the only concept that more or less compares to the factors that distinguish real war from war on paper. . . . The good general must know friction in order to overcome it whenever possible, and in order not to expect a standard of achievement in his operations which this very friction makes impossible. . . . Friction . . . is the force that makes the easy so difficult.**

Visitors who wish to understand any decison made in battle would do well to keep this in mind.

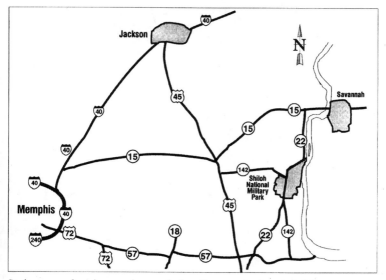

Strip map showing main roads leading to the battlefield.

---

*U.S. Grant, *Personal Memoirs of U. S. Grant,* 2 vols. (New York: Charles Webster nd Co., 1885), vol. I, 351 n.

**Clausewitz, *On War,* pp. 119–21.

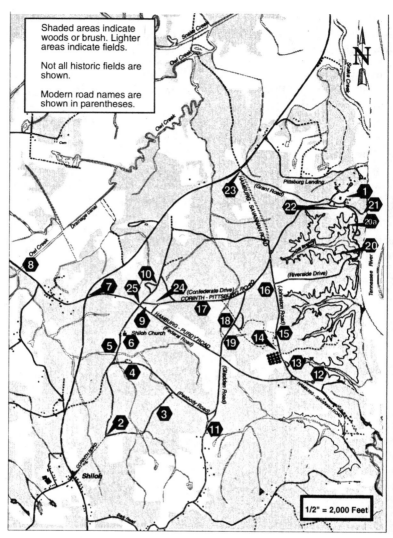

Base map showing the location of all stops.

GUIDE TO THE BATTLE OF SHILOH

The main entrance to the Shiloh National Military Park is off Tennessee State Route 22.

The tour begins at the National Park Service Visitor Center. Here you can gain your initial orientation to the battlefield. The Visitor Center is located just above Pittsburg Landing, used by the river steamers that supported the Union forces.

Stop in the vicinity of the Visitor Center parking lot. Park and walk past the cemetery down to the landing used by the Union army. The readings here will give you an overview into Union operations and General Grant's perspective of events leading up to the Battle of Shiloh.

STOP 1, THE STRATEGIC SITUATION

Narrative of Maj. Gen. U. S. Grant, USA, Commanding Army of the Tennessee

When I reassumed command on the 17th of March I found the army divided, about half being on the east bank of the Tennessee at Savannah, while one division was at Crump's Landing on the west bank about four miles higher up, and the remainder at Pittsburg landing, five miles above Crump's. The enemy was in force at Corinth, the junction of the two most important railroads in the Mississippi valley—one connecting Memphis and the Mississippi River with the East, and the other leading south to all the cotton states. Still another railroad connects Corinth with Jackson, in west Tennessee. If we obtained possession of Corinth the enemy would have no railroad for the transportation of armies or supplies until that running east from Vicksburg was reached. It was the great strategic position at the West between the Tennessee and the Mississippi rivers and between Nashville and Vicksburg.

Maj. Gen. Ulysses S. Grant, Commander, Army of the Tennessee, in an 1861 photo. (U.S. Army Military History Institute)

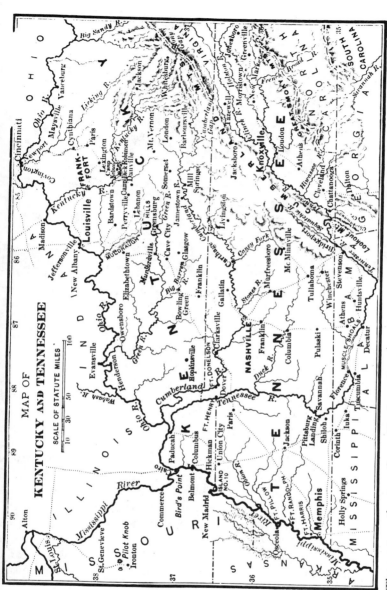

The western theater of war. (*Battles and Leaders of the Civil War*)

Lithograph depicting Pittsburg Landing. Note the lack of trees—to be expected during a period in which steam-powered boats used wood to fuel their boilers. (*Harper's Weekly*, May 3, 1862)

I at once put all the troops at Savannah in motion for Pittsburg landing, knowing that the enemy was fortifying at Corinth and collecting an army there under [Gen. A. Sidney] *Johnston.** It was my expectation to march against that army as soon as [Maj. Gen. D. C.] Buell, who had been ordered to reinforce me with the Army of the Ohio, should arrive; and the west bank of the river was the place to start from. Pittsburg is only about twenty miles from Corinth, and Hamburg landing, four miles further up the river, is a mile or two nearer. I had not been in command long before I selected Hamburg as the place to put the Army of the Ohio when it arrived. The roads from Pittsburg and Hamburg to Corinth converge some eight miles out. This disposition of the troops would have given additional roads to march over when the advance commenced, within supporting distance of each other.

Before I arrived at Savannah, [Maj. Gen. W. T.] Sherman,

---

*Editors' note: The convention used in this book is that all Confederate names are italicized. Union names are in standard type.

who had joined the Army of the Tennessee and been placed in command of a division, had made an expedition on steamers convoyed by gunboats to the neighborhood of Eastport, thirty miles south, for the purpose of destroying the railroad east of Corinth. The rains had been so heavy for some time before that the low-lands had become impassable swamps. Sherman debarked his troops and started out to accomplish the object of the expedition; but the river was rising so rapidly that the back-water up the small tributaries threatened to cut off the possibility of getting back to the boats, and the expedition had to return without reaching the railroad. The guns had to be hauled by hand through the water to get back to the boats.

On the 17th of March the army on the Tennessee River consisted of five divisions, commanded respectively by Generals C. F. Smith, [John A.] McClernand, L. Wallace, [Stephen A.] Hurlbut, and Sherman. General W. H. L. Wallace was temporarily in command of Smith's division, General Smith . . . being confined to his bed. Reinforcements were arriving daily and as they came up they were organized, first into brigades, then into a division, and the command given to General [B. M.] Prentiss, who had been ordered to report to me. General Buell was on his way from Nashville with 40,000 veterans. On the 19th of March he was at Columbia, Tennessee, eighty-five miles from Pittsburg.

When all reinforcements should have arrived I expected to take the initiative by marching on Corinth, and had no expectation of needing fortifications, though this subject was taken into consideration. [Col. J. B.] McPherson, my only military engineer, was directed to lay out a line to intrench. He did so, but reported that it would have to be made in rear of the line of encampment as it then ran. The new line, while it would be nearer the river, was yet too far away from the Tennessee, or even from the creeks, to be easily supplied with water, and in case of attack these creeks would be in the hands of the enemy.

The fact is, I regarded the campaign we were engaged in as an offensive one and had no idea that the enemy would leave strong intrenchments [at Corinth] to take the initiative when he knew he would be attacked where he was if he remained. This view, however, did not prevent every precaution being taken and every effort made to keep advised of all movements of the enemy.

A "Hardened Killer" in the inexperienced Union army. The "man" is holding a Belgian musket and has a Colt revolver. *(The Truth about Shiloh)*

Johnston's cavalry meanwhile had been well out toward our front, and occasional encounters occurred between it and our outposts. On the 1st of April this cavalry became bold and approached our lines, showing that an advance of some kind was contemplated. On the 2d *Johnston* left Corinth in force to attack my army. On the 4th his cavalry dashed down and captured a small picket guard . . . stationed some five miles out from Pittsburg on the Corinth road. Colonel [Ralph P.] Buckland sent relief to the guard at once and soon followed in person with an entire regiment, and General Sherman followed Buckland taking the remainder of a brigade. The pursuit was kept up for some three miles . . . and after nightfall Sherman returned to camp and reported to me by letter what had occurred.

At this time a large body of the enemy was hovering to the west of us, along the line of the Mobile and Ohio railroad. My apprehension was much greater for the safety of Crump's landing than it was for Pittsburg. I had no apprehension that the enemy could really capture either place. But I feared it was possible that he might make a rapid dash upon Crump's and destroy our transports and stores, most of which were kept at that point, and then retreat before Wallace could be reinforced. Wallace's position I regarded as so well chosen that he was not removed.

At this time I generally spent the day at Pittsburg and returned to Savannah in the evening. I was intending to remove my headquarters to Pittsburg, but Buell was expected daily and would come in at Savannah. I remained at this point, therefore, a few days longer than I otherwise should have done. . . .

On Friday the 4th . . . I was very much injured by my horse falling with me, and on me, while I was trying to get to the front where firing had been heard. . . . For two or three days after I was unable to walk except with crutches.

On the 5th General [William] Nelson, with a division of Buell's army, arrived at Savannah, and I ordered him to move up the east bank of the river, to be in a position where he could be ferried over to Crump's landing or Pittsburg as occasion required. I had learned that General Buell himself would be at Savannah the next day, and desired to meet me on his arrival. Affairs at Pittsburg landing had been such for several days that I did not want to be away during the day. I determined, therefore, to take a very early breakfast and ride out to meet Buell. . . . While I was at breakfast, however, heavy firing was heard in the direction of Pittsburg landing, and I hastened there, sending a hurried note to Buell informing him of the reason why I could not meet him at Savannah. On the way up the river I directed the dispatch boat to run in close to Crump's landing, so that I could communicate with General Lew Wal-

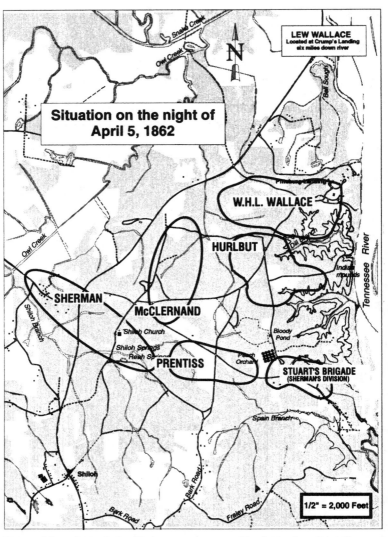

General location of the Union camps near Pittsburg Landing (Stop 1).

lace. I found him waiting on a boat apparently expecting to see me, and I directed him to get his troops in line ready to execute any orders he might receive. He replied that his troops were already under arms and prepared to move.

Up to that time I had felt by no means certain that Crump's landing might not be the point of attack. On reaching the front, however, about eight A.M., I found that the attack on Pittsburg was unmistakable, and that nothing more than a small guard, to protect our transports and stores, was needed at Crump's. Captain Baxter, a quartermaster on my staff, was accordingly directed to go back and order General Wallace to march immediately to Pittsburg by the road nearest the river. . . .

Some two or three miles from Pittsburg landing was a log meeting-house called Shiloh. It stood on the ridge which divides the waters of Snake and Lick creeks, the former emptying into the Tennessee just north of Pittsburg landing, and the latter south. This point was the key to our position and was held by Sherman. His division was at that time wholly raw, no part of it ever having been in an engagement, but I thought the deficiency was more than made up by the superiority of the commander.

McClernand was on Sherman's left, with troops that had been engaged at Forts Henry and Donelson and were therefore veterans so far as western troops had become such at that stage of the war. Next to McClernand came Prentiss with a raw division, and on the extreme left, Stuart with one brigade of Sherman's division. Hurlbut was in rear of Prentiss, massed, and in reserve at the time of the onset. The division of General C. F. Smith was on the right, also in reserve. . . .

The position of our troops made a continuous line from Lick Creek on the left to Owl Creek, a branch of Snake Creek, on the right, facing nearly south and possibly a little west. The water in all these streams was very high at the time and contributed to protect our flanks. The enemy was compelled, therefore, to attack directly in front. This he did with great vigor, inflicting heavy losses on the National side, but suffering much heavier on his own. [U. S. Grant, *Personal Memoirs of U. S. Grant,* 2 vols. (New York: Charles Webster and Company, 1885), vol. I, pp. 330–39 and passim.]

As you leave the Visitor Center parking lot, check your mileag at the stop sign next to an artillery battery and an Illinoi monument.

Drive down Confederate Drive 3.4 miles to Fraley Field. Con federate Road is one of the main roads through the park. Tak care not to bear off on the intervening crossroads. After the roa turns sharply to the left, park in front of the stone marker. Wall to the west (toward the rear of your car) down a small trail (ap proximately 100 yards).

STOP 2A, THE CONFEDERATE PLAN

Here you will be able to see an open field with two markers This is Fraley Field. The blue marker shows the initial Union posi tion held by a small unit of skirmishers. The red marker acros the field marks the location from which the Confederates initiall attacked.

Fraley Field was the first point of Confederate contact with th Union forces. The Union Army of the Tennessee was encampe south and west of Pittsburg Landing awaiting the arrival of Genera Buell's Army of the Ohio. These combined forces would then at tack south to seize the key railroad junction at Corinth, Mississippi about 22 miles distant.

Gen. Albert Sidney *Johnston*, the commander of the Confeder ate Army of the Mississippi, determined to attack before the Unior armies could link up. He counted on surprising them in thei camps, scattered between the Tennessee River and Owl Creek. H issued a detailed and complex order to his inexperienced subordi nate commanders.

The Confederate army had no common command and contro organization coming into this battle. Two corps *(Polk* and *Bragg* were organized with divisions and subordinate brigades. The othe two *(Hardee* and *Breckinridge)* had no divisions, with brigade com manders operating directly under the corps commanders. Thi confused command and control system would have a great impac on the inexperienced Confederates during the upcoming battle.

Union pickets, pushing forward of the camps, reported enem activity on April 4 and 5. Knowing that their troops were, for th most part, extremely inexperienced, the Union senior com

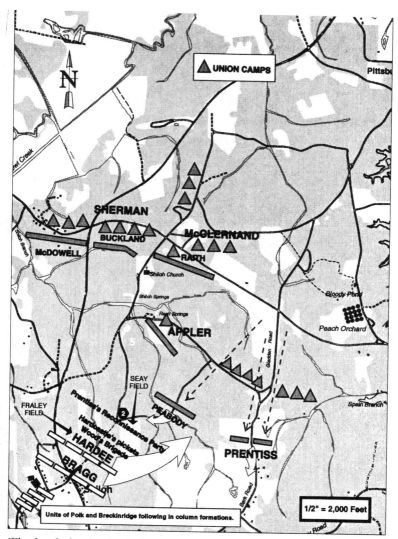

The battle begins in Fraley Field (Stop 2A).

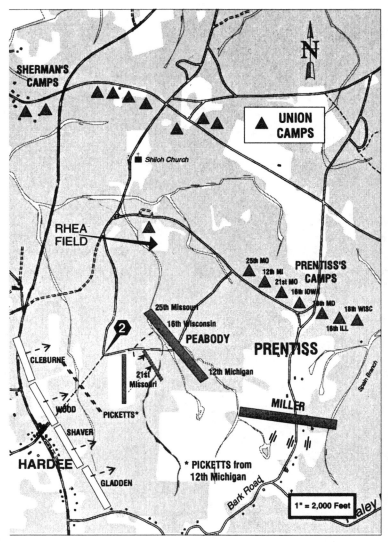

The battle shifts to Seay Field. (Stop 2B)

manders attributed the reports to exaggeration and overactive imagination.

This set the stage for the lead elements of *Hardee's* Confederate Corps (in actuality a collection of brigades) to clash with the forward positions of Prentiss's Union division at Fraley Field.

Report of Gen. G. T. Beauregard, CSA, Commanding Army of the Mississippi

On . . . [March] 2, having ascertained conclusively from the movements of the enemy on the Tennessee River and from reliable sources of information, that his aim would be to cut off my communications in West Tennessee with the Eastern and Southern States, by operating from the Tennessee River, between Crump's Landing and Eastport as a base, I determined to foil his designs by concentrating all my available forces at and around Corinth.

Meanwhile, having called on the Governors of the States of Tennessee, Mississippi, Alabama, and Louisiana to furnish additional troops, some of them . . . soon reached this vicinity, and with two divisions of General *Polk's* command from Columbus, and a fine corps of troops from Mobile and Pensacola, under Major-General [Braxton] *Bragg*, constituted the Army of the Mississippi. At the same time General *Johnston*, being at Murfreesboro, on the march to form a junction of his forces with mine, was called on to send at least a brigade by the railroad, so that we might fall on and crush the enemy, should he attempt an advance from under his gunboats.

The call on General *Johnston* was promptly complied with. His entire force was also hastened in this direction, and by April 1 our united forces were concentrated along the Mobile and Ohio Railroad from Bethel to Corinth and on the Memphis and Charleston Railroad from Corinth to Iuka.

It was then determined to assume the offensive, and strike a sudden blow at the enemy, in position under General Grant on the west bank of the Tennessee, at Pittsburg, and in the direction of Savannah, before he was re-enforced by the army under General Buell, then known to be advancing for that purpose by rapid marches from Nashville via Columbia. About the same time General *Johnston* was advised that such an opera-

Gen. Albert Sidney *Johnston*, Commander, Army of the Mississippi. (U.S. Army Military History Institute)

tion conformed to the expectations of the President [Jefferson Davis].

By a rapid and vigorous attack on General Grant it was expected he would be beaten back into his transports and the river, or captured, in time to enable us to profit by the victory and remove to the rear all the stores and munitions that would fall into our hands in such an event before the arrival of General Buell's army on the scene. It was never contemplated, however, to retain the position thus gained and abandon Corinth, the strategic point of the campaign.

Want of general officers needful for the proper organization of divisions and brigades of an army brought thus suddenly together and other difficulties in the way of an effective organization delayed the movement until the night of the 2d instant [April 2], when it was heard, from a reliable quarter, that the junction of the enemy's armies was near at hand. It was then, at a late hour, determined that the attack should be attempted at once, incomplete and imperfect as were our preparations. . . . Accordingly, that night at 1 A.M. the preliminary orders to the commanders of corps were issued for the movement.

On the following morning the detailed orders of movement . . . were issued. [*O.R.*, X, pt. 1, p. 385.]

Special Orders HDQRS. Army of the Mississippi, No. 8

CORINTH, MISS., APRIL 3, 1862

I. In the impending movement the corps of this army will march, assemble, and take order of battle in the following manner, it being assumed that the enemy is in position about a mile in advance of Shiloh Church, with his right resting on Owl Creek and his left on Lick Creek.

1st. The Third Corps, under Major-General *Hardee,* will advance as soon as practicable on the Ridge road from Corinth to what is known as the Bark road, passing about half a mile northward of the workhouse. The head of this column will bivouac, if possible, tonight at Mickey's house, at the intersection of the road from Monterey to Savannah. The cavalry, thrown well forward during the march, to reconnoiter and prevent surprise, will halt in front of the Mickey house, on the Bark road.

2d. Major *Waddell,* aide-de-camp to General *Beauregard,* with two good guides, will report for service to Major-General *Hardee.*

3d. At 3 o'clock A.M. to-morrow the Third Corps, with the left in front, will continue to advance by the Bark road until within sight of the enemy's outposts or advanced positions, when it will be deployed in line of battle, according to the na-

ture of the ground, its left resting on Owl Creek, its righ
toward Lick Creek, supported on that flank by one-half of it
cavalry, the left flank being supported by the other half. Th
interval between the extreme right of this corps and Lick Cree
will be filled by a brigade or division, according to the exten
of the ground, from the Second Corps.

These troops during the battle will also be under the com
mand of Major-General *Hardee*. He will make the proper dis
position of the artillery along the line of battle, rememberin,
that the rifled guns are of long ranges and should be place
on any commanding position in rear of the infantry to fir
mainly on the reserves and second line of the enemy, but wi
occasionally be directed on his batteries and heads of column:

II. The Second Corps, under Maj. Gen. Braxton *Bragg*
will assemble on Monterey, and move thence as early as pract
cable, the right wing, with left in front, by the road from Mon
terey to Savannah, the head of the column to reach the vicinit
of Mickey's house, at the intersection of the Bark road, befor
sunset. The cavalry with this wing will take position on th
road to Savannah, beyond Mickey's as far as Owl Creek, havin
advanced guards and pickets well to the front.

The left wing of this corps will advance at the same time
also left in front, by the road from Monterey to Purdy, th
head of the column to reach by night the intersection of tha
road with the Bark road. This wing will continue the movemen
in the morning as soon as the rear of the Third Corps sha
have passed the Purdy road, which it will then follow.

The Second Corps will then form the second line of battl
about 1,000 yards in rear of the first line. It will be formed, i
practicable, with regiments in double columns at half distanc
disposed as advantageously as the nature of the ground wi
admit and with a view to facility of deployment, the artiller
placed as may seem best to Major-General *Bragg*.

III. The First Corps, under Major General *Polk*, with th
exception of the detached division at Bethel, will take up it
line of march by the Ridge road, hence to Pittsburg, half a
hour after the rear of the Third Corps shall have passed Cor
inth, and will bivouac to-night in rear of that corps, and on to
morrow will follow the movements of said corps with the sam

interval of time as to-day. When its head of column shall reach the vicinity of the Mickey house it will be halted in column or massed on the line of the Bark road, according to the nature of the ground, as a reserve.

Meantime one regiment of its cavalry will be placed in observation on the road from *Johnston's* house to Stantonville, with advance guards and pickets thrown out well in advance toward Stantonville. Another regiment or battalion of cavalry will be posted in the same manner in the road from Monterey to Purdy, with its rear resting on or about the intersection of that road with the Bark road, having advanced guards and pickets in the direction of Purdy.

The forces at Bethel and Purdy will defend their positions, as already instructed, if attacked; otherwise they will assemble on Purdy, and thence advance with advanced guards, flankers, and all other prescribed military precautions, by the road thence to Monterey, forming a junction with the next of the First Corps at the intersection of that road with the Bark road leading from Corinth.

IV. The reserve of the forces will be concentrated, by the shortest and best routes at Monterey as soon as the rear of the Second Corps shall have moved out of that place. Its commander will take up the best position whence to advance, as required, either in the direction of Mickey's or of Pratt's house, on the direct road to Pittsburg, if that road is found practicable, or in the direction of the Ridge road to Hamburg, throwing all its cavalry on the latter road as far as its intersection with the one to Pittsburg, passing through Guersford, on Lick Creek. This cavalry will throw well forward advanced guards and vedettes* toward Guersford and in the direction of Hamburg, and during the impending battle, when called to the field of combat, will move by the Guersford road. A regiment of the infantry reserve will be thrown forward to the intersection of the Gravel Hill road with the ridge road to Hamburg, as a support to the cavalry. The reserve will be formed of *Breckinridge's* (commanded temporarily by Col. R. *Trabue*), *Bowen's*, and *Statham's* brigades as now organized, the whole under command of Brigadier General *Breckinridge*.

---

*A vedette is a mounted sentry placed in advance of the outposts of an army.

V. General *Bragg* will detach the 51st and 52d Regiments of Tennessee Volunteers, *Blount's* Alabama, and *Desha's* Arkansas battalion, and *Bains'* battery from his corps, which, with two of *Carroll's* regiments now en route for these headquarters, will form a garrison for the post and depot of Corinth.

VI. Strong guards will be left at the railroad bridges between Iuka and Corinth, to be furnished in due proportion from the commands at Iuka, Burnsville, and Corinth.

VII. Proper guards will be left at the camps of the several regiments of the forces in the field. Corps commanders will determine the strength of these guards.

VIII. *Wharton's* regiment of Texas cavalry will be ordered forward at once to scout on the road from Monterey to Savannah between Mickey's and its intersection with the Pittsburg-Purdy road. It will annoy and harass any force of the enemy moving by the latter way to assail *Cheatham's* division at Purdy.

IX. The chief engineer of the forces will take all due measures and precautions and give all requisite orders for the repair of the bridges, causeways, and roads on which our troops may move in the execution of these orders.

X. The troops, individually so intelligent, and with such great interests involved in the issue, are urgently enjoined to be observant of the orders of their superiors in the hour of battle. Their officers must constantly endeavor to hold them in hand and prevent the waste of ammunition by heedless timeless firing. The fire should be slow, always at a distinct mark. It is expected that much and effective work will be done with the bayonet.

By command of General A. S. *Johnston:*

THOMAS JORDAN, *Assistant Adjutant-General*

[*O.R.,* X, pt. 1, pp. 392–95.]

The movement, after some delay, commenced, the troops being in admirable spirits. It was expected we should be able to reach the enemy's lines in time to attack him early on the

5th instant. The men, however, for the most part, were unused to marching, and the roads, narrow and traversing a densely-wooded country, became almost impassable after a severe rainstorm on the night of the 4th, which drenched the troops in bivouac; hence our forces did not reach the intersection of the roads from Pittsburg and Hamburg, in the immediate vicinity of the enemy, until late Saturday afternoon.

It was then decided that the attack should be made on the next morning, at the earliest hour practicable, in accordance with the orders of movement; that is, in three lines of battle, the first and second extending from Owl Creek, on the left, to Lick Creek, on the right, a distance of about 3 miles, supported by the third [line] and the reserve.

The first line, under Major-General *Hardee,* was constituted of his corps, augmented on his right by *Gladden's* brigade, of Major-General *Bragg's* corps, deployed in line of battle, with their respective artillery following immediately by the main road to Pittsburg and the cavalry in rear of the wings.

The second line, composed of the other troops of *Bragg's* corps, followed the first at a distance of 500 yards in the same order as the first.

The army corps under General *Polk* followed the second line, at a distance of about 800 yards, in lines of brigades deployed, with their batteries in rear of each brigade, moving by the Pittsburg road, the left wing supported by cavalry. The reserve, under Brigadier-General *Breckinridge,* followed closely the third line in the same order, its right wing supported by cavalry. These two corps constituted the reserve, and were to support the front lines of battle by being deployed, when required, on the right and left of the Pittsburg road, or otherwise acting according to the exigencies of the battle.

At 5 A.M. on the 6th instant, a reconnoitering party of the enemy having become engaged with our advance pickets, the commander of the forces gave orders to begin the movement and attack as determined upon, except that *Trabue's* brigade, of *Breckinridge's* division, was detached and advanced to support the left of *Bragg's* corps and line of battle when menaced by the enemy, and the other two brigades were directed to advance by the road to Hamburg to support *Bragg's* right; and at the same time *Maney's* regiment, of *Polk's* corps, was advanced by the same road to re-enforce the regiment of cavalry and battery of four pieces already thrown forward to watch and guard Greer's, Tanner's, and Borland's Fords, on Lick Creek.

At 5.30 A.M. our lines were in motion, all animated, evidently, by a promising spirit. The frontline was engaged at once, but advanced steadily, followed in due order, with equal resolution and steadiness, by the other lines, which were brought successively into action with rare skill, judgment, and gallantry by the several corps commanders as the enemy made a stand, with his masses rallied for the struggle for his encampments.

Like an Alpine avalanche our troops moved forward, despite the determined resistance of the enemy, until after 6 P.M., when we were in possession of all his encampments between Owl and Lick Creeks but one; nearly all of his field artillery; about 30 flags, colors, and standards; over 3,000 prisoners, including a division commander (General Prentiss), and several brigade commanders; thousands of small-arms; an immense supply of subsistence, forage, and munitions of war, and a large amount of means of transportation—all the substantial fruits of a complete victory, such, indeed, as rarely have followed the most successful battles; for never was an army so well provided as that of our enemy.

The remnant of his army had been driven in utter disorder to the immediate vicinity of Pittsburg, under the shelter of the heavy guns of his iron-clad gunboats, and we remained undisputed masters of his well-selected, admirably-provided cantonments, after over twelve hours of obstinate conflict with his forces, who had been beaten from them and the contiguous covert, but only by a sustained onset of all the men we could bring into action.

Our loss was heavy. . . . Our commander-in-chief, General A. S. *Johnston*, fell mortally wounded, and died on the field at 2:30 P.M., after having shown the highest qualities of the commander and a personal intrepidity that inspired all around him and gave resistless impulsion to his columns at critical moments.

The chief command then devolved upon me, though at the time I was greatly prostrated and suffering from the prolonged sickness with which I had been afflicted since early in February. The responsibility was one which in my physical condition I would have gladly avoided, though cast upon me when our forces were successfully pushing the enemy back upon the Tennessee River, and though supported on the immediate field by such corps commanders as Major-Generals *Polk, Bragg,* and *Hardee,* and Brigadier-General *Breckinridge,* commanding the reserve.

It was after 6 P.M., . . . when the enemy's last position was carried, and his forces finally broke and sought refuge behind a commanding eminence covering the Pittsburg Landing, not more than half a mile distant, and under the guns of the gunboats, which opened on our eager columns a fierce and annoying fire with shot and shell of the heaviest description. [*O.R.,* X, pt. 1, pp. 385–87.]

Report of Maj. A. B. Hardcastle, CSA, Third Mississippi Infantry Battalion, Third Brigade, Third Corps

On the evening of the 5th I occupied a post of picket with the body of my battalion a quarter of a mile in front of our brigade, No. 190 [*sic*], 8 flankers on the right and 22 on the left, deployed at intervals of 12 paces. We covered the front of the brigade. An advance party of 7 men, under command of Lieutenant *Hammock,* were posted 200 yards in front of my center. Another party, under the command of Lieutenant *McNulty,* of 8 men, were posted 100 yards in front of my center; three-quarters were deployed. Indications of the enemy's approach were made known to these officers by singular beats on the drum in the enemy's lines just before dawn.

About dawn the cavalry vedettes fired three shots, wheeled, and galloped back. Lieutenant *Hammock* suffered the enemy to approach within 90 yards. Their lines seemed about 350 yards long and to number about 1,000. He fired upon them and joined his battalion with his men. Lieutenant *McNulty* received the enemy with his fire at about 100 yards, and then joined his battalion with his men, when the vedettes rode back to my main position. At the first alarm my men were in line and all ready. I was on a rise of ground, men kneeling. The enemy opened a heavy fire on us at a distance of about 200 yards, but most of the shots passed over us. We returned the fire immediately and kept it up. Captain *Clare,* aide to General *Wood,* came and encouraged us. We fought the enemy an hour or more without giving an inch.

Our loss in this engagement was: killed, 4 privates; severely wounded, 1 sergeant, 1 corporal, and 8 privates; and slightly wounded, color-sergeant and 9 privates.

At about 6:30 A.M. I saw the brigade formed in my rear and I fell back. Captain *Hume's* company, bearing the colors, formed promptly at the command halt. I formed and took position in the brigade line of battle near the right. We advanced, dressing to the right, I charged the first camp of the enemy. I was ahead of my battalion a short distance and lost myself from it by going too far to the left. During my separation of about an hour I fought with the Sixteenth Alabama Regiment and changed front. The battalion had moved a little to the right toward an open field and were there occupied firing on the enemy running across the field. When I rejoined them they were marching forward in line against the enemy on a changed front. We halted on the right of our brigade and received a heavy fire from the enemy. We replied briskly and continued firing for some time. The enemy were driven off by a combined movement from our left. [*O.R.*, X, pt. 1, pp. 602–3.]

Walk back to your car, then proceed approximately 50 yards beyond the car (east) to Seay Field, the open field on the right.

STOP 2B, SEAY FIELD

THE FIRST DAY

Union pickets falling back from Fraley Field joined their regiment (the Twenty-first Missouri), which hurriedly formed in Seay Field to face the attacking Confederates.

Report of Brig. Gen. B. M. Prentiss, USA, Commanding Sixth Division, Army of the Tennessee

Saturday evening, pursuant to instructions, . . . the usual advance guard was posted, and in view of information received from the commandant thereof, I sent forward five companies of the Twenty-fifth Missouri and five companies of the Twenty-first Missouri, under command of Col. David *Moore.* I also, after consultation with Col. David Stuart, commanding a brigade of General Sherman's division, sent to the left one company of the Eighteenth Wisconsin Infantry, under command of Captain Fisk.

At about 7 o'clock the same evening Colonel *Moore* returned, reporting some activity in the front—an evident reconnaissance by cavalry. This information received, I proceeded to strengthen the guard stationed on the Corinth road, extending the picket lines to the front a distance of a mile and a half, at the same time extending and doubling the lines of the grand guard.

At 3 o'clock on the morning of Sunday, April 6, Col. David *Moore,* Twenty-first Missouri, with five companies of his infantry regiment, proceeded to the front, and at break of day the advance pickets were driven in, whereupon Colonel *Moore* pushed forward and engaged the enemy's advance, commanded by General *Hardee.* At this stage a messenger was sent to my headquarters, calling for the balance of the Twenty-first Missouri, which was promptly sent forward. This information received, I at once ordered the entire force into line, and the remaining regiments of the First Brigade, commanded by Col. Everett Peabody, consisting of the Twenty-fifth Missouri, Sixteenth Wisconsin, and Twelfth Michigan Infantry, were advanced well to the front. I forthwith at this juncture communicated the fact of the attack in force to Major-General Smith and Brig. Gen. S. A. Hurlbut.

Shortly before 6 o'clock, Col. David *Moore* having been severely wounded, his regiment commenced falling back, reaching our front line at about six o'clock, the enemy being close upon his rear. Hereupon the entire force, excepting only the Sixteenth Iowa, which had been sent to the field the day previous without ammunition, and the cavalry, which was held in readiness to the rear, was advanced to the extreme front and thrown out alternately to the right and left.

Shortly after 6 o'clock the entire line was under fire, receiving the assault made by the entire force of the enemy, advancing in three columns simultaneously upon our left, center, and right. This position was held until the enemy passed our right flank, this movement being effected by reason of the falling back of some regiment to our right not belonging to this division.

Perceiving the enemy was flanking me, I ordered the division to retire in line of battle to the color line of our encampment, at the same time communicating to Generals Smith and Hurlbut the fact of the falling back, and asking for reinforcements. [*O.R.,* X, pt. 1, p. 278.]

Report of Lieut. Col. Humphrey M. Woodyard, USA, Twenty-first Missouri Infantry, First Brigade, Sixth Division, Army of the Tennessee

On the morning of the 6th of April, before sunrise, General Prentiss ordered Colonel *Moore*, with five companies of our regiment, to sustain the pickets of the Twelfth Michigan Infantry. The colonel had not proceeded more than half a mile when he met the pickets coming in, with many killed and wounded. Colonel *Moore* immediately dispatched Lieutenant Menn for the remaining five companies. General Prentiss, being in camp, ordered me to join Colonel *Moore*.

We marched some 300 yards together, after I formed the

junction, in a nearly westerly direction, by flank movement, four ranks, when the head of the column came to the northwest corner of a cotton field [Seay Field]. We were here fired upon, and Colonel *Moore* received a severe wound in the right leg and Lieutenant Menn was wounded in the head. I then assumed command of the regiment, and formed a line of battle on the brow of a hill on the cotton field, facing nearly west. I held this position for some half or three-quarters of an hour and kept the enemy in check. He fell back and endeavored to outflank me.

Discovering this, I moved my line to the north of the field again. I was then joined by four companies of the Sixteenth Wisconsin Infantry. Having no field officers with them, I ordered them to a position east of the field, and as soon as this was done joined them with my command. This line of battle formed, facing south, behind a small incline, enabling my men to load and be out of range of the enemy's fire. The position proved a strong one, and we managed to hold it for upwards of an hour. Finding they could not dislodge us, the enemy again tried to outflank us and deal a cross-fire. I then fell back in good order, firing as we did so, to the next hill.

Colonel Peabody, commanding First brigade, here came up with the Twenty-fifth Missouri Regiment. I requested him to bring his men up to the hill on our right, as it would afford protection to his men and be of assistance to my command. He did so, but the enemy coming by heavy main center and dealing a cross-fire from our right and left, we could not maintain this position for over thirty minutes. We gradually began to fall back and reached our tents, when the ranks got broken in passing through them.

We endeavored to rally our men in the rear of the tents and formed as well as could be expected, but my men got much scattered, a great many falling into other regiments. . . . [*O.R.,* X, pt. 1, p. 283.]

Report of Col. David Moore, USA, Twenty-first Missouri Infantry, First Brigade, Sixth Division, Army of the Tennessee

In pursuance of the order of Brig. Gen. B. M. Prentiss, commanding Sixth Division, Army of West Tennessee, I on

Brig. Gen. Benjamin M. Prentiss, Commander, Sixth Division, Army of the Tennessee. (U.S. Army Military History Institute)

Saturday [April 5] proceeded to a reconnaissance on the front of the line of General Prentiss' division and on the front of General Sherman's division. My command consisted of three companies from the Twenty-first Missouri Regiment. . . . A thorough reconnaissance over the extent of three miles failed to discover the enemy. Being unsuccessful . . . I returned to my encampment about 7 o'clock P.M.

On Sunday morning, the 6th instant, at about 6 o'clock, being notified that the picket guard of the First Brigade, Sixth Division, had been attacked and driven in, by order of Col. Everett Peabody, commanding the First Brigade, Sixth Division, I advanced with five companies of my command a short distance from the outer line of our encampment. I met the retreating pickets of the First Brigade bringing in their wounded. Those who were able for duty I . . . compelled to return to their posts, and learning that the enemy was advancing in force I sent for the remaining five companies of my regiment, which companies having joined me, I ordered an advance and attacked the enemy, who was commanded by Brigadier-General *Ruggles,* of the rebel army. A terrific fire was opened upon us from the whole front of the four or five regiments forming the advance of the enemy, which my gallant soldiers withstood during thirty minutes, until I had communicated the intelligence of the movement against us to my commanding general.

About this time, being myself severely wounded (the bone of the leg below the knee being shattered), I was compelled to retire from the field, leaving Lieutenant-Colonel Woodyard in command. [*O.R.,* X, pt. 1, p. 282.]

Get back in your car and continue to drive for 0.4 mile on the one-way road (Reconnoitering Road) until you reach Shaver's Brigade marker (on the right side of the road). Pull off the road onto the shoulder.

STOP 3, THE CONFEDERATES ATTACK

Hearing fighting in the vicinity of Fraley's Field, Union General Prentiss attempted to form his Sixth Division into line of battle in front of his encampments, approximately 500 yards north of where you now stand. The Union troops, still in the process of learning

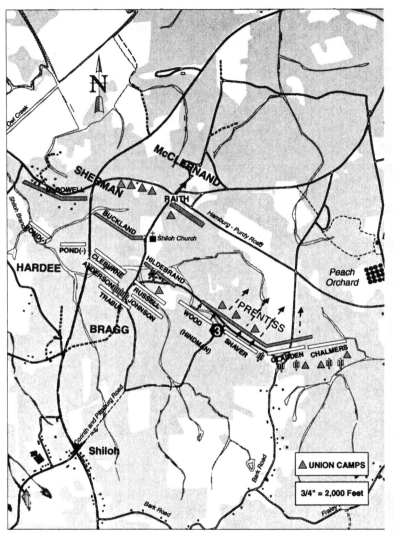

The Confederate attack develops (Stop 3). As the Confederate attack develops, units of *Hardee, Bragg,* and *Polk* become intermingled. *Hardee* moves to take command of the Confederate left, *Polk* the center, and *Bragg* the right.

their drill formations—which was the only way that soldiers could be moved in battle—now found themselves under fire for the very first time. *Hardee's* units surged forward to the attack, eventually overwhelming the disorganized Union troops.

Note the terrain. It was nearly the same in 1862. In the confusion of battle it was difficult for commanders to see and understand what was happening when there was such limited visibility.

Report of Lieut. Gen. William J. Hardee, CSA, Commanding Third Corps, Army of the Tennessee

About 10 o'clock on . . . April 5, my corps reached the outposts and developed the line of the enemy. It was immediately deployed in line of battle about a mile and a half east of Shiloh Church, where Lick Creek and Owl Creek approach most nearly. The right was extended toward Lick Creek and the left rested near Owl Creek, which streams at that point are rather more than 3 miles apart. . . . The storm of the preceding night rendered the roads so miry that the different commands were not collected at Shiloh until 4 or 5 o'clock in the afternoon. This rendered it necessary to postpone the attack until the next day.

Some of the troops having failed to provide themselves with provisions, or having improvidently consumed or lost them, the propriety of returning to Corinth without attacking the enemy was urged and considered, but the commanding general determined, regardless of all objections, to force a battle the succeeding morning.

By the order of battle our troops were arranged in two parallel lines, the first, under my command, being composed of my corps, consisting of the brigades of Brigadier Generals *Hindman [Shaver]*, *Wood*, and *Cleburne*, numbering 6,789 effective men, and the brigade of Brigadier-General *Gladden*, which was attached to my command. . . . In the arrangement of my line of battle two brigades were intrusted to Brigadier General *Hindman;* his own, under the immediate command of Colonel *Shaver*, who conducted his command to my satisfaction, and the other under command of Brigadier-General *Wood*. [*O.R.*, X, pt. 2, pp. 567–68.]

Report of Col. R. G. Shaver, 7th Arkansas Infantry, CSA, Commanding First Brigade, Hindman's Division, Third Army Corps, Army of the Mississippi

On the morning of April 5 ... my command ... was moved forward to the first line, and deployed to the right of the corps ... Third Confederate on the right, Seventh Arkansas on the left, Sixth Arkansas on the right center, and Second Arkansas on the left center. In this position the command remained for the day and night.

Between daylight and sunrise on the ... 6th I received orders to advance in the direction of the enemy, and when I had advanced about a mile my skirmishers were fired upon by the enemy's, which was returned briskly and with effect, and resulted in the enemy's skirmishers being gradually driven back. A steady advance was made, the enemy's skirmishers meanwhile contesting the ground, but no very persistent resistance was offered until my command had advanced to within about a half mile of the enemy's encampments. As we were descending the second ridge from the enemy's encampment a brisk fire was opened upon us, but being returned with determination by my skirmishers the enemy quickly retired, suffering my command to reach the crest of the ridge without material opposition.

In passing the declivity of the second ridge and ascending the ridge in front of the enemy's encampment my command was subjected to a galling fire and my skirmishers driven in. Pressing forward, the crest of the ridge overlooking the enemy's line and encampment was soon reached, the enemy found in heavy force, and the battle commenced. The enemy's fire was terrific and told with terrible effect, and was returned with a spirited determination and energy that threw the enemy into confusion in the end.

The conflict was very sanguinary. In the mean time Captain *Swett's* battery took position on my right and opened a destructive fire on the enemy's lines and camps. It soon became apparent that unless something was done to relieve Captain *Swett* his battery would be rendered useless, as his men were falling fast, and I so stated to General *Hindman*. I was ordered to immediately charge the enemy's line and camp. The order to charge was given and promptly and cheerfully responded to by the officers and men. The enemy broke and fled in dismay, my men pursuing them through their camps and to the ravine beyond. Here the order was given to halt and reform the line. Colonel *Marmaduke,* in pursuit of the enemy having become detached to the right, was ordered to rejoin the command. The camp captured, . . . after reforming my line I was ordered to make an oblique change of front to the left, with the view of making an attack upon an encampment to the left and the rear of the camp just captured, but before making any considerable advance I was ordered to make a flank movement to the left, reform my line, as at first, and dislodge the enemy, who were in strong force in a woods some 300 yards in front and supported on their right by a battery. [*O.R.,* X, pt. 1, pp. 573–74.]

Narrative of Pvt. Henry M. Stanley, CSA, Sixth Arkansas Infantry, Hindman's Brigade, Hardee's Corps, Army of the Mississippi

"Forward, gentlemen, make ready," urged Captain *Smith.* In response we surged forward, for the first time marring the alignment. We trampled recklessly over the grass and young sprouts. Beams of sunlight stole athwart our course. . . . Nothing now stood between us and the enemy.

"There they are!" was no sooner uttered than we cracked into them with levelled muskets. "Aim low, men! commanded Captain *Smith.* I tried hard to see some living thing to shoot at, for it appeared absurd to be blazing away at shadows. . . . Still advancing, firing as we moved, I at last saw a row of little globes of pearly smoke streaked with crimson, breaking-out with spurtive quickness from a long line of blue figures in front; and simultaneously, there broke upon our ears an appalling crash of sound, the series of fusillades, following one another with startling suddenness, which suggested . . . a mountain upheaved, with huge rocks tumbling and thundering down a slope. . . . Again and again these loud and quick explosions were repeated, seemingly with increased violence, until they rose to the highest pitch of fury and in unbroken continuity. All the world seemed involved in one tremendous ruin! . . .

We plied our arms, loaded, and fired, with . . . nervous haste. . . . My nerves tingled, my pulses beat double-quick, my heart throbbed loudly and almost painfully; but, amid all the excitement, my thoughts . . . took all sound, and sight, and self into their purvue. . . . I was angry with my rear rank, because he made my eyes smart with the powder of his musket; and felt like cuffing him for deafening my ears! . . .

We continued advancing, step by step, loading and firing as we went. To every forward step they took a backward move loading and firing as they slowly withdrew. Twenty thousand muskets were being fired at this stage. . . . After a steady exchange of musketry, which lasted some time, we heard the order: "Fix Bayonets! On the double-quick!" . . .

There was a simultaneous bound forward. . . . The Federal appeared inclined to await us; but, at this juncture, our men raised a yell, thousands responded to it, and burst out into the wildest yelling it has ever been my lot to hear. It drove all sanity and order from among us. It served the double purpose of relieving pent-up feelings and transmitting encouragement along the attacking line. . . . It reminded me that there [were about four hundred companies like the *Dixie Greys* who shared our feelings. Most of us, engrossed with the musket-work, had forgotten the fact; but the wave after wave of human voices louder than all other battle-sounds together, penetrated to every sense, and stimulated our energy to the utmost.

"They fly!" was echoed from lip to lip. It accelerated our pace, and filled us with a noble rage. . . . It deluged us with rapture, and transfigured each Southerner into an exulting victor. At such a moment, nothing could have halted us. Those savage yells, and the sight of thousands of racing figures coming towards them, discomfited the blue-coats; and when we arrived upon the place where they had stood, they had vanished.

Then we caught sight of their beautiful array of tents [Henry M. Stanley, *The Autobiography of Sir Henry Morton Stanley* (Boston: Houghton Mifflin, 1909), pp. 187–88.]*

---

*Private Stanley survived the war and later became famous as the journalist who finally caught up with the lost missionary in Africa: "Dr. Livingston, I presume."

Report of Col. Francis Quinn, Twelfth Michigan Infantry, Commanding Sixth Division, Army of West Tennessee

At 3 o'clock A.M. of that day several companies were ordered out from the First Brigade of this division to watch, and endeavor, if possible, to capture, a force of the enemy who were prowling near our camp. Our brave boys marched out, . . . met the enemy, and immediately a sharp firing commenced, our little force giving ground.

About daylight the dead and wounded began to be brought in. The firing grew closer and closer till it became manifest a heavy force of the enemy was upon us. The division was ordered into line of battle by General Prentiss, and immediately advanced in line about one-quarter of a mile from the tents, where the enemy were met in short firing distance. Volley after volley was given and returned and many fell on both sides, but their numbers were too heavy for our forces. I could see to the right and left. They were visible in line, and every hill-top in the rear was covered with them. It was manifest they were advancing in not only one but several lines of battle. The whole division fell back to their tents and again rallied, and although no regular line was formed, yet from behind every tree a deadly fire was poured out upon the enemy, which held them in check for about one-half hour, when, re-enforcements coming to their assistance, they advanced furiously upon our camp, and we were forced to again give way. At this time we lost four pieces of artillery. The division fell back about one-half mile, very much scattered and broken. Here we were posted, being drawn up in line behind a dense clump of bushes, when General Prentiss rode up and proposed heroically for us to fight our way back to our tents, but finally gave this up and formed the line for defense where it was. [*O.R.*, X, pt. 1, p. 280.]

Drive 0.3 mile to a T in the road. Turn left for 0.4 mile to Rhea Field. (This is called Rea Field on some maps/sources.) Park next to the artillery piece, off the road. Walk up to the vicinity of the artillery and look in the direction the guns are pointing, toward the woods and thickets, and then toward your left, across the field.

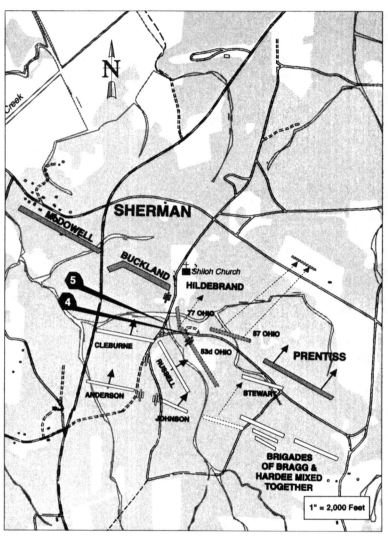

Sherman's defense, Rhea Field (Stops 4 and 5).

STOP 4, RHEA FIELD

At this time *Hardee's* units are attacking Prentiss's Sixth Division in the vicinity of Stop 3. In the area west (in the direction the single cannon is pointing) of your position, *Bragg's* Confederate units were deploying into the attack on the left (west) of *Hardee's* force. To your direct front (toward the Confederate Burial Trench) the Confederate brigades of *Anderson, Russell,* and *Johnson,* as well as part of *Cleburne's* brigade, attacked the Fifty-third Ohio Infantry, which was trying to form and fight in front of its camp on Rhea Field. (The stone marker in the middle of the field indicates the camp of the Fifty-third Ohio.) Actions described at this stop include those at Rhea Field and to the east and north of your current location.

In 1862 this field was much larger, extending nearly to Shiloh Church (Stop 6A). Both artillery and infantry could then see over the small trees and bushes in the creek beds, from Shiloh Church to your present location. This was a factor in the actions described in the next three stops.

Report of Brig. Gen. Charles Clark, CSA, Commanding First Division, First Corps, Army of the Mississippi

On Sunday morning . . . the two brigades [*Russell* and *Stewart*] the Second in front, marched to the field as ordered by Major-General *Polk* in line of battle, the center on the Pittsburg road, *Stanford's* battery attached to and following the Second [brigade] in the road and *Bankhead's* battery the First.

When within about 1,000 yards of the enemy's camps the left flank of each line, while passing through a field, was exposed to a fire of round shot and shell from a battery of the enemy, but no casualties occurred, although the battery continued to fire upon us for thirty minutes. When we arrived within 300 yards of Major-General *Bragg's* line, General A. Sidney *Johnston* ordered me to send the Second Brigade [*Stewart*] by a flank movement to the right, to support the forces there engaged, and to remain with the First Brigade in position and await orders. He led the Second Brigade in person and I did not see it afterwards.

In a few moments I was ordered to move to the edge of the open fields in front, and was there met by Major-General

Bragg, who informed me that the battery on the left and front of my line was enfilading his troops, and directed me to charge it with one of my regiments. The Eleventh Louisiana (Col. Sam F. *Marks*) being the most convenient, I led it forward. The battery was concealed from us by a ridge and distance of about 300 yards. The battalion moved up the ascent, with fixed bayonets, at a double-quick, and when on the crest of the ridge we were opened upon by the enemy's battery with shot and canister, and by a large infantry support with musketry at easy range. Our men were compelled to fall back behind the ridge where they were promptly reformed.

In the mean time Colonel *Russell* brought forward the other three regiments, and with the whole brigade I again charged. The enemy retreated. We pursued them at double-quick some 500 yards, when we met a large force in position upon whom we opened fire. A brisk interchange of musketry continued for about fifteen minutes, when the enemy commenced retiring, covering their retreat with skirmishers. [*O.R.,* X, pt. 1, pp. 414–15.]

Report of Colonel R. M. Russell, CSA, Commanding First Brigade, First Division, First Corps, Army of the Mississippi

On the morning of the 6th the First Army Corps . . . was drawn up in columns of brigades a short distance in front of the enemy's encampment, near a ravine, covered with briers and brushwood, waiting for the order to advance. Soon after daylight the attack had been made by the right of our army, under Major-General *Hardee,* and the First [Corps] was held as a supporting corps. While in this position the enemy opened fire upon us with solid shot and shell with field batteries posted in strong positions on the hills in front. The Second Brigade commanded by Brigadier-General *Stewart,* moved to the right

Pending this movement I received orders to charge through the enemy's encampment and take it at all hazards. . . I immediately ordered the regiments on the left to charge and started to advance those on the right, but was ordered by General *Clark* to go forward with the left and he would give the order to the right wing.

I placed myself at their head, and we moved rapidly for

ward until we had passed through a part of the first encampment, the enemy all the while pouring a shower of Minie and musket balls from the hills above, until suddenly he opened his batteries with grape and canister with such sure aim and terrible effect that the advancing line was forced to give way and retire behind the thicket and ravine, where I reformed it preparatory to a second advance. I found afterward that instead of two regiments advancing, but seven companies had succeeded in passing the almost impenetrable undergrowth and joined in the first charge.

The line being reformed, the order was again given to charge through the camp, which was done in gallant style and with complete success.

At this point I sent my acting brigade adjutant to the right to see where the Twelfth and Thirteenth Regiments were, with a view to getting all the brigade together again; but he reported that three other regiments had forced their way between, and it would be impossible to accomplish this.

I then moved forward with those I had up to the top of the hill, where we met with the most obstinate and determined resistance. The enemy's batteries, supported by a heavy force of infantry, rapidly thinned our ranks and held our troops back in a hotly contested conflict, which lasted nearly an hour. They were finally forced to give way and fall back, closely pursued by our eager troops.

Continuing to advance, we soon encountered a battery, two pieces of which were taken and sent to the rear. Pushing still farther forward, a force was found partially concealed in the bushes in front of our left and extending beyond that flank. Fearing they were some of our Louisiana troops, I caused the firing to cease and halted the line, and sent forward to ascertain their true character. Conflicting reports were brought back.

Just at this time the troops that were on the right were seen to retire. I rode down the line to ascertain the cause. I found them to be the Fifth Tennessee Regiment, of General *Stewart's* brigade, and was informed that they had orders to fall back. This compelled me to retire a short distance. . . . [*O.R.*, X, pt. 1, pp. 416–17.]

Report of Brig. Gen. Alexander P. Stewart, CSA, Commanding Second Brigade, First Division, First Corps

While our left was moving through an open field a fire o artillery was opened upon it. . . . We continued to advance unti General A. S. *Johnston* came up and directed me to move m brigade to the right, to support General *Bragg* [to the east and north of Rhea Field]. I faced the command to the right and moved in a direction oblique to the former front, until we reached an open woods in front of one of the enemy's camps from which he had already been driven. General *Johnston* having gone to some other part of the field, and finding no one to give me directions, after halting a few minutes I moved the brigade forward through the camp and beyond it, where I me a staff officer, who directed me to move to the left and then forward. I executed the order, and in doing so lost sight o *Neely's* regiment, which did not hear the order to move to the left. The other three regiments were pushed forward across a small stream and up the side of a hill, where I directed them to lie down until I could bring up the Fourth Tennessee. I rode back for it, passing through the left of *Stanford's* battery, which had become engaged with one of the enemy's to our right and front.

On bringing up the Fourth I found that the other three regiments had moved forward up the hill. Just then a staff officer informed me that General *Bragg* desired the battery in our front [McAllister's Illinois battery] to be taken. I turned to the Fourth; told them what was wanted; asked if they would take the battery, and received the reply, "Show us where it is we will try!"

The regiment moved forward, under a severe fire of canister, from which it lost 31 men killed and 160 wounded, charged and carried the battery, and drove the enemy into the thick woods beyond it, where the Twelfth Tennessee . . . formed on its left. The entire regiment behaved admirably. [*O.R.*, X, pt 1, p. 427.]

Report of Lt. Col. O. F. Strahl, CSA, Fourth Tennessee Infantry, Stewart's Brigade, First Division, First Corps, Army of the Mississippi

The position occupied by this regiment . . . was on the right of the Second Brigade, First Division, First Army Corps, and moved forward in the second line of battle until about 10 A.M., when it came up with the first [line], which was driven back by a battery of the enemy [McAllister] in front, placed on the opposite side of an old field, on a hill. Here we were thrown into some confusion by the first line of battle falling back through ours; but we soon rallied, and formed in front under a very heavy fire of grape and shell from the enemy's guns, which were about 800 yards distant.

We were here separated from the rest of our brigade. . . . Our men here were ordered to fall flat on their faces in order to protect themselves from the enemy's fire, and while remaining here General *Stewart* rode up and told me that General *Bragg* said that the battery must be taken, and asked me if I would do it. I told him we would try, and immediately ordered the men forward, bearing to the left, in order to avoid the open field in front, and marched through a thicket of small timber at double-quick. We continued to march at double-quick until we were within 30 paces of the enemy's guns, when we halted, fired one round, and rushed forward with a yell, and the battery was ours. We took 2 prisoners at the battery, who did not have time to escape nor courage to fight.

During the whole time of this charge the battery played upon us with grape and canister, making sad havoc in our ranks, killing 31 men and wounding about 160. The battery, however, according to the report of the prisoner taken there, was supported by seven regiments of infantry—four Ohio regiments and three Illinois.

After taking the battery I found I was in advance of our lines near a quarter of a mile, and heavily pressed both on the right and left by the enemy's infantry. I immediately dispatched my adjutant for aid, and in a short time had the pleasure of seeing our troops coming up in double-quick to support me.

While remaining here we were called on to support one of our own batteries that had been placed on the same ground that the enemy's formerly occupied. While supporting this battery we were in a very heavy fire from the enemy, who made a desperate effort to take it. . . . The enemy were repulsed.

I then marched the regiment a short distance to the rear, had the men to wipe out their guns, many of them being so dirty they could not load, fill their cartridge boxes, and replenish their canteens with water. We then marched forward into line, and continued in line until after dark, when we fell back, in order to get out of reach of the shells from the gunboats. We slept near where we took the enemy's battery, in their camp, and took supper and breakfast at their expense. [*O.R.*, X, pt. 1, pp. 431–32.]

Report of Col. Jesse Hildebrand, USA, Third Brigade, Fifth Division, Army of the Tennessee

Early on the morning of Sunday, 6th instant, our pickets were fired on, and shortly after 7 o'clock the enemy appeared in force, presenting himself in columns of regiments at least four deep. He opened upon our camp a heavy fire from infantry, which was immediately followed by shell. Having formed my brigade in line of battle, I ordered an advance. The Seventy-seventh and Fifty-seventh Regiments were thrown forward to occupy a certain position, but encountered the enemy in force within 300 yards of our camp. Unfortunately we were not supported by artillery, and consequently were compelled to retire under cover of our camp, the engagement becoming general along the entire front of my command.

A battery [Taylor's, commanded by Captain Barrett] having been brought to support our right, the Fifty-seventh and Seventy-seventh Regiments stood side by side for four hours, contending with a force of not less than four to one. The battery having been forced from its position, and the infantry both on our right and left, having fallen back, it became necessary that the two regiments . . . should fall back, lest their retreat be effectually cut off.

The Fifty-third Regiment, after forming in line of battle under my order, fired two rounds and immediately fell back into the woods. It appears from the report of Colonel Appler that, apprehending a flank movement on his left, he ordered a retreat, but subsequently rallied in rear of the Eighteenth Illinois. This regiment became separated from my command, and its movements throughout the balance of the day were general. [*O.R.*, X, pt. 1, p. 262.]

Report of Lieut. Col. Robert A. Fulton, USA, Fifty-third Ohio Infantry, Third Brigade, Fifth Division

Shortly after daylight on the morning of the 6th the regiment was formed on the color line under order and direction of Colonel Appler. After remaining here for a time they were moved to the left of our camp, forming a line of battle perpendicular to the first line. Soon after Colonel Appler ordered the regiment to face about and wheel to the right and take position in rear of the camp [east side of Rhea Field], which maneuver was executed under fire of the rebel skirmishers [*Cleburne's* Fifteenth Arkansas].

The new line of battle was formed just in rear of our camp, in the edge of the woods. A section of Waterhouse's battery took position in the woods to our right. General Sherman and staff rode up to the open field in front of the left wing, and were fired upon by the rebel skirmishers, now advancing through the thicket in front of our camp, killing an orderly. General Sherman, riding back, ordered Colonel Appler to hold his position; he would support him. A battery opened upon us. The section of artillery on our right, after firing two shots, limbered up and went to the rear.

A line of rebel infantry advanced to within 50 yards and were fired into by the left wing and recoiled. Advancing again, they were met by a fire from the regiment, under which they again fell back. At this time Colonel Appler gave the command, "Fall back and save yourselves." Hearing this order, the regiment fell back in disorder, passing around the flanks of the Illinois Forty-ninth.

Here, in connection with the company officers and the adjutant, I succeeded in rallying the regiment, and was about to station them at the crossing of the creek, above the Big Springs, to repel the force who were turning the flank of the Fifty-seventh Ohio, when Colonel Appler, by direction, he says, of a staff officer of General McClernand, moved the regiment by the left flank up the ravine and afterward by the right flank, taking position on the hill to the left of Shiloh Chapel, and near the front of General Sherman's headquarters.

The regiment remained in this position for some time exposed to a galling fire, which could not be returned without endangering the regiment in front, who were hotly engaged. Colonel Appler here abandoned the regiment, giving again the order, "Fall back and save yourselves." Companies A and F . . . remained in the front, and soon after became hotly engaged, in connection with the Seventeenth Illinois. This regiment retreating, the two companies fell back after them, making as much resistance as possible. They afterwards joined the Forty-eighth Ohio [Buckland's brigade], and with them aided in repelling the final assault made Sunday evening, and joined me again at night. [*O.R.*, X, pt. 1, pp. 264–65.]

Return to your car and continue to drive for 0.1 mile to the intersection. Turn right, cross the bridge over Shiloh Branch Creek, and stop next to *Cleburne's* Brigade marker on the left. Pull off the road onto the shoulder.

STOP 5, CLEBURNE'S ASSAULT

As the Confederate brigades of *Johnson* and *Russell* attacked toward the Fifty-third Ohio camp (Stop 4), *Hardee's* Third brigade, commanded by Irish-born Brig. Gen. Patrick *Cleburne*, forced its way through the thick ravine formed by Shiloh Branch Creek toward the crossroads at Shiloh Church. In the dense thickets two regiments, the Sixth Mississippi and Twenty-third Tennessee—accompanied by *Cleburne*—split off and attacked the Fifty-third Ohio and Waterhouse's Illinois battery position (in the vicinity of Stop 4). *Cleburne* rode back around the morass and rejoined the remaining four regiments of his brigade, which were moving against Buckland's brigade of Sherman's division as they continued to attack toward the crossroads at Shiloh Church, approximately 350 yards straight ahead (north) of your present position.

Meanwhile, on other parts of the battlefield *Hardee's* and *Bragg's* units were pushing Prentiss's regiments out of their encampments in the center of the Union position. No actions had yet begun on the Union left flank (Stuart's brigade).

Report of Brig. Gen. P. R. Cleburne, CSA, Commanding Second Brigade, Hardee's Corps, Army of the Mississippi

My brigade was formed in line of battle on the left of your *[Hindman's]* division. . . . Twenty-third Tennessee on the right, Sixth Mississippi next, Fifth Tennessee next, Twenty-fourth Tennessee on the left, Fifteenth Arkansas deployed as skirmishers in front of the line, with their reserve near the left, and the Second Tennessee *en echelon* 500 yards in rear of my left flank, with a strong line of skirmishers covering the interval between its left and that of the Twenty-fourth Tennessee.

In this formation, soon after daylight, I advanced with the division against the enemy, keeping the proper distance from and regulating my movements by those of General *Wood's* brigade . . . on my right. I remained myself near the right of my brigade so as to preserve, as far as possible, my connection with the division. *Trigg's* battery followed near the right of my brigade, but was under the control of the chief of artillery, and left me after the first encounter.

I advanced some distance through the woods without opposition. The enemy first showed himself about 400 yards off toward my left flank. I ordered Captain *Trigg* to send a howitzer in this direction and wake him up with a few shells. Continuing to move forward, the Fifth Arkansas engaged the enemy's skirmishers and drove them in on their first line of battle. My skirmishers then fell back on their reserve.

I was soon in sight of the enemy's encampments, behind the first of which he had formed his line of battle. He was very advantageously posted and overlapped my left flank by at least a brigade. His line was lying down behind the rising ground on which their tents were pitched, and opposite my right he had made a breastwork of logs and bales of hay. Everywhere his musketry and artillery at short range swept the open spaces between the tents in his front with an iron storm that threatened certain destruction to every living thing that would dare to cross them. An almost impassable morass, jutting out from the foot of the height on which the enemy's tents stood, impeded the advance of my center, and finally caused a wide opening in my line. The Fifth Tennessee and the regiments on its left kept to the left of this swamp, and the Sixth Mississippi and Twenty-third Tennessee advanced on its right. My own horse bogged down in it and threw me, and it was with great difficulty I got out.

My brigade was soon on the verge of the encampments and the battle began in earnest. *Trigg's* battery, posted on some high ground in the woods in my rear, opened over the heads of my men, but so thick were the leaves, he could only see in one direction, while the enemy were playing on him from several. The result was he was unable to accomplish much, and was ordered to a new position. I had no artillery under my command from this time forward.

The Sixth Mississippi and Twenty-third Tennessee charged through the encampments on the enemy. The line was necessarily broken by the standing tents. Under the terrible fire much confusion followed, and a quick and bloody repulse was the consequence.

The Twenty-third Tennessee was with difficulty rallied about 100 yards in the rear; again and again the Sixth Mississippi, unaided, charged the enemy's line, and it was only when the regiment had lost 300 officers and men killed and wounded, out of an aggregate of 425, that it yielded and retreated in disorder over its own dead and dying. . . . The field officers were both wounded. It would be useless to enlarge on the courage and devotion of the Sixth Mississippi. The facts as recorded speak louder than any words of mine.

Col. Mat. *Martin*, former commander of the Twenty-third Tennessee, arrived on the field just as his old regiment broke; though not then on duty, he voluntarily assisted me in rallying and inspiring the men with renewed determination, and remained with it until severely wounded at a subsequent period of the day.

While my right was reforming, I galloped around the morass to my left, which, after a desperate fight and heavy loss, caused chiefly by the fact that the enemy flanked me on the left, had driven him back at all points, and was now in possession of his first line of encampments.

Here the Second Tennessee, coming up on the left, charged through a murderous cross-fire. . . . Here the Twenty-fourth Tennessee won a character for steady valor, and its commander, Lieutenant-Colonel *Peebles*, showed that he possessed all the qualifications of a commander in the field.

Here the Fifteenth Arkansas inflicted heavy loss upon the

enemy and lost many good men and its major, T. T. *Harris*, [who] scorned to pay any regard to his personal safety [and] . . . moved up within pistol range of the enemy and was shot dead while firing on them with his revolver.

Finding my advance on the left wing for the present unemployed, I galloped back to my right. About half of the Twenty-third Tennessee and 60 men of the Sixth Mississippi had reformed. With these I advanced directly to my front, through the enemy's encampment, the enemy having retreated as soon as my left had broken their right. Colonel *Patterson*, of the Eighth Arkansas, connected his regiment with my remnants of two regiments, and remained fighting with me until about 12 or 1 o'clock. [*O.R.*, X, pt. 1, pp. 581–82.]

Report of Col. Ben. J. Hill, CSA, Fifth Tennessee Infantry, Cleburne's brigade, Hardee's Corps, Army of the Mississippi

At daylight Sunday morning we were ordered to advance with the balance of your brigade, the Sixth Mississippi . . . on my right and the Twenty-fourth Tennessee . . . on my left. We advanced some 3 miles, when our pickets commenced a sharp and lively skirmish. We continued to advance and drove them before us to within 500 yards of the Federal encampment. They opened a terrific fire upon our columns. A deep ravine, full of green briers and grape-vines, separated us from Colonel Thornton's [Sixth Mississippi] regiment. My right was exposed to a severe flank fire from a battery and from musketry and other small arms. We were at the foot of a long hill, upon which the enemy were hidden.

The Fifteenth Arkansas . . . was in advance of us and deployed as skirmishers, but was soon called in to sustain the Twenty-fourth Tennessee, on the left, which it performed gallantly and promptly. The firing was constant and continuous for half or three-quarters of an hour, when one of the aides of General *Beauregard* came to me and said the battery on the right [Taylor's battery] must be charged and silenced at all hazards. I gave the word and my brave boys promptly responded. . . . We charged, dispersed the enemy, and silenced the battery. As the enemy retreated my marksmen had better opportunity for trying their skill, and well did they improve it, as was proven by the number of the enemy who there fell. We continued on at double-quick for near a mile, crossing their first encampment, and formed line of battle at the foot of the next hill [Stop 17]. [*O.R.*, X, pt. 1, p. 587.]

Report of Maj. Ezra Taylor, USA, First Illinois Light Artillery, Chief of Artillery, Fifth Division, Army of the Tennessee

By instructions from the general [Sherman] commanding the division, the Morton Battery, Captain Behr commanding, was placed on the Purdy road, in rear of McDowell's brigade; Taylor's battery, Captain Barrett commanding, to the right and in advance of the chapel, on the road leading to Corinth; Capt. A. C. Waterhouse's battery near the left of the division. . . .

The enemy appearing in large masses, and opening a battery to the front and right of the two guns, advanced across . . . [the] Creek. I instructed Captain Waterhouse to retire the two guns to the position occupied by the rest of his battery. About . . . [this] time the enemy appeared in large force in the open field [Rhea Field] directly in front of the position of this battery, bearing aloft, as I supposed, the American flag, and their men and officers wearing uniforms so similar to ours that I hesitated to open fire on them until they passed into the woods, and were followed by other troops who wore a uniform not to be mistaken. I afterwards learned that the uniform jackets worn by these troops were black. As soon as I was certain as to the character of the troops I ordered the firing to commence, which was done in fine style and with excellent precision. After instructing the battery to be cool and watch all the movements of the enemy, who was throwing large forces into the timber on the left of its position, I went to the position occupied by Taylor's battery and ordered Captain Barrett to open fire with shell, which was done promptly, causing the enemy to take shelter in the timber, under cover of which he advanced to within 150 yards of the guns, when they opened a tremendous fire of musketry, accompanied by terrific yells, showing their evident desire to intimidate our men; but the only effect it had on the men of this battery was to cause them promptly to move their guns by hand to the front and pouring into them a shower of canister, causing both the yelling and the firing of the enemy to cease for a time.

In the meantime the enemy was pushing our force on the left of both of these batteries. . . . Seeing Waterhouse's battery limbering to the rear, and fearing the result of a too hasty retreat, I hastened to the position, and finding him retiring, I at once ordered him to unlimber and contest every foot of ground, while I sent a messenger to find another battery to come to their assistance. My order was promptly obeyed, and they were soon throwing canister among the enemy; but their bravery alone could not drive back the masses who were swarming around their left and pushing back the infantry and opening a flank fire of musketry and a battery, which they had succeeded in planting in the timber in front, they were compelled to retire under a galling fire, leaving three guns and their entire camp and garrison equipage on the field. . . .

. . . After five hours' hard fighting in these two positions . . . their ammunition became exhausted, and I instructed them to retire out of range and get a new supply, after which our section engaged the enemy for half an hour, driving him to the corner of the timber. [*O.R.*, X, pt. 1, pp. 273–74.]

Drive straight ahead (north) for 0.2 mile to Shiloh Church. Park at the church and walk across the road to Taylor's Battery. Face south—the direction the guns are pointing.

STOP 6A, SHILOH CHURCH

The surprised Union forces of Prentiss's and Sherman's divisions struggled to hold their positions as *Hardee's* three brigades and two of *Polk's* brigades charged into their disorganized position. Prentiss's units began to break, some of them moving to the rear. *Hardee's* losses, however, had been heavy, and *Bragg's* second wave of attackers began pushing into the fight, adding to the confusion.

Report of Brig. Gen. William T. Sherman, USA, Commanding Fifth Division, Army of the Tennessee

Shortly after 7 A.M., with my entire staff, I rode along a portion of our front, and when in the open field before

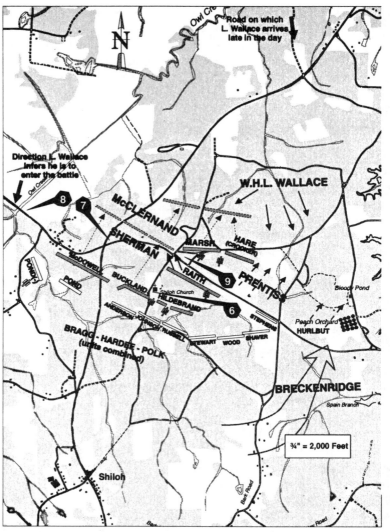

Shiloh Church (Stops 6–9).

Brig. Gen. William T. Sherman, Commander, Fifth Division, Army of the Tennessee. (U.S. Army Military History Institute)

Sherman's division became engaged along its line of camps, centered on Shiloh Church. The battery shown is Taylor's Battery. Note the openness of the terrain depicted by the artist. *(Frank Leslie's Illustrated Famous Leaders and Battle Scenes of the Civil War)*

Appler's regiment the enemy's pickets opened a brisk fire on my party killing my orderly. . . . The fire came from the bushes which line a small stream that rises in the field in front of Appler's camp and flows to the north along my whole front. This valley afforded the enemy a partial cover, but our men were so posted as to have a good fire at him as he crossed the valley and ascended the rising ground on our side.

About 8 A.M. I saw the glistening bayonets of heavy masses of infantry to our left front in the woods beyond the small stream . . . and became satisfied for the first time that the enemy designed a determined attack on our whole camp. All the regiments of my division were then in line of battle at their proper posts. I rode to Colonel Appler and ordered him to hold his ground at all hazards, as he held the left flank of our first line of battle. I informed him that he had a good battery on his right and strong supports to his rear. General McClernand had promptly responded to my request, and had sent me three regiments, which were posted to protect Waterhouse's battery and the left flank of my line.

The battle began by the enemy opening a battery in the woods to our front and throwing shells into our camp. Taylor's [Shiloh Church] and Waterhouse's [Rhea Field] batteries promptly responded, and I then observed heavy battalions of infantry passing obliquely to the left across the open field in Appler's front; also other columns advancing directly upon my division. Our infantry and artillery opened along the whole line and the battle became general. Other heavy masses of the enemy's forces kept passing across the field to our left and directing their course on General Prentiss, whose line of camps was almost parallel with the Tennessee River and about 2 miles back from it. Very soon the sound of musketry and artillery announced that General Prentiss was engaged, and about 9 A.M. I judged that he was falling back. About this time Appler's regiment broke in disorder, soon followed by fugitives from Mungen's regiment, and the enemy pressed forward on Waterhouse's battery, thereby exposed. . . . Although our left was thus turned and the enemy was pressing on the whole line, I deemed Shiloh so important that I remained by it, and renewed my orders to Colonels McDowell and Buckland to hold their ground, and we did hold those positions till about 10 o'clock A.M., when the enemy got his artillery to the rear of our left flank, and some change became absolutely necessary.

Two regiments of Hildebrand's brigade—Appler's and Mungen's—had already disappeared to the rear, and Hildebrand's own regiment was in disorder, and therefore I gave directions for Taylor's battery, still at Shiloh, to fall back as far as the Purdy and Hamburg road, and for McDowell and Buckland to adopt that road as their new line. [*O.R.*, X, pt. 1, pp. 249–50.]

Report of Capt. Samuel E. Barrett, USA, Battery B (Taylor's Battery), First Illinois Light Artillery, Sherman's Division, Army of the Tennessee

We were stationed near the outposts, and on the alarm being given, at about 7:30 o'clock on Sunday morning, the battery was promptly got in readiness, and in ten minutes thereafter commenced firing on the right of the log church, some hundred yards in front of General Sherman's headquarters, where the attack was made by the enemy in great force.

The enemy once charged on the battery, but were repulsed with great loss. The enemy, however, succeeded in turning our left flank, and, finding the battery in a critical condition, I

retired to the open field [¾ mile north of Shiloh Church] occupied by the First Brigade, First Division, and awaited orders,
which were soon received, to go into battery on the upper end
of the field. This movement was promptly executed, and we
engaged for two hours a rebel battery (masked) in the camp
of the Forty-fifth Regiment Illinois Infantry, suffering a loss of
one man killed and 3 wounded.

As the firing had been very rapid all the morning my supply of ammunition became exhausted, and I retired to an open
field some half mile in the rear, where, finding my baggage
wagons, I refilled my caissons and gun-limbers. I remained on
this field most of the day and the day following until about 4
o'clock P.M. when I was ordered to move forward and go into
battery near the point we occupied when the attack was made
on the preceding day. . . .

My camp and garrison equipage was almost totally ruined,
much of it being plundered and the remainder destroyed.
[*O.R.*, X, pt. 1, pp. 275–76.]

Report of Col. Ralph P. Buckland, USA, Commanding Fourth Brigade, Fifth Division, Army of the Tennessee

Between 6 and 7 o'clock on Sunday morning I was informed that our pickets were fired upon. I immediately gave
orders for forming the brigade on the color line, which was
promptly done. About this time I was informed that the pickets
were being driven in. I ordered the Forty-eighth Regiment,
Colonel Sullivan, to advance in support of the pickets, which
he did, but discovered that the enemy had advanced in force
to the creek, about 80 to 100 rods in front. I immediately
ordered the brigade to advance in line of battle.

We had marched about 30 to 40 rods when we discovered
the enemy, and opened fire upon him along the whole line,
which checked his advance and caused him to fall back. Discovering that he was pushing a column up a narrow ravine,
which extended from the left of the Seventy-second Regiment
to the flat at the creek, bearing somewhat to the right, I ordered the Seventy-second to change front, so as to form a line
parallel to the ravine extending down to the flat, Company B
forming an angle across the head of the ravine. In this position
our line was maintained for more than two hours under a

deadly fire from the enemy. Officers and men behaved with great coolness and bravery, keeping up a constant stream of fire upon the enemy. He several times recoiled and rallied, but did not advance his line after the action commenced until we were ordered to fall back upon the Purdy road, which we did in good order. . . .

We formed a line again on the Purdy road, but the fleeing mass from the left broke through our lines, and many of our men caught the infection and fled with the crowd. Colonel Cockerill became separated from Colonel Sullivan and myself and was afterwards engaged with part of his command at McClernand's camp. Colonel Sullivan and myself kept together and made every effort to rally our men, but with very poor success. They had become scattered in all directions. We were borne considerably to the left, but finally succeeded in forming a line and had a short engagement with the enemy, who made his appearance soon after our line was formed. The enemy fell back, and we proceeded to the road where you found us. At this point I was joined by Colonel Cockerill, and we there formed line of battle and slept on our arms Sunday night. [*O.R.*, X, pt. 1, pp. 266–67.]

Walk 150 yards south in the direction the artillery pieces are pointing to the open field on the right. Cross the field to the Tennessee Monument.

STOP 6B, TENNESSEE MONUMENT

Report of Col. William B. Bate, CSA, Second Tennessee Infantry, Reorganized and Assigned to Second Brigade, Third Corps, Army of the Mississippi

The regiment . . . on the morning of the 5th, at 10 o'clock, after a severe night march, assumed position in General *Hardee's* line of battle upon the left of your brigade, 400 yards in the rear, with instructions to observe that relative position (either in motion or stationary) to the left wing of General *Hardee's* line, so as to protect it against any movement of the enemy in that direction. We remained at the post assigned until the general advance early Sunday morning, when we moved in conformity to the order of the day previous.

An idealized lithograph entitled "Charge of General Grant." Although often forward with front line commanders throughout the first day's fighting, Grant did *not* lead a charge against the attacking Confederates, leaving the tactical operations to his subordinate commanders. (U.S. Army Military History Institute)

On approaching the hill near the encampment of the enemy, where the left wing, which I was ordered to protect, was engaged, I found the skirmishers which had previously been thrown out in front and on our left . . . driven in, and receiving orders . . . to advance, I did so, when the firing became general both in front and to the left of us, to which we replied persistently until the enemy was driven back from his position. The charge of my regiment at this point was most gallantly done, but resulted in a serious loss of my men . . . under the enemy's crossfire. . . .

Being thus cut up, I reformed the regiment about 40 yards in rear of our line of battle and reorganized (some companies being without officers) in the best and most rapid manner. . . . Having received no further orders, I moved the regiment to the right and then to the front, with the view of taking a battery which was then playing upon us. Having made a hasty reconnaissance in person of our front and left, I moved the regiment briskly (and they did it in fine style) to the charge, when I received a severe wound in the left leg.

In the hurry I had neglected to communicate to Lieutenant-Colonel *Goodall* the result of my reconnaissance and purpose of movement, he being at the time on the right of the regiment and I on its left. When [I was] wounded, Colonel *Goodall* immediately took command of the regiment and very properly halted and held it in position until he could communicate with our commanders. . . . Colonel *Goodall* was cool, courageous, and efficient on the field, and proved his services to be most invaluable. [*O.R.*, X, pt. 1, p. 585.]

Walk back to the car and turn right (north) out of the parking lot at Shiloh Church. Drive 0.3 mile to the intersection where the Raith Monument is located. Turn left for 0.4 mile to the McDowell's Headquarters marker on the right side of the road. Stop short of the stop sign and pull off onto the shoulder. Stand with the McDowell's Headquarters marker to your back. You are looking south into the attacking Confederates.

STOP 7, McDOWELL'S HEADQUARTERS

As the Confederates drove Sherman's troops from the area around Shiloh Church, he was forced to take decisive action to restore the situation. He ordered his brigades to withdraw to the Purdy-Hamburg Road, where you are now located. Col. John A. McDowell, the right flank brigade of the division, was ordered to fall back on line with Buckland's regiments withdrawing from the vicinity of Shiloh Church. There was considerable confusion while Sherman's forces endeavored to establish a new line. Wounded in the hand during the initial skirmish, Sherman was in the thick of the fighting throughout the morning, with at least three horses shot out from under him and his enlisted orderly killed.

Meanwhile, other actions were occurring elsewhere on the battlefield. In the center of the line (vicinity Stop 18, Hornets' Nest) remnants of the divisions of Prentiss, W. H. L. Wallace, and Hurlbut were working to establish a defensive line. Prentiss fell back through Wallace's and Hurlbut's advancing divisions, reorganized his five to six hundred troops, and was joined by the Twenty-third Missouri Infantry from Pittsburg Landing. He then advanced to rejoin Wallace and Hurlbut in the Hornets' Nest. On the east flank near the Tennessee River, Col. David Stuart's small brigade desperately fought to defend its isolated position against the Confederate right.

These actions will be covered later, but it is necessary to understand that they were happening at the same time that Sherman's and McClernand's brigades on the Union right flank were engaged.

Report of Brig. Gen. William T. Sherman (continued)

I rode across the angle and met Behr's battery at the crossroads, and ordered it immediately to unlimber and come into battery, action right. Captain Behr gave the order, but he was almost immediately shot from his horse, when the drivers and gunners fled in disorder, carrying off the caissons and abandoning five of the six guns without firing a shot. The enemy pressed on, gaining this battery, and we were again forced to choose a new line of defense. Hildebrand's brigade had substantially disappeared from the field, though he himself bravely remained. McDowell's and Buckland's brigades still retained their organization, and were conducted by my aides so as to join on General McClernand's right, thus abandoning my original camps and line.

This was about 10:30 A.M., at which time the enemy had made a furious attack on General McClernand's whole front. Finding him pressed, I moved McDowell's brigade directly against the left flank of the enemy, forced him back some distance, and then directed the men to avail themselves of every cover—trees, fallen timber, and a wooded valley to our right. We held this position for four long hours, sometimes gaining and at other times losing ground, General McClernand and myself acting in perfect concert and struggling to maintain this line.

While we were so hardly pressed two Iowa regiments [Fifteenth and Sixteenthth Iowa] approached from the rear, but could not be brought up to the severe fire that was raging in our front, and General Grant, who visited us on that ground, will remember our situation about 3 P.M; but about 4 P.M. it was evident that Hurlbut's line had been driven back to the river, and knowing that General [Lew] Wallace was coming from Crump's Landing with re-enforcements, General McClernand and I, on consultation, selected a new line of defense, with its right covering the bridge by which General Wallace had to approach. We fell back as well as we could, gathering, in addition to our own, such scattered forces as we could find, and formed a new line. . . .

My division was made up of remnants perfectly new, nearly all having received their muskets for the first time at Paducah. None of them had ever been under fire or beheld heavy columns of an enemy bearing down on them as they did on us. . . . They knew nothing of the value of combination and organization. When individual fears seized them the first impulse was to get away. To expect of them the coolness and steadiness of older troops would be wrong. [*O.R.*, X, pt. 1, p. 250.]

Report of Col. John A. McDowell, USA, Sixth Iowa Infantry, First Brigade, Fifth Division, Army of the Tennessee

At the first alarm of the enemy's attack . . . the line of the First Brigade was formed, as per previous orders, to hold the Purdy road and the right front. Two companies of the Sixth Iowa were detached to defend the bridge crossing Owl Creek [Stop 8] and one of the 12-pounder howitzers of the Morton Battery placed to command the crossing on the hill at the right of our encampment.

About 8 o'clock the line was thrown forward to the brow of the hill, and the remaining guns of the Morton battery brought up to command the several openings to the front, and from this position several shots were fired on the enemy's masses, not then formed into line, and the Fortieth Illinois Infantry were ordered forward and to the left to support the right of the Fourth Brigade, in which position they became warmly engaged, when the order came to fall back to the Purdy road.

This was accomplished with difficulty, from the extended front of our line, at that time three-quarters of a mile in length, on and over a broken and wooded surface, and at the time when the only passable (the main) road was filled by the teams of the brigade. Yet the change of position and front was just accomplished when the order to send the battery to the center was received. The five guns were immediately dispatched. The other, from the position of guarding the bridge, not coming up in time, remained with the brigade, as the passage by the road had in the meantime been cut off.

In this position and front a few rounds were exchanged, and the skirmishers were again thrown forward. When it was known that we were cut off from the center by the enemy in force on the center and across the road and by a large force in the old field on our left and their cavalry to the left and rear, the howitzer was placed on our left front under cover, and the enemy driven from the field by a few discharges of canister. Soon after, at about 10 o'clock, Major Sanger brought the order to move to the center and rear. This was accomplished as soon as possible under the annoyance of the enemy's skirmishers. Here our front was again changed to the former front of the general line of engagement. [*O.R.*, X, pt. 1, pp. 254–55.]

Report of Capt. John Williams, USA, Sixth Iowa Infantry, First Brigade, Fifth Division, Army of the Tennessee

On Sunday morning, when the attack was made on General Grant's center, the regiment was immediately brought into line of battle, and was then moved about 50 yards to the front along the edge of the woods. Company I was thrown out as skirmishers, and Companies E and G were moved to the left and front of our line to support a battery just placed there. We were in this position for more than two hours, when we were ordered to fall back to the rear of our camp on the Purdy road.

The battle at this time was raging fiercely in the center and extending gradually to the right. The line was slowly yielding to a vastly superior force, and it now became evident that we must change our position or be entirely cut off from the rest of the army. The regiment then marched by the left flank about 600 yards; crossed an open field about 150 yards wide; took a position in the edge of the woods, and formed a new line of battle, which was again succeeded by another line nearly perpendicular to the former, the right resting close to the Purdy road.

It was here Lieutenants Halliday and Grimes were wounded and carried from the field . . . [and] that Companies D and K, on picket duty at Owl Creek, joined the regiment by a circuitous route, the enemy having already got between them and the regiment.

The regiment did not remain here long, however, but moved by the left flank in an easterly direction about half a mile, over a broken and open field, and again entered the woods. A new line was formed, and the regiment moved forward to meet the advancing foe. The line of battle—at this time diagonal to the enemy's—was immediately changed to front them, and it was here that the regiment withstood a shower of leaden hail and bullets which now was pouring in upon it with deadly effect. Notwithstanding a vastly superior force and with no support, the regiment gallantly maintained this position for more than two hours, and when it became apparent that no succor was coming to it, and after the enemy had already turned our right flank and began pouring a galling cross-fire upon it, the regiment was ordered to retire. It fell back in good order and was assigned to the support of batteries near the river. . . .

In regard to the bravery, coolness, and intrepidity of both officers and men too much cannot be said. Where all did so well to particularize would seem invidious; . . . the officers, with one or two exceptions, are deserving of the highest praise. The men were at all times cool and as free from fear or confusion as if they were on dress parade.

The list of casualties . . . fully attests the severity of the contest.

Killed	64
Wounded	100
Missing	47
Total	211

Total number engaged less than 650.*
[*O.R.*, X, pt. 1, pp. 256–57.]

Logically and chronologically, you should next drive to Owl Creek, approximately 0.5 mile west of where you are now, at McDowell's Headquarters. Because the National Park Service has closed off the Purdy-Hamburg Road access to the Shiloh Battle-

---

*Final figures show 183 casualties (*O.R.*, X, pt. 1, p. 103).

field Park, it is easiest to explain the significance of the Purdy
Road/Owl Creek location from the present site.

Should you desire to see the area, you will need to return to
the entrance/exit to Shiloh Battlefield Park. Turn left on Route
22 and drive 1.8 miles. Turn right on Purdy Road and drive 0.5
mile. Stop just before crossing the drainage canal ditch and pull
off the road. Read the Stop 8 readings.

STOP 8, OWL CREEK

(To be read at Stop 7 or at optional Stop 8 [off the battlefield
park])

Owl Creek bounded the western portion of the battlefield. Today it is a modern canal, but in 1862 it was a meandering stream
in flood and therefore an unfordable obstacle. For that reason
Grant anchored his right flank here.

The Owl Creek/Purdy Road area could have been the site of a
decisive event in the battle. Grant's only reserve, Brig. Gen. Lew
Wallace's veteran division, was at Crump's Landing, approximately
6 miles to the north of Pittsburg Landing. Wallace (who later wrote
the novel *Ben Hur*) and some of his staff contended that they were
ordered to join the right flank of the Union army in this vicinity
(the intersection of Purdy Road and Owl Creek).

Grant's staff officers, on the other hand, claimed that Wallace
had been ordered to move south to Pittsburg Landing, using the
shortest route. This would have brought his six thousand experi-
enced soldiers onto the battlefield where and when they were badly
needed. For reasons that have become the subject of great controversy, Wallace's division marched and countermarched, causing his
command to miss the entire first day of battle. It was dark by the
time they reached the Union final defensive line (Stop 24).

Narrative of Gen. U. S. Grant, USA, Commanding Army of the Tennessee

On reaching the front . . . about eight A.M. [on April 6], I
found that the attack on Pittsburg was unmistakable, and that
nothing more than a small guard to protect our transports and
stores was needed at Crump's [Landing]. Captain Baxter, a
quartermaster on my staff, was accordingly directed to go back
and order General [Lewis] Wallace to march [from Crump's]

GENERAL LEW WALLACE.

Maj. Gen. Lew Wallace, Commander, Third Division, Army of the Tennessee. (U.S. Army Military History Institute)

immediately to Pittsburg [Landing] by the road nearest t[h]e river. Captain Baxter made a memorandum of this order.

About one P.M., not hearing from Wallace and being muc[h] in need of reinforcements, I sent two more of my staff, Colon[el] McPherson and Captain Rowley, to bring him up with his di[vi]sion. They reported finding him marching towards Pur[dy,] Bethel, or some point west from the river, and farther fro[m] Pittsburg by several miles than when he started. The road fro[m] his first position to Pittsburg Landing was direct and near t[he] river. Between the two points a bridge had been built acr[oss] Snake Creek by our troops, at which Wallace's command h[ad] assisted, expressly to enable the troops at the two places [to] support each other in case of need. Wallace did not arrive [in] time to take part in the first day's fight.

General Wallace has since claimed that the order delivere[d] to him by Captain Baxter was simply to join the right of t[he] army, and that the road over which he marched would ha[ve] taken him to the road from Pittsburg to Purdy where it cross[es] Owl Creek on the right of Sherman; but this is not where [I] had ordered him nor where I wanted him to go.

I never could see . . . why any order was necessary furth[er] than to direct him to come to Pittsburg Landing, without spe[ci]fying by what route. His was one of three veteran divisions th[at] had been in battle and its absence was severely felt. Later [in] the war General Wallace would not have made the mistake th[at] he committed on the 6th of April 1862.

I presume his idea was that by taking the route he did [he] would be able to come around on the flank or rear of t[he] enemy, and thus perform an act of heroism that would r[e]bound to the credit of his command, as well as to the bene[fit] of his country. [*Memoirs,* II: 336–38.]

Report of Maj. Gen. Lewis Wallace, USA, Commanding Third Division, Army of the Tennessee

Sunday morning, 6th instant, my brigades, three in nu[m]ber, were encamped, the first at Crump's Landing, the seco[nd] 2 miles from that Landing, the third at Adamsville, 2½ mi[les] farther out on the road to Purdy. . . . Hearing heavy and co[n]tinuous cannonading in the direction of Pittsburg Landi[ng] early Sunday morning, I inferred a general battle, and, in a[n] ticipation of an order from General Grant to join him at that place, had the equipage of the several brigades loaded in wagons for instant removal to my first camp on the river. The First and Third brigades were also ordered to concentrate at the camp of the Second, from which proceeded the nearest and most practicable road to the scene of battle.

At 11:30 o'clock the anticipated order arrived, directing me to come up and take position on the right of the army and form my line of battle at a right angle with the river. As it also directed me to leave a force to prevent surprise at Crump's Landing, the Fifty-sixth Ohio and Sixty-eighth Ohio regiments were detached for that purpose. . . .

Selecting a road that led directly to the right of the lines as they were established around Pittsburg Landing on Sunday morning, my column started immediately, the distance being about six miles. The cannonading, distinctly audible, quickened the steps of the men. Snake Creek, difficult of passage at all times, on account of its steep banks and swampy bottoms, ran between me and the point of junction. Short way from it Captain Rowley, from General Grant, and attached to his staff, overtook me. From him I learned that our lines had been beaten back; that the right, to which I was proceeding, was then fighting close to the river, and that the road pursued would take me in the enemy's rear, where, in the unfortunate condition of the battle, my command was in danger of being entirely cut off.

It seemed, on his representation, most prudent to carry the column across what is called the "River road," which, following the windings of the Tennessee bottoms, crossed Snake Creek by a good bridge close to Pittsburg Landing. This movement occasioned a counter march, which delayed my junction with the main army until a little after night fall. The information brought me by Captain Rowley was confirmed by Colonel McPherson and Captain Rawlins, also of the general's staff, who came up while I was crossing to the River road. About 1 o'clock at night my brigades and batteries were disposed, forming the extreme right, and ready for battle. [O.R., X, pt. 1, pp. 169–70.]

Major and Aide-de-Camp W. R. Rowley to Col. John A. Rawlins, Assistant Adjutant-General, April 4, 1863

I was an aide-de-camp on the staff of General U. S. Grant, with the rank of captain, and on the morning of the 6th of April I accompanied the general, together with the other members of his staff, from Savannah to Pittsburg Landing. When the steamer upon which we were embarked arrived near to Crump's Landing General Grant directed that it should be run close in to the shore, as he wished to communicate with General Wallace, who was standing upon the commissary boat lying at that place. General Grant called to General Wallace, saying, "General, you will get your troops under arms *immediately,* and have them ready to move at a moment's notice." General Wallace replied that it should be done, adding (I think) that the necessary orders had already been given. This was between the hours of 7 and 8 o'clock A.M. We passed on up the river, meeting the steamer *Warner,* which had been sent by General W. H. L. Wallace (as I understood) with a messenger to inform General Grant that a battle has been commenced. The *Warner* rounded to and followed us back to Pittsburg Landing.

Upon reaching the Landing General Grant immediately mounted his horse and rode upon the bank, and after conversing a moment with some officers turned to Captain Baxter assistant quartermaster, and ordered him to proceed *immediately* to Crump's Landing, and direct General Wallace to march with his division up the river and into the field on the right of our line as rapidly as possible.

This order was given to Captain Baxter about the hour of 8 o'clock. I think not later than that. We immediately rode to the front. At about 11 o'clock General Grant expressed considerable solicitude at the non-appearance of General Wallace and sent an orderly to the extreme right to see if he could see anything of him, remarking that it could not *possibly* be many minutes before he would arrive.

Shortly after the hour of 12 o'clock m. [noon], as we were riding towards the right of the line, a cavalry officer rode up and reported to General Grant, stating that General Wallace has positively refused to come up unless he should receive *written* orders. After hearing the report General Grant turned to me, saying, "Captain, you will proceed to Crump's Landing and say to General Wallace that it is my orders that he bring his division up *at once,* coming up by the River road, crossing Snake Creek on the bridge (which General Sherman would protect), and form his division on the extreme right, when he would receive further orders; and say to him that it is *important* that he should make haste." Adding, "It has just been reported to me that he has refused to come up unless he receives a *written* order. If he should require a written order of you, you will give him one," at the same time asking me if I had writing materials in my haversack. I started at once, when the general called to me again, saying, "You will take with you the captain (referring to the cavalry officer before mentioned, who was still sitting there on his horse—his name I do not recollect), and two orderlies, and see that you do not spare horse flesh." This was at the hour of 12:30 o'clock m. [noon], as near as I can recollect.

I proceeded at once to General Wallace's camp, back of Crump's Landing, and being well mounted, it took me but a short time to reach it. Upon arriving there I found no signs of a camp, except one baggage wagon that was just leaving. I inquired of the driver as to where General Wallace and his troops were; he replied that they had gone up to the fight. I inquired what road they took; to which he replied by pointing to a road, which I understand to be the Purdy road.

While sitting there upon my horse I could hear the firing upon the battle-field quite distinctly. I then took the road pointed out by the teamster and rode a distance of between 5 and 6 miles, as I judged, when I came up with the rear of General Wallace's division; they were at a rest, sitting on each side of the road, some with their arms stacked in the middle of the road. I passed the entire division (except the cavalry), all being at a halt. When I reached the head of the column I found General Wallace sitting upon his horse, surrounded by his staff, some of whom were dismounted and holding their horses by the bridles.

I rode up to General Wallace and communicated to him General Grant's orders as I had received them, and then told him that it had been reported to him (i.e., General Grant) that he had refused to march without written orders; at which he seemed quite indignant, saying that it was a "damned lie!" that he had never refused to go without a written order, in proof

of which he said, "Here you find me on the road." To which I
replied that I had certainly found him on *a* road, but I hardly
thought it the road to Pittsburg Landing. It certainly was not
the road that I had come down from there on, and that I had
traveled farther since I had left his camp than I had in coming
from the battle-field to the camp, and judging from the sound
of the firing, we were still a long distance from the battle-field.
To which the general replied that this was the road his cavalry
had brought him, and the *only road* he knew anything about.
He then ordered one of his aides to ride ahead and bring
the cavalry back. I then asked him where this road came into
Pittsburg Landing; to which he replied that it crossed the creek
at a mill (I think he called it Veal's Mill) and intersected the
Corinth and Pittsburg Landing road in front of where General
McClernand's camp was. I then told him that I thought it would
be impossible for him to get in upon that road, as the enemy
now had possession of those camps, and that our line of battle
was to the rear of them. At this moment his cavalry came back,
and General Wallace rode forward to communicate with them.
When he came back he remarked that it was true that the
enemy was between us and our army; that the cavalry had been
close enough to hear the musketry. The order was then given
to counter-march; upon which I remarked to General Wallace
that I would ride on and inform General Grant that he was
coming; to which he replied, "No, captain; I shall be obliged
to keep you with me to act as guide, as none of us know the
River road you speak of." I accordingly remained.

The march toward the old camp was continued to a point
about one-half mile north of it, where the troops filed to the
right and came into the River road. At the point of filing off
we were met by Lieutenant-Colonel (now Major-General) Mc-
Pherson and Major Rawlins, members of General Grant's staff,
who had also come to look after General Wallace. The march
was continued up the River road until the battlefield was
reached, which was just as it was getting dark and after the
fighting for the day was over.

Of the character of the march after I overtook General
Wallace I can only say that to *me* it appeared intolerably slow,
resembling more a reconnaissance in the face of an enemy
than a forced march to relieve a hard-pressed army. So strongly
did this impression take hold of my mind, that I took the liberty

of repeating to General Wallace that part of General Grant's order enjoining haste. The same idea seemed to have taken possession of the minds of Colonel McPherson and Major Rawlins, as on the march from the camp to the battle-field Major Rawlins on several occasions rode back for the purpose of trying to hurry up the troops and to ascertain what was the cause of the delay. I have no means of judging as to what distance General Wallace was from the battle-field when I found him, except that I could hear the firing much more distinctly at the camp he had left than I could at the point where I found him. [*O.R.*, X, pt. 1, pp. 178–80.]

Both sides of this controversy are presented in Appendix II.

Turn your car around, and drive back the same way you came (east) for 0.5 mile to a stop sign at an intersection. Turn left and park off the road on the shoulder near the Raith Monument. Face toward the rear of your car (south). In the distance you can see Shiloh cemetery. Shiloh Church (Stop 6) is just south of the cemetery.

STOP 9, RAITH MONUMENT

Sherman's division had been severely handled in the vicinity of Shiloh Church. His leftmost brigade, under Colonel Hildebrand, had disintegrated, and many of its troops were running back to Pittsburg Landing. The remainder of the division had fallen back along a line just north of your location.

At this position Sherman's troops fell into a loose defensive line with Maj. Gen. John A. McClernand's division. McClernand's Third Brigade (Raith) was somewhat forward of the rest of the division and was ordered to fall back into line. On the Third Brigade's right was Buckland's weakened brigade of Sherman's division. Sherman's (and the Union's) right flank brigade, Col. John A. McDowell commanding, was beyond Buckland.

The Confederates continued to push against the Union line as it attempted to form. The Southern units were intermingled to an extent from the earlier fighting around Shiloh Church (see map to understand how the various Confederate corps were already mixed together), but the commanders maintained their forward momentum, trying to overwhelm Union units before these could

The Line of Battle

Watercolor showing action in McClernand's division area in the first da of the battle. The Eleventh Illinois was part of the Second Brigade (McClernand's First Division. (U.S. Army Military History Institute)

organize a solid defensive position. The fighting was intense, an casualties were heavy.

Report of Lieut. Abram H. Ryan, USA, Seventeenth Illinois Infantry, Acting Adjutant-General, Third Brigad First Division, Army of the Tennessee

On the morning of the 6th . . . I was sent for by Colon Rearden, . . . commanding brigade. Upon reporting to him h stated that owing to ill-health he was unable to command th brigade. While conversing with him heavy firing was heard i the front and on our left. Colonel Rearden ordered me t report to Colonel Raith, Forty-third Regiment Illinois Volur teer Infantry (next senior officer of the brigade), his condition and request him to assume command, and then to report to Major-General McClernand the condition of the brigade. These orders were complied with.

On rejoining the brigade it was advanced to the encampment of General Sherman's division. When all was ready for action I rode to the front, near Taylor's battery, and found nothing intervening between us and the enemy except a line of skirmishers and Taylor's battery. While reconnoitering my horse received a ball through the neck, forcing me back to the main line. I reported to Captain Barrett, commanding battery, that his [infantry] support had left him, and, pointing out the position of the brigade, told him to call upon it if hard pressed.

Returning to the brigade I reported to Colonel Raith the condition of affairs, who directed me to find the position of the Second Brigade, which I found on our left and rear, commanded by Colonel Marsh, of the Twentieth Regiment Illinois Volunteer Infantry, and with it Major-General McClernand, supervising its movements. On reporting to him he ordered the Third Brigade to fall back and form on the right of the Second. Returning to the brigade, and not finding Colonel Raith, I gave the necessary orders for the movement. The right of the brigade retained its position, the left falling back in good order, though fighting the enemy step by step. They understood what the movement was for, and executed it accordingly.

Upon reaching the ground that the Second Brigade had occupied we discovered that it had changed its position. We, however, retained the position, hotly pressed by the enemy, till in danger of being flanked on the left, Colonel Raith being engaged in another portion of the field. Seeing no support, I gave the necessary orders and fell back, fighting the enemy step by step, and formed on a line with some troops in our rear. Major Schwartz here requested that a portion of the brigade be detached to support his battery. The Seventeenth Illinois Regiment was detailed for that purpose, and remained until the battery limbered up and changed position. A few minutes afterward Colonel Raith fell mortally wounded. I accompanied him a short distance to receive orders, etc.

When I returned the Twenty-ninth and Forty-ninth Regiments had fallen to the rear, having expended their ammunition. The remainder of the brigade continued the fight until their ammunition gave out likewise, when they were ordered to the rear for a new supply. On gaining the encampment of the First Brigade, First Division, Lieutenant _____ [name not given] of Taylor's battery requested a detail of men to assist in working the battery, many of his own men having fallen. I immediately detailed 20 men from the Seventeenth Illinois Regiment, and reported them to Captain Barrett, commanding battery. Searching through the encampment of the Eighth Illinois Regiment, I found ammunition and carried it to the brigade, but it proved to be of a wrong caliber. Learning that it could be used by the Eleventh Regiment Illinois Volunteer Infantry, I turned it over to Colonel Ransom, commanding.

After waiting a while, and no ammunition coming up, I fell back to meet the train. As I could do no further good remaining with the train, I rode forward to hurry up ammunition. Meeting with Lieut. C. C. Williams, brigade quartermaster, he gallantly volunteered to bring forward a train, designating a field where to meet the regiments.

When I returned I found that the regiments had been separated. Halting the advance, I eventually succeeded in getting the Seventeenth, Forty-third, and Forty-ninth Regiments into line, when Quartermaster Williams returned with the ammunition train, under the direction of Lieutenant Jones, ordnance officer, First Division, who, supplying the men with whatever was necessary, gallantly moved with his train to the front. . . .

I cannot close this report . . . without referring to some of the officers and men in this brigade. To Colonel Raith . . . who fell early in the action, while gallantly and bravely discharging the duties of brigade commander . . . we cannot but admire the heroism and patriotism always exhibited by him, even to the shedding of his last drop of blood upon the altar of his adopted country. . . .

The brigade went into action with . . . about 1,650 men; reported loss, killed, wounded, and missing, 834 men.* [*O.R.*, X, pt. 1, pp. 139–40.]

---

*Final returns adjust this figure to 535 (*O.R.*, X, pt. 1, p. 100).

Report of Lieut. Col. Adolph Engelmann, USA, Forty-third Illinois Volunteer Infantry, Third Brigade, First Division, Army of the Tennessee

On Sunday morning . . . at the request of Col. J. Raith then commanding the regiment, I called upon General McClernand for permission to fire off the guns of our men, which were still loaded from the evening of April 4, when the pieces had been loaded in expectation of an attack by the enemy. The permission was granted, but the general directed that we should keep a sharp lookout for any engagement in front of us, and that in case anything be heard he be instantly informed of it.

But two of our companies had discharged their guns when the colonel, hearing the distant report of fire-arms, ordered firing to cease and the regiment to get ready for action, and also directed me to report the facts to General McClernand. The general then sent me to Colonel Rearden, commanding Third Brigade, with orders for him to hold the brigade in readiness for action. Colonel Rearden, however, was ill, and requested me to inform Colonel Raith that he, being the next oldest and only colonel in the brigade now present, should assume command. In the meantime Colonel Raith had formed the Forty-third Regiment, the command of which now devolved upon me, whilst Colonel Raith, without any aides or even any mounted orderlies to assist him, found himself suddenly in command of a brigade, of which as yet but one regiment had got ready for the engagement, and the enemy already within a few hundred yards of our lines, but still concealed by the forest and steadily driving our own troops in front of us toward our lines. . . .

I proceeded to the encampment of the Forty-ninth Regiment Illinois Volunteers . . . some distance to our left, with orders for that regiment to turn out instantly, brisk firing being then heard within a short distance from its color line, but those from whom it proceeded still concealed by the forest. My orders to turn out were met by the inquiry, "For what purpose?" And to my response, "That it was to meet the enemy which was engaged with our troops but a short distance in front," they said that the firing then heard was none other than our own men firing off their pieces. The infatuation that no enemy was about was so general that I was also to a great extent affected by it, and [I] rode forward in the direction from which the firing proceeded to obtain certainty. Not more than 200 yards in front of the Forty-ninth I came upon our own lines, then briskly engaged with the enemy. Hastening back to the Forty-ninth, I found that as yet little heed had been given to my previous orders to turn out. Upon communicating these facts to the officers that regiment was speedily paraded, but only in time to find itself pressed hard in front and flanked on the left by vastly superior numbers. . . .

Having thoroughly aroused the Forty-ninth, I hastened back to my own regiment. The color line immediately in front of the encampment being but a poor position to await the enemy in, the regiment was ordered about 100 yards forward, where it took a position sheltered by the brow of a hill and to the left of a battery stationed on the right [Waterhouse] and that distance to the front of our encampment. The two flank companies were now thrown out as skirmishers forward and to the left of our lines, the enemy crowding upon us in apparently great numbers from that direction. The enemy still advancing, so that we would soon have been exposed to a raking flank fire from the left, and now two right companies (F and D) were detached, to remain as a support of the battery.

At this time large numbers of our own troops belonging to the divisions [of] Sherman and Prentiss, heretofore in front of us, retired through our lines, and it was impossible to induce them to rally upon us, while the remaining companies changed direction on the eighth company to the rear, and firing by the rear rank for some time, gallantly withstood a vastly superior force of the enemy.

Being here compelled to give way by the enemy passing beyond our right and left flanks and crowding upon us in front, we fell back upon the battery. This having exhausted its ammunition and lost several of its horses, being exposed to a galling fire both from large masses of infantry and two of the enemy's batteries—one placed in position near the [Shiloh] meeting-house and the other near the encampment of the Forty-ninth—withdrew, leaving two of its pieces on the field, the efforts of our men to draw them away by hand proved unavailing on the soft and ascending ground. The enemy steadily advancing and the position being very unfavorable for infantry, the brigade, which here had become united, fell back toward the road [Purdy Road] leading east and west through the encampment of the First Division. The brigade was rallied by its gallant commander, Col. Julius Raith, and formed in support of several pieces of Schwartz's battery, here placed in position, and after a short pause the enemy again pressed upon us in vastly superior numbers. Here Major Schwartz was wounded and Colonel Raith received a Minie ball through his right thigh.

The resistance here for some time was desperate, the [infantry] support to the right of the battery having fallen back and the artillerists being also compelled to abandon their pieces. However, the Forty-third Regiment maintained its position to the left of the battery for some time, till the enemy's fire, flanking from the right, compelled it again to fall back. Here again some of the men assisted Lieutenant Nispel, of Schwartz's battery, in the attempt to take off one of the pieces by hand, but were again defeated by the softness of the soil, after having dragged it a distance of about a quarter of a mile, Colonel Raith having been given in charge of 4 men to carry him from the field, suffering intensely, the bone being completely shattered. After being carried a short distance, overcome by pain, he insisted on being left on the field, telling the men that they could be of more service to the regiment in the ranks than carrying off a disabled officer. At his urgent entreaties and commands they left him, and Colonel Raith laid thus exposed through the entire day and stormy night that followed, with no other assistance than was given him by the passing enemy, who on the following morning carried him into a tent, from which some hours afterward, the position having again fallen into our possession, he was removed to the river bank, and on Sunday morning into the steamer *Hannibal,* where his leg was amputated on Wednesday morning; but he was too much exhausted from exposure and loss of blood, and died on Friday evening. . . . In him the army lost one of its bravest officers.

Having fallen back through the timber in front of the encampment of the First Division . . . [the regiment] again formed in line forward of and to the right of General Oglesby's headquarters. The ammunition of the regiment being almost completely exhausted, I sent one of the officers, with several men, to procure a supply, but before that officer could rejoin us the regiment was ordered forward by Captain Hammond, of General Sherman's staff, and advanced in double-quick past the battery planted in front of General Oglesby's encampment. Being placed in the center of the line of attack, it advanced steadily and fearlessly upon the enemy's batteries, then planted near General McClernand's headquarters. Within a short distance of the enemy the regiments to our right and left came to a halt and opened their fire. The Forty-third still advanced closer upon the enemy, but reduced in numbers, and its supports having come to a halt, it too had to stop, it being impossible for it to advance alone on the dense masses in front.

The ammunition now being entirely exhausted, the men gathered a scant supply from the killed and wounded of the enemy, who here covered the ground thickly. The troops of the enemy opposed to us having been armed with the Enfield rifle, their ammunition being of English make and excellent quality, it could be used in our muskets. The men being cheered on by General McClernand, who was present in the thickest of the fight, for a long period maintained a fearful contest, that cost great numbers on both sides. Our lines again giving way, the regiment retired down the branch on which the conflict had raged, and in the open field below again formed on the right of the Twentieth Illinois Regiment.

Being altogether out of ammunition, I again sent for a supply, but none being found, and the supply which had been promised . . . failing to arrive, we were again compelled to retire as the enemy advanced. We now fell back by degrees, and a new line being formed, we found ourselves posted between the Forty-sixth Illinois and Thirteenth Missouri, our position being midway between the encampments of the Forty-sixth and Ninth Illinois [the vicinity of Stop 23]. We here succeeded in getting a fresh supply of ammunition. The men, totally exhausted, lay heedless to the shower of shot and shell that passed over their heads. In this position we passed the night. [*O.R.*, X, pt. 1, pp. 143–45.]

Drive straight ahead (north) for 0.3 mile and turn left onto a small loop road at Indiana monument. Park on the shoulder beside the Confederate artillery piece from Bankhead's Battery. Look to the left (south) down the road toward the Raith Monument (Stop 9).

STOP 10, McCLERNAND'S BATTLE

The three Confederate corps of *Hardee*, *Bragg*, and *Polk* had by this time become inextricably intermingled in the thick broken terrain over which they had moved and attacked the Union forces. The Confederate corps had broken down, and the generals had lost contact with many of the units. Gen. Albert S. *Johnston* was forward in the thick of combat on the far right, leaving *Beauregard* and his staff officers to try to coordinate different parts of the battlefield. Confederate units by now were scattered all over the area, many waiting for their orders.

Prentiss's remnants joined with elements from W. H. L. Wallace's and Hurlbut's divisions along a wagon road later called the Hornets' Nest. On the Union left flank, Stuart's lone brigade had been compelled to withdraw. Maj. Gen. John A. McClernand's division now faced the powerful, if disjointed, Confederate attack falling against his position on the Union right. Obviously he himself could not see all of the activities described in his report (following). The terrain forced him to rely on reports of his subordinates.

Report of Maj. Gen. John A. McClernand, USA, Commanding First Division, Army of the Tennessee

Early on the morning . . . of the 6th of April, hearing sharp firing at short intervals on my left and front, in the direction of Sherman's and Prentiss' divisions, I sent a messenger to General Sherman's headquarters to inquire into the cause of it. Soon after my messenger returned with General Sherman's request that I should send a battalion of my cavalry to join one of his, for the purpose of discovering the strength and design of the enemy.

Before my cavalry had reached General Sherman's camp his was seen retiring to the rear of his line, which was now being formed nearly parallel with and within a short distance of the left of my camp. Hastening forward, General Sherman informed me that the enemy had attacked him in large force and that he desired support. At the same time the firing in the direction of General Prentiss' division indicated a partial abatement of the resistance offered by his division.

Before my left, consisting of the Third Brigade [Raith], could form for the support of General Sherman, the enemy

Maj. Gen. John A. McClernand, Commander, First Division, Army of the Tennessee. (U.S. Army Military History Institute)

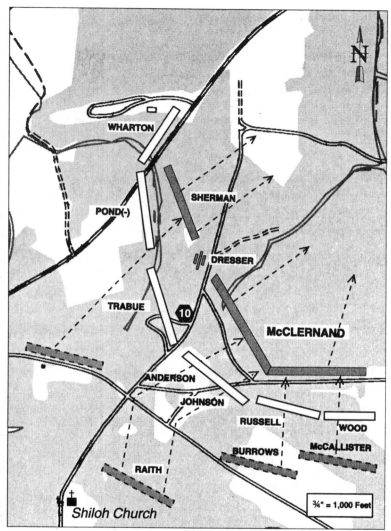

The Confederate attack on the Union right, approximately midday,
April 6, 1862 (Stop 10).

had pierced General Prentiss' line, afterward taking him and a number of his men prisoners, and rapidly forcing back General Sherman's left wing, was pressing upon my left with a mass five regiments deep, bearing the American flag. Discovering that this honored emblem was not borne by General Prentiss' retiring forces, but was used by the enemy as a means of deception, I ordered the Third Brigade to form line of battle, fronting the enemy's advance, nearly at a right angle with General Sherman's line; but before this order had been fully executed the enemy had approached within short musket-range and opened a deadly fire upon us. . . . While the line was being formed Captain Stewart, of my staff, brought information that the enemy, whose fire he had wonderfully escaped, were advancing in line of battle in strong force to the left of the brigade.

Colonel Raith, having completed his line, ordered a charge upon the enemy, in which he fell mortally wounded while encouraging his men by his heroic and daring example. The charge, although successful in repulsing the enemy in front, left the flanks of his command liable to be turned by the superior numbers of the enemy, which was only prevented by changing the fronts of the two flank regiments. . . .

The situation of the Third Brigade at this juncture was most critical. Generals Prentiss' and Sherman's divisions had retired, leaving the brigade exposed to combined attack. The enemy in front was recovering from the disorder of his repulse, and the forces of *Beauregard* and *Polk* were sweeping around on the right and left. In obedience to my order the brigade fell back . . . about 300 yards, and reformed in front of my headquarters, joining the Second Brigade, under command of Col. C. C. Marsh . . . and the First Brigade, under command of Col. A. M. Hare . . . the Eleventh Iowa being formed as a reserve, to support the center and left. Burrows' Ohio battery was advanced to the center, at a point on the Corinth road near my headquarters; Schwartz's battery, in support of Sherman, to the right, and McAllister's battery to the left, to command the approach across a field.

While this disposition was being completed the enemy were rapidly advancing at all points, supported by several batteries. The action, both by infantry and artillery, became general all along the line, and the conflict was desperate. In the course of twenty minutes Schwartz's battery had silenced the enemy's battery in front, and to repel the enemy, whose left was still bearing back General Sherman's division on my right, Major Schwartz, chief of my staff, joined the Thirty-fourth and Forty-third Illinois and boldly charged the enemy, receiving a severe wound in the leg, which caused him to be taken from the field. Our resistance, however, was overborne by superior numbers, which still continued to flank the right of my line. All of Schwartz's battery except one caisson was brought off—a portion of it by hand.

Burrows' battery opened a brisk fire from its position at the center, but from the near approach of the enemy, and the deadly fire opened on it both by infantry and artillery, was soon lost, including 70 horses* killed. . . . The underbrush and trees bear abundant and impressive evidence of the sanguinary character of this engagement.

McAllister's battery opened from the corner of . . . [Review] field . . . and by a well-directed and effective fire kept the enemy from crossing it until his battery was nearly surrounded and his support forced back, when, after silencing a battery in the woods on the opposite side of the field, he withdrew three of his pieces along the Corinth road towards Pittsburg Landing. The fourth piece was left behind for want of horses to take it off, but was recovered next day. In this engagement Captain McAllister was four times slightly wounded, but kept the field. . . .

Wholly unsupported on the left, and still outflanked on the right by increasing numbers, to save my command from being surrounded I ordered it to fall back about 200 yards and reform at a right angle with the center of my camp. The order was promptly and successfully executed, save by the Forty-third Illinois, which had failed to receive it. This gallant regiment still continued the conflict until it was surrounded, and cut its way through the enemy to the right and rear of my third line. [*O.R.*, X, pt. 1, pp. 114–16.]

Drive around the one-way loop for 0.6 mile to the stop sign. Continue straight to intersection. Turn left on Federal Road.

---

*This is the actual figure. A Union battery had a total of eighty-four horses assigned to it.

Drive 0.8 mile to intersection, turn right on *Gladden* Road for 0.6 mile to *Gladden's* Monument (Spain Field). Park next to the monument. Look in the direction from which you just came (north).

STOP 11, GLADDEN'S ATTACK

Shortly after portions of *Hardee's* corps initiated the battle in the vicinity of Rhea Field (Stop 2), *Gladden's* brigade of *Bragg's* corps attacked Miller's brigade of Prentiss's division. For an hour and a half the surprised Union troops inflicted heavy initial casualties on the attacking force, but then broke at 9:00 A.M. and scattered across the battlefield. Many found their way back to Pittsburg Landing, (about 2½ miles), where they remained demoralized and disorganized for the remainder of the day.

Report of Gen. Braxton Bragg, CSA, Second Corps, Army of the Mississippi

But few regiments of my command had ever made a day's march. A very large proportion of the rank and file had never performed a day's labor. Our organization had been most hasty, with great deficiency in commanders, and was therefore very imperfect. The equipment was lamentably defective for field service, and our transportation, hastily impressed in the country, was deficient in quantity and very inferior in quality. . . .

The road to Monterey (11 miles) [present-day town of Micier, Tenn.] was found very bad, requiring us until 11 o'clock on the 4th to concentrate at that place. . . . The commanders of divisions and brigades were assembled at night, the order of battle was read to them, and the topography of the enemy's position was explained, as far as understood by us. Orders were then given for the troops to march at 3 A.M., so as to attack the enemy early on the 5th.

About 2 A.M. a drenching rain-storm commenced, to which the troops were exposed, without tents, and continued until daylight, rendering it so dark and filling the creeks and ravines to such an extent as to make it impracticable to move at night. Orders were immediately sent out to suspend the movement until the first dawn of day. Continued firing by volleys and single shots was kept up all night and until 7 A.M. next morning

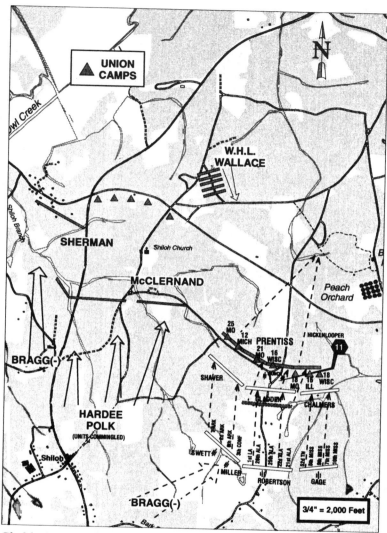

Gladden's attack (Stop 11).

by the undisciplined troops of our front, in violation of positive orders. Under such circumstances little or no rest could be obtained by our men, and it was 7 o'clock in the morning before the road was clear so as to put my command in motion, though it had been in ranks and ready from 3 A.M., in the wet and cold, and suffering from inaction.

At this juncture the commanding general arrived at our position. My column . . . moved on without delay until arriving near where the Pittsburg road leaves the Bark road, when a message from Major-General *Hardee* announced the enemy in his front and that he had developed his line. As promptly as my troops could be brought up in a narrow road, much encumbered with artillery and baggage wagons, they were formed . . . about 800 yards in rear of *Hardee's* line, my center resting on the Pittsburg road, my right brigade, *Gladden's,* of *Withers'* division, thrown forward to the right of the first line, Major-General *Hardee's* force not being sufficient for the ground to be covered. In this position we remained, anxiously awaiting the approach of our reserves to advance upon the enemy, now but a short distance in our front. . . .

The night was occupied by myself and a portion of my staff in efforts to bring forward provisions for a portion of the troops then suffering from their improvidence. Having been ordered to march with five days' rations, they were found hungry and destitute at the end of three days. This is one of the evils of raw troops, imperfectly organized and badly commanded. . . . In this condition we passed the night, and at dawn of day prepared to move.

The enemy did not give us time to discuss the question of attack, for soon after dawn they commenced a rapid musketry fire on our pickets. The order was immediately given by the commanding general and our lines advanced. Such was the ardor of our troops that it was with great difficulty they could be restrained from closing up and mingling with the first line. Within less than a mile the enemy was encountered in force at the encampments of his advanced positions, but our first line brushed him away, leaving the rear nothing to do but to press on in pursuit. In about one mile more we encountered him in strong force along most of the entire line. His batteries were posted on eminences, with strong infantry supports.

Finding the first line was now unequal to the work before

it, being weakened by extension and necessarily broken by the nature of the ground, I ordered my whole force to move up steadily and promptly to its support. The order was hardly necessary, for subordinate commanders, far beyond the reach of my voice and eye in the broken country occupied by us, had promptly acted on the necessity as it arose, and by the time the order could be conveyed the whole line was developed and actively engaged.

From this time, about 7:30 o'clock, until night the battle raged with little intermission. All parts of our line were not constantly engaged, but there was no time without heavy firing in some portion of it. My position for several hours was opposite my left center (*Ruggles'* division) immediately in rear of *Hindman's [Shaver's]* brigade, *Hardee's* corps.

In moving over the difficult and broken ground the right brigade of *Ruggles'* division, Colonel *Gibson* commanding, bearing to the right, became separated from the two left brigades *[Anderson* and *Pond]*, leaving a broad interval.

Three regiments of Major General *Polk's* command opportunely came up and filled this interval. Finding no superior officer with them, I took the liberty of directing their movements in support of *Hindman*, then, as before, ardently pressing forward and engaging the enemy at every point.

On the ground which had come under my immediate observation we had already captured three large encampments and three batteries of artillery. It was now about 10:30 o'clock.

Our right flank . . . had pressed forward ardently under the immediate direction of the commanding general and swept all before it. Batteries, encampments, store-houses, munitions in rich profusion, were ours, and the enemy, fighting hard and causing us to pay dearly for our successes, was falling back rapidly at every point. His left, however, opposite our right, was his strongest ground and position, and was disputed with obstinacy.

It was during this severe struggle that my command suffered an irreparable loss in the fall of Brigadier-General *Gladden*, commanding First Brigade, *Withers'* division, mortally, and Col. D. W. *Adams*, Louisiana Regular Infantry, his successor, severely, wounded. Nothing daunted, however, by these losses, this noble division, under its gallant leader, *Withers*, pressed on with the other troops in the vicinity and carried all before them. *Their progress, however, under the obstinate resistance made was not so rapid as was desired in proportion to that of the left, where the enemy was less strong; so that, instead of driving him, as we intended, down the river, leaving the left open for him to pass, we had really enveloped him on all sides and were pressing him back upon the landing at Pittsburg* [emphasis added].*

Meeting at about 10:30 o'clock upon the left center with Major-General *Polk,* my senior, I promptly yielded to him the important command at that point, and moved toward the right, in the direction in which Brigadier-General *Hindman,* of *Hardee's* line, had just led his division. Here we met the most obstinate resistance of the day. . . . [*O.R.,* X, pt. 1, pp. 463–66.]

Report of Col. Z. C. Deas, CSA, Twenty-second Alabama Infantry, Commanding First Brigade (Gladden), Second Division, Second Corps, Army of the Mississippi

On the morning of April 6 this brigade . . . under command of Brigadier-General *Gladden,* moved out of camp, marching in line of battle, and shortly after 7 o'clock came upon the enemy, when the engagement commenced. One of their batteries was playing upon us with effect, but in a short time *Robertson's* battery was brought on our side, which soon silenced theirs. We then charged, driving the enemy flying through their camp. In this charge several colors were captured.

Just before this charge was made General *Gladden,* while gloriously sustaining the reputation won in Mexico at the head of the immortal Palmetto Regiment, received a wound from a cannon-ball, which proved fatal.

Beyond this camp the brigade (now under the command of Colonel *Adams*) was halted, and after a time a battery sta-

---

*Memorandum for the commanders of the corps and of the reserve.

HEADQUARTERS ARMY OF THE MISSISSIPPI, *Corinth, April 3, 1862*

In the approaching battle every effort should be made to turn the left flank of the enemy so as to cut off his line of retreat to the Tennessee River and throw him back on Owl Creek, where he will be obliged to surrender. Every precaution must also be taken on our part to prevent unnecessary exposure of our men to the enemy's gunboats.

By command of General A. S. *Johnston:*

THOMAS JORDAN, *Assistant Adjutant-General*

[*O.R.,* X, pt. 1, p. 397]

tioned near their next camp opened upon us, which was responded to by *Robertson's*, and after a sharp contest silenced.

Orders were now received to move forward in support of General *Chalmers*, and while here the gallant *Adams*, when encouraging his men by his reckless daring and apparent contempt of the missiles of death flying thick around him, received a severe wound in the head.

The command of the brigade now devolved upon me. Without instructions, without a staff officer, or even one of my own regiment mounted to assist me, I moved forward to aid where I could, and before proceeding far came up with General *Breckinridge*, who was warmly engaged on my right. I immediately advanced to his assistance. The fire here was very severe, and I sent back for the Twenty-sixth Alabama to come up (which they failed to do), and also for a battery, which was brought up promptly, and with this assistance, after a hard and long-continued struggle, we succeeded in driving the enemy back.

At this point General *Bragg* came up and ordered me to change direction, obliquing to the left. In a short time I came upon the enemy again, drawn up some distance in front of another camp, and after a short but very sharp engagement drove them before me, pursuing them to their camp, where I assisted in capturing a large number. Here, in the hot pursuit, the Twenty-first and Twenty-fifth Alabama became separated from me in the woods, and before I had time to find them I received an order from General *Withers* to form on the extreme left, where I remained until night came on, and then attempted to get back to the camp I had left, but got into a different one. My men being now completely exhausted, and not having had anything to eat since morning, I encamped here for the night. . . . At daylight on the morning of the 7th I sent Capt. R. J. *Hill* to hunt for General *Withers'* division and also to get information. [*O.R.*, X, pt. 1, pp. 538–39.]

Turn around and drive back on the same road for 0.6 mile to the intersection (stop sign). Turn right on Federal Road for 0.8 mile. At the Y in the road, bear left to Stuart's Headquarters Monument (circle). Park off the pavement. Stand with Stuart's Monument to your back and face Girardey's Confederate artillery pieces.

STOP 12, THE ATTACK AGAINST STUART

The extreme left of the Union position was held by the small (about two thousand) brigade of Col. David Stuart, of Sherman's division. Hearing the sounds of fighting to the west, Stuart formed his regiments and moved them from one place to another, not knowing where he could expect the Confederates to attack. *Bragg's* engineer officer, scouting for gaps in the Union line near the Tennessee River, observed this movement after the battle had opened on the Union right and reported to *Johnston's* headquarters that a "division" was moving to a position where they could flank the Confederate attack.

Johnston ordered Brig. Gen. John C. *Breckinridge's* reserve corps to cover the Confederate flank. In addition, the brigades of *Chalmers* and *Jackson*, which had overrun Prentiss's camps, were pulled out of the Confederate main attack and marched against Stuart's troops. This would have significant consequences later in the battle.

About 900 yards south is the initial position of *Gage's* Confederate artillery battery. You will see this battery numerous times in the remainder of the fighting on the Confederate right flank. This site is also the position of a Union field hospital, one of the few established on the battlefield itself. This tent hospital became the model for later field hospitals.

Report of Col. David Stuart, USA, Commanding Second Brigade, Fifth Division, Army of the Tennessee

The brigade . . . occupied the extreme left of the advance, General Prentiss' division on my right and front. In obedience to General Sherman's orders I kept a company . . . in the vicinity of the ford of Lick Creek, on the Hamburg road, and another . . . in the vicinity of the Bark road (coming in on the hills opposite . . . the encampment), as picket guards, and on his order on Saturday sent six companies out on the Hamburg road with a squadron of cavalry sent forward by General McClernand to reconnoiter beyond Hamburg. . . .

At 7:30 o'clock on Sunday morning I received a verbal message from General Prentiss that the enemy were in his front in force. Soon after my pickets sent in word that a force, with artillery, were advancing on the Back [Bark] road. In a very short time I discovered the Pelican flag advancing in the

Col. David Stuart, Commander, Second Brigade, Fifth Division (Sherman),
Army of the Tennessee. (U.S. Army Military History Institute)

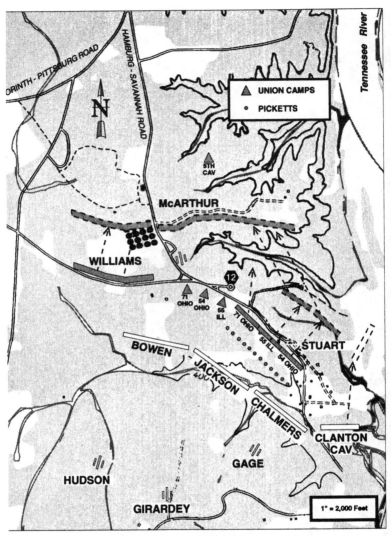

The Confederate attack on the Union left, approximately 10:30 A.M., April 6, 1862 (Stop 12). *The tent-shaped symbols indicate the locations of the Union camps.*

Scene in a Union field hospital. The only Union field hospital on the battlefield was located near Colonel Stuart's brigade headquarters on the left of the Union position. *(Battles and Leaders of the Civil War)*

rear of General Prentiss' headquarters. I dispatched my adjutant . . . to General Hurlbut, who occupied with his division the rear in the center, to inform him that General Prentiss' left was turned, and to ask him to advance his forces. The reply was that he would advance immediately. Within fifteen minutes General Hurlbut sent forward a battery [Mann's Missouri Battery], which took position on the road. . . .

A regiment . . . formed in line on the right of this battery. Observing these dispositions, and expecting that the remainder of General Hurlbut's division would be up quickly, I established my line of battle accordingly, with the right of the Seventy-first Ohio resting opposite the eastern extremity of the camp of the Fifty-fifth Illinois, the Fifty-fifth Regiment next, on the left, and the Fifty-fourth beyond, facing the south. I had two companies of the Fifty-fifth Illinois and two companies of the Fifty-fourth Ohio detached as skirmishers on the hills . . . across the . . . ravine where the enemy was endeavoring to plant a battery.

Stuart's brigade holding the Union left flank against Confederate attempts to flank the Union line and drive the federal units away from Pittsburg Landing. Stuart's outnumbered force made Confederate commanders think a much larger force was on the Union left, drawing off Southern units from the Hornets' Nest battle at a critical time. (*The Truth about Shiloh*)

From a convenient position on the brow of the bank north of the creek with my glass I could observe all their movements. Having succeeded in planting their battery in a commanding position they opened a fire of shell upon us, under cover of which the infantry advanced upon us diagonally from the left of Prentiss' division and also from the right of their battery. I hastened . . . to the battery I had left half an hour before in front of Colonel Mason's tent to order them farther to the east, in front of my headquarters, where they would have had a splendid fire as well upon the enemy's battery as upon the advancing infantry, [but] the battery had left without firing a gun and the battalion on its right had disappeared.

For above a quarter of a mile to my right no soldier could be seen, unless fugitives, making their way to the rear. A large body of the enemy's troops were advancing due north toward Mason's [Seventy-first Ohio] camp, and I saw that the position of my brigade was inevitably flanked by an overwhelming and unopposed force. Hastening back to my brigade I found the enemy rapidly advancing on its front. The Seventy-first Ohio had fallen back, under the shelling of the enemy's guns, to some position . . . about 150 yards in the rear, and reformed on a ridge of ground very defensible for infantry, but I could not find them and had no intimation as to where they had gone. Before I could change position the Fifty-fifth Illinois and Fifty-fourth Ohio were engaged, but as soon as possible I withdrew them to a position on the brow of a hill, and formed a line. . . . At this point I had not to exceed 800 men of the Fifty-fifth Illinois and Fifty-fourth Ohio. I saw nothing more of the Seventy-first Regiment through the fight.

The enemy's force [*Chalmers's* Brigade] of five regiments of infantry and a battery of four guns, which had been moving on our right flank, were here brought to a stand and formed a line of battle; a body of [enemy] cavalry were sent off on our right toward our rear, to harass or cut off our retreat [and] a part of the force which had attacked our first front was . . . flanking us on our . . . left. Against this . . . force (moving through a ravine just . . . in the rear of our extreme left) I sent a detachment of four companies of Zouaves, Fifty-fourth Ohio . . . by whom they were held in check during the fight.

This engagement opened, the enemy's line and ours being established at a distance of about 150 yards apart. . . . We fought and held them for upwards of two hours. The enemy's lines were within the edge of a grove, pretty well defended by trees; the space between us was an open, level, and smooth field. The disposition of their forces was made deliberately, and occupied fully fifteen minutes after we came upon the ground.

Inadequate as I knew my force to be, I was encouraged to fight it and hold my position, first with the object of detaining the enemy's forces from advancing toward the river, and secondly because I received a message from General [John] McArthur, who appeared in person somewhere in my vicinity, to hold my position, and that he would support me on my right.

I could not find the Seventy-first Ohio . . . and had less than 800 men under my command. During the action we observed a battery [*Gage*] planted south east of us, in a commanding position, to enfilade our line. It was, however, employed with little beyond threatening effect, the firing being too high. We had received no support on our right, as promised by General

McArthur. We had emptied the cartridge boxes of the killed and wounded, and our ammunition was exhausted. Our fire was so slacked from this cause and our losses that I was apprehensive of a forward movement by the enemy, who could easily have overwhelmed us. . . . I gave the order to fall back through the ravine and reform on a hill to our right. . . . When we reached it, the enemy had advanced on our left with their battery and were on a commanding position within 600 yards. They opened a fire of shell upon us, which compelled me to move on still farther, sheltering the command as well as possible by ravines and circuitous paths till we reached a cavalry [Fifth Ohio Cavalry] camp, where the brigade was re-formed. . . .

Finding I was beyond the line of the enemy . . . I ordered the brigade to march to the rear, toward the Landing, in preference to sending for ammunition, which I apprehended would not reach us. Within a quarter of a mile of the batteries the brigade was halted by an officer of General Grant's staff, who stated that ammunition was being sent back, and ordered that every fragment of regiments moving toward the Landing should be stopped. [*O.R.*, X, pt. 1, pp. 257–59.]

Report of Brig. Gen. James R. Chalmers, CSA, Commanding Second Brigade, Second Division, Second Corps

At dawn the First Brigade of this division, under command of Brigadier-General *Gladden,* filed past me, and we, falling into its rear, moved forward until our march was arrested by the column of Major General *Hardee,* the rear of which had not got in motion when we reached its encampment. After some delay we moved on to a position about 2 miles in front of the enemy's line. On reaching the ground I found our line of battle deployed, and General *Gladden's* brigade (which it was first intended should be held in reserve in the second line on my right) was deployed into line of battle, and thrown forward into the first line, on the right of Major-General *Hardee's* command, to fill the interval between his right and Lick Creek. . . . There being still a vacancy between the right of General *Gladden's* brigade and the creek, my brigade was extended *en echelon* in the rear . . . and to the right of General *Gladden,* and held in line by battalions at half distance doubled on the center.

Upon examination of the country it was apparent to me that our progress would be much retarded if we attempted to move by battalions in double column on the center, and, upon the suggestion being made to Brigadier-General *Withers* and Major-General *Bragg,* it was ordered that the supporting line should move by the right of companies to the front.

In this order we commenced the march early on the morning of the 6th. The space between Owl and Lick Creeks was about a half mile narrower where we first deployed . . . than it was in front of the enemy's line, and as the space between General *Gladden's* left and Lick Creek increased as we advanced, it became necessary that my brigade should move up into the front line, on the right of General *Gladden.* . . . Skirmishers from each regiment were at once thrown forward.

In obedience to orders from General *Withers* the right of this brigade was advanced by a gradual left wheel. . . . When we arrived in sight our line of battle was formed, and the brigade moved steadily forward. . . . When within about 150 yards of the enemy the line was halted and a heavy firing ensued. . . . After several rounds were discharged the order to charge bayonets was given, and the Tenth Mississippi Regiment (about 360 strong) . . . dashed up the hill, and put to flight the Eighteenth Wisconsin Regiment, numbering nearly 1,000 men. The order to charge having been given from the right flank, where I was then stationed, was not heard down the line, and consequently the Tenth Mississippi moved alone in the first charge, though I was quickly followed by the Ninth and Seventh Mississippi, when the whole line of the enemy broke and fled, pursued by these three regiments, through their camps and across a ravine about half a mile to the opposite hill, where they were halted by command of General *Johnston.* . . .

When the orders were received from General *Withers* to move on, skirmishers were thrown out in front of the whole line. . . . Our orders were to swing around, with our right resting on the creek bottom, [Lick Creek] and to drive the enemy before us toward Pittsburg, and we accordingly moved forward, advancing most rapidly on the right and gradually wheeling the whole line. In this order we were marching when our skir-

mishers developed the enemy [Fifty-fourth Ohio Infantry] con
cealed behind a fence, in thick undergrowth, with an open field
or orchard in his front. The width of this orchard was about
350 . . . yards, and behind it was a very steep and perfectly
abrupt hill, at the foot of which ran a small branch. [This action
occurred approximately 1,000 yards southeast of where you
are now located.] At the base of this hill ran the Hamburg and
Pittsburg road, skirting the orchard at its base and then turn
ing to the right. . . . The ground from the branch to the fence
where the enemy was concealed, was a gradual ascent, and our
line was in full view of the enemy from the time it crossed the
stream. The Ninth Mississippi was now on the left and there
was a space of about 30 yards between its left and the Hamburg
and Pittsburg road. As soon as I discovered the position of the
enemy I ordered up *Gage's* battery, which until now had not
been engaged, and put it in position on the hill above the
branch.

My line moved on across the orchard in most perfect order
and splendid style, and to my great surprise not a shot was
fired until we came within about 40 yards of the fence, then a
heavy fire was opened on us in front, and at the same time a
column was seen coming at double-quick down the Hamburg
and Pittsburg road, with the evident intention of getting in our
rear and cutting off the whole brigade. As soon as this column
was fairly in sight . . . *Gage's* battery opened a well-directed fire
on its head, and it was scattered in confusion, and at the same
moment our infantry made a charge in front, and after a hard
fight drove the enemy from his concealment, though we suf
fered heavily in killed and wounded.

After this fight our ammunition was exhausted, and, the
wagons being some distance behind, we lost some time before
it was replenished. As soon . . . as the ammunition could be
distributed we moved on, with the right resting on the edge of
the Tennessee River bottom, with the same orders as before
[*O.R.*, X, pt. 1, pp. 547–49.]

**Turn around and drive back on the same road. Bear to the
right for 0.3 mile to the loop on the right. Stop at the Johnston
Monument.**

thograph showing Gen. A. S. *Johnston* falling from his horse after receiving a mortal wound at Shiloh. In fact, *Johnston's* wound was behind his ee, causing him to bleed to death as his staff tried to find and treat his und. *(The Life of General Albert Sidney Johnston)*

TOP 13, JOHNSTON'S DEATH

As the fighting raged around the Hornets' Nest, Confederate rces on either flank continued to drive the Union defenders orthward toward Pittsburg Landing. On the Union right flank e troops of Sherman and McClernand continued to withdraw nder pressure toward Pittsburg Landing. On the Union left flank uart's brigade continued to use the broken terrain to slow the onfederate attack and inflict casualties. Brig. Gen. John A. IcArthur's brigade (W. H. L. Wallace's division) had moved to elp restore Stuart's precarious situation on the flank closest to e Tennessee River. These two brigades continued to face the onfederate brigades of *Chalmers* and *Jackson*, now joined by *Breckridge's* Reserve Corps. The Confederate advance was slow in taking shape as the commanders tried to mount a coordinated attack the difficult terrain.

Gen. Albert Sidney *Johnston*, moving with *Bowen's* brigade of *reckinridge's* Corps, heard intense fighting in the vicinity of the each Orchard (Stop 14). He sent one of his aides to rally the tackers and carry the position with the bayonet. *Breckinridge* reorted that all efforts to get the troops to make the charge had

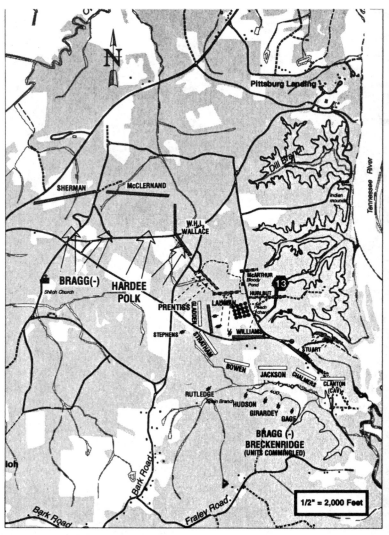

Johnston leads the assault on the Peach Orchard (Stop 13).

iled. *Johnston* moved up to the brigade and addressed them, say-
g that he would lead the charge himself, a declaration that had a
lvanizing effect on the troops. With a shout they moved forward.
acArthur's line crumbled, allowing the attackers to bypass Stu-
t's brigade. As the attack against the Peach Orchard pushed the
efenders back, *Johnston* continued to observe and send orders
om behind *Statham's* brigade, which had led the attack. No one
oticed that the general had been struck by bullets, as many as
ur times. Only one had broken the skin, a minié ball that hit him
the back of the right knee. *Johnston* reeled in the saddle. Only
en did aides notice that his boot had filled with blood. They
ould not find the wound, and *Johnston* had ordered his personal
hysician to stay and treat the wounded in Prentiss's overrun
mps. With a tourniquet in his pocket that could have saved his
e, *Johnston* bled to death.

Report of Brig. Gen. John K. Jackson, CSA, Commanding Third Brigade, Withers's Division, Second Corps, Army of the Mississippi

The brigade [in the aggregate 2,208] was ordered to take
position in the second line, on the left of General *Chalmers'*
brigade, whose right rested on Lick Creek Swamp. The regiments were first drawn up in line of battle . . . with the battery
on the extreme left. The infantry were then broken by the
right of companies to the front, and ordered to hold themselves in readiness to move at a moment's notice. My brigade
. . . thus bivouacked on Saturday night.

On Sunday morning the order was given for an advance.
The infantry and artillery commenced the movement about
daylight, moving by right of companies to the front through
the forest, with a view to a rapid formation at any moment by
company into line. The order received and extended was that
the second line should follow up the advance of the first line
at a distance of about 1,000 yards in its rear and support it as
occasion required, at the same time bearing off well to the
right and resting upon the left of General *Chalmers'* brigade,
gradually sweeping around by a protracted wheel of the whole
line to the left, the march being rapid by the eagerness of the
men to press upon the enemy, which they were urged to do
fiercely and furiously. I found that the first line was soon

warmly engaged; that solid shot and shell from a battery of the enemy were passing over the first line and occasionally wounding one of my men. Advancing rapidly, I found that the engagement was between *Gladden's* brigade and the enemy, and that the latter had been driven from their camps [Stop 11].

Following on, I came up with General *Gladden's* brigade just beyond this camp, formed in squares. Just here heavy firing was heard to the left, and by order of General *Johnston* my brigade was moved in that direction, by the left flank, up a ravine. Before proceeding far another order was received to change direction and move to the right, as the enemy were deployed there. During this time Captain *Girardey* used his battery with effect upon a battery of the enemy which was playing on us from the brow of the hill opposite. [*O.R.*, X, pt. 1 pp. 553–54.]

Narrative of Col. William Preston Johnston, CSA, son of General Albert Sidney Johnston, Commanding Army of the Mississippi

General *Johnston* was with the right of *Statham's* brigade confronting the left of Hurlbut's division, which was behind the crest of a hill, with a depression filled with chaparral in it front. *Bowen's* brigade was further to the right in line with *Statham's*, touching it near this point. The Confederates held the parallel ridge in easy musket-range; and "as heavy fire as I ever saw during the war," says [Tennessee] Governor [Isham G.] *Harris,* was kept up on both sides for an hour or more. It was necessary to cross the valley raked by this deadly ambuscade and assail the opposite ridge in order to drive the enemy from his stronghold. When General *Johnston* came up and saw the situation, he said to his staff: "They are offering stubborn resistance here. I shall have to put the bayonet to them."

It was the crisis of the conflict. The Federal key was in his front. If his assault were successful, their left would be completely turned, and the victory won. He determined to charge. He sent Governor *Harris,* of his staff, to lead a Tennessee regiment; and, after a brief conference with *Breckinridge,* whom he loved and admired, that officer, followed by his staff appealed to the soldiers. As he encouraged them with his fine voice and manly bearing, General *Johnston* rode out in front and slowly down the line. His hat was off. His sword rested in its scabbard. In his right hand he held a little tin cup, the memorial of an incident that had occurred earlier in the day. Passing through a captured camp, he had taken this toy, saying, "Let this be my share of the spoils today." It was this plaything which, holding it between two fingers, he employed more effectively in his natural and simple gesticulation than most men could have used a sword. His presence was full of inspiration. He sat his thoroughbred bay, "Fire-eater," with easy command. His voice was persuasive, encouraging, and compelling. His words were few; . . . "Men! They are stubborn; we must use the bayonet." When he reached the center of the line, he turned. "I will lead you!", he cried, and moved toward the enemy. The line was already thrilling and trembling with that irresistible ardor which in battle decides the day. With a mighty shout *Bowen's* and *Statham's* brigades moved forward at a charge. A sheet of flame and a mighty roar burst from the Federal stronghold. The Confederate line withered; but there was not an instant's pause. The crest was gained. The enemy were in flight.

General *Johnston* had passed through the ordeal seemingly unhurt. His horse was shot in four places; his clothes were pierced by missiles; his boot sole was cut and torn by a minie; but if he himself had received any severe wound, he did not know it. At this moment Governor *Harris* rode up from the right. After a few words, General *Johnston* sent him with an order to Colonel *Statham,* which having delivered, he speedily returned. In the meantime, knots and groups of Federal soldiers kept up a desultory fire as they retreated upon their supports, and their last line, now yielding, delivered volley after volley as they sullenly retired.

By the chance of war, a minie-ball from one of these did its fatal work. As he sat there, after his wound, Captain *Wickham* says that Colonel *O'Hara,* of his staff, rode up, and General *Johnston* said to him, "We must go to the left, where the firing is heaviest," and then gave him an order, which *O'Hara* rode off to obey. Governor *Harris* returned, and, finding him very pale, asked him, "General, are you wounded." He answered, in a very deliberate and emphatic tone: "Yes, and, I fear, seriously."

These were his last words. *Harris* and *Wickham* led his horse back under cover of the hill, and lifted him from it. They searched at random for the wound, which had cut an artery in his leg, the blood flowing into his boot. When his brother-in-law, *Preston,* lifted his head, and addressed him with passionate grief, he smiled faintly, but uttered no word. . . . In a few moments he was dead.

His wound was not necessarily fatal. General *Johnston's* own knowledge of military surgery was adequate for its control by an extemporized tourniquet had he been aware . . . of its nature. Dr. D. W. *Yandell,* his surgeon, had attended his person during most of the morning; but, finding a large number of wounded men . . . at one point, General *Johnston* had ordered *Yandell* to stop there, establish a hospital, and give them his services. . . . Had *Yandell* remained with him, he would have had little difficulty with the wound.

Governor *Harris,* and others of General *Johnston's* staff promptly informed General *Beauregard* of his death, and General *Beauregard* assumed command, remaining at Shiloh Church, awaiting the issue of events. [William Preston Johnston, "Albert Sidney Johnston at Shiloh," in Robert Johnson and Clarence Buel, eds., *Battles and Leaders of the Civil War,* 4 vols. (New York: The Century Co., 1884–1888), vol. I, pp. 564–65.]

Report of Col. Joseph Wheeler, CSA, Nineteenth Regiment Alabama Infantry, Third Brigade, Second Division, First Corps, Army of the Mississippi

When the first line opened the engagement a few of our men were wounded by the scattering shots of the enemy. We were then ordered forward and entered the more advanced Federal camps behind the first line. We were then directed to move about a mile to the right and front, where we formed in the first line of battle, in which we continued during the remainder of the day. At this point General A. S. *Johnston* ordered the regiment, with his own lips, to charge the camps of the Fifty-ninth [Fifty-fifth] Illinois Regiment, to do which it was necessary to pass down a deep ravine and mount a steep hill to the other side.

This duty was performed . . . under a heavy fire from a screened foe, with rapidity, regularity, and cool gallantry. But little resistance was offered after reaching the camps, the en

he Peach Orchard. This lithograph shows Hurlbut's Division repulsing
ne of the Confederate attacks, before finally having to withdraw back
)ward Pittsburg Landing. Note the log houses in the vicinity. This illustra-
on is from a sketch of the time. *(The American Soldier in the Civil War)*

emy fled before us to the crest of another ravine back of us,
and about 200 yards from their camp. After forming in line in
the face of the enemy we were ordered to lie down, while the
artillery was placed in position to our rear and fired over our
heads sufficient to shake their line.

The regiment then moved forward rapidly, driving the enemy before it and dislodging him from every place he attempted to make a stand, taking several prisoners and killing
and wounding a large number. [*O.R.*, X, pt. 1, p. 558.]

**Take the right fork from the Johnston Monument. At the yield
ign, turn right and drive north 0.1 mile. Turn left and park near
he Peach Orchard. Walk into the Peach Orchard to the four
rtillery pieces of Mann's Battery.**

TOP 14A, THE PEACH ORCHARD

While the Confederate attacks were pushing McArthur's Union
roops back and flanking *Stuart's* isolated brigade, intense pressure
ontinued to build against the federal troops in the Hornets' Nest.
bout the same time *Johnston* had ordered *Statham's* and part of

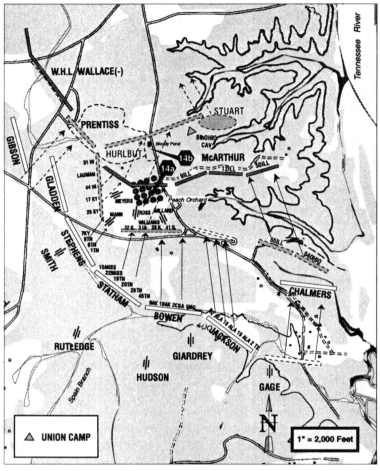

Union forces withdraw under pressure from the Peach Orchard, approximately midafternoon, April 6, 1862 (Stop 14).

Stephen's brigades against Hurlbut's Union forces holding a line in front of the Peach Orchard. The federal infantry fell back through the Orchard, but the artillery batteries continued to fire until the very last minute, inflicting heavy casualties on the attacking Confederates. So heavy was the firing in the Peach Orchard that the bullets hitting peach blossoms made it seem that it was snowing at times.

The log cabin located near the Peach Orchard is the only surviving structure from the time of the battle. It was moved to its current site a few weeks after the fighting to replace a cabin that had burned during the battle.

Report of Maj. Gen. B. F. Cheatham, CSA, Commanding Second Division, First Corps, Army of the Mississippi

Early on the morning of the 6th instant the division was formed for action on either side of the Pittsburg road, immediately to the rear of the First Division, First Corps, commanded by Brig. Gen. Charles *Clark.*

Advancing about the distance of a mile I was directed by Major-General *Polk* to deploy the Second Brigade *[Stephens's]* to the left as a support to General *Bragg's* left wing, then hotly engaged with the forces of the enemy. Taking the position as ordered, I remained here for half an hour and until ordered by General *Beauregard* to proceed with the Second Brigade to the extreme right of our line to ascertain the point where the firing was heaviest and there engage the enemy at once.

At about 10 A.M. I reached the front of an open field lying east of the center of the Federal line of encampments and discovered the enemy in strong force, occupying several log houses. His line extended behind a fence and occupied an abandoned road. He was advantageously located. I here directed Captain *Smith* to move his pieces forward and open on the enemy, which was done with the utmost promptness and under a fire that disabled a number of his horses before he could unlimber and come into battery. For nearly an hour the firing was kept up with the enemy's battery—superior to ours in the caliber and range of its guns—with a result highly creditable to the skill and gallantry of Captain *Smith,* his officers and men.

About this time General *Breckinridge,* with his command, came up and took position on my right, and opened upon the enemy a heavy fire of musketry, and a few moments afterward I was directed by Colonel *Jordan,* assistant adjutant-general to General *Beauregard,* to charge quick time across the open field, about 300 yards in width, flanked on one side by a fence and dense thicket of forest trees and undergrowth. So soon as the brigade entered the field the enemy opened upon us from his entire front a terrific fire of artillery and musketry, but failed altogether to check our movement until we reached the center of the field, when another part of the enemy's force, concealed and protected by the fence and thicket to our left [center of the Hornets' Nest], opened a murderous cross-fire upon our lines, which caused my command to halt and return their fire.

After a short time I fell back to my original position, and moving a short distance to the right, with General *Breckinridge* on my right, we together attacked the enemy, about 5,000 strong, admirably posted, and were actively and continuously engaged for three hours [part of the Hornets' Nest Battle].

In the charge first mentioned the Second Brigade lost many of its bravest and best officers and men. Major *Welborn,* of the Seventh Regiment Kentucky Volunteers, and Capt. Jo. B. *Freeman,* of the Sixth Tennessee Volunteers, fell, mortally wounded. Captain *Persons,* of the Sixth Tennessee, and Lieut. Robert *Thomas,* adjutant of the Ninth Tennessee, after exhibiting the most determined spirit and a high degree of skill as officers, fell dead. [*O.R.,* X, pt. 1, pp. 438–39.]

Report of Brig. Gen. Stephen A. Hurlbut, USA, Commanding Fourth Division, Army of the Tennessee

On Sunday morning . . . about 7.30 A.M., I received a message from Brigadier-General Sherman that he was attacked in force . . . upon his left. I immediately ordered Col. J. C. Veatch, commanding the Second Brigade, to proceed to the left of General Sherman. This brigade . . . was in march in ten minutes, arrived on General Sherman's line rapidly, and went into action. I must refer to Colonel Veatch's report for the particulars of that day. Receiving in a few moments a pressing request for aid from Brigadier-General Prentiss, I took command in person of the First and Third Brigades. As we drew near the rear and left of General Prentiss' line his regiments, in broken masses, drifted through my advance, that gallant officer making every effort to rally them.

I formed my line of battle—the First Brigade thrown to the front on the southerly side of a large open field [the field directly south of the Peach Orchard], the Third Brigade continuing the line with an obtuse angle around the other side of the field and extending some distance into the brush and timber; Mann's battery was placed in the angle of the line, Ross' battery some distance to the left, and the Thirteenth Ohio Battery on the right and somewhat advanced in cover of the timber, so as to concentrate the fire upon the open ground in front—and waited for the attack. A single shot fired from the enemy's batteries struck in Myers' Thirteenth Ohio battery, when officer and men, with a common impulse of disgraceful cowardice, abandoned the entire battery, horses, caissons, and guns, and fled, and I saw them no more until Tuesday. I called for volunteers from the artillery. The call was answered, and 10 gallant men from Mann's battery and Ross' battery brought in the horses, which were wild, and spiked the pieces. The attack commenced on the Third Brigade, through the thick timber, and was met and repelled by a steady and continuous fire, which rolled the enemy back in confusion, after some half hour of struggle, leaving many dead and wounded.

The glimmer of bayonets on the left and front of the First Brigade showed a large force of the enemy gathering [*Chalmers's* and *Jackson's* Brigades], and an attack was soon made on the Forty-first Illinois and Twenty-eighth [Illinois] on the left of the brigade, and on the Thirty-second Illinois and Third Iowa on the right. At the same time a strong force of very steady and gallant troops formed in columns, doubled on the center, and advanced over the open field in front. They were allowed to approach within 400 yards, when fire was opened from Mann's and Ross' batteries, and from the two right regiments of the First Brigade and the Seventeenth and Twenty-fifth Kentucky, which were thrown forward slightly, so as to flank the column. Under this withering fire they vainly attempted to deploy, but soon broke and fell back under cover, leaving not less than 150 dead and wounded as evidence how our troops maintained their position. The attack on the left was also repulsed, but as the ground was covered with brush the loss could not be judged.

General Prentiss having succeeded in rallying a considerable portion of his command, I permitted him to pass to the front of the right of my Third Brigade, where [in the "Hornets' Nest"] they redeemed their honor by maintaining that line for some time while ammunition was supplied to my regiments. A series of attacks upon the right and left of my line were readily repelled, until I was compelled to order Ross' battery to the rear, on account of its loss in men and horses. During all this time Mann's battery maintained its fire steadily, effectively, and with great rapidity, under the excellent handling of Lieut. E. Brotzmann.

For five hours these brigades maintained their position under repeated and heavy attacks, and endeavored, with their thin ranks, to hold the space between Stuart and McClernand, and did check every attempt to penetrate the line, when, about 3 o'clock, Colonel Stuart, on my left, sent me word that he was driven in, and that I would be flanked on the left in a few moments. It was necessary for me to decide at once to abandon either the right or left. I considered that Prentiss could, with the left of General McClernand's troops, probably hold the right, and sent him notice to reach out toward the right and drop back steadily parallel with my First Brigade, while I rapidly moved General Lauman's from the right to the left, and called up two 20-pounder pieces of Major Cavender's battalion, to check the advance of the enemy upon the First Brigade. These pieces were taken into action by Dr. Cornyn, the surgeon of the battalion, and Lieutenant Edwards, and effectually checked the enemy for half an hour, giving me time to draw off my crippled artillery and to form a new front with the Third Brigade [Lauman's].

In a few minutes two Texas regiments crossed the ridge separating my line from Stuart's former one, while other troops also advanced. Willard's battery was thrown into position . . . and opened with great effect upon the "Lone Star" flags, until their line of fire was obstructed by the charge of the Third Brigade, which, after delivering its fire with great steadiness, charged full up the hill and drove the enemy 300 or 400 yards.

Perceiving that a heavy force was closing on the left, between my line and the river, while heavy fire continued on the right, I ordered the line to fall back. The retreat was made quietly and steadily and in good order. I had hoped to make a stand on the line of my camp, but masses of the enemy were pressing rapidly on each flank, while their light artillery was closing rapidly in the rear.

On reaching the 24-pounder siege guns in battery near the river [Pittsburg Landing]. I again succeeded in forming a line of battle in rear of the guns, and, by direction of Major-General Grant, I assumed command of all troops that came up. Broken regiments and disordered battalions came into line gradually upon my division. [*O.R.,* X, pt. 1, pp. 203–4.]

Report of Col. John D. Martin, CSA, Second Confederate Infantry, commanding Second Brigade (Bowen), Reserve Corps, Army of the Mississippi

After a march of 2 miles our knapsacks, etc., were left. Soon after again reaching the road the roar of artillery broke upon the ear. We were then ordered to the scene of action at double-quick for nearly 2 miles, when the scene of battle lay before and below us. We were here formed in line of battle, the First Missouri and my regiment in front and the Ninth and Tenth Arkansas Regiments in the rear. We were led by General A. S. *Johnston,* who told us a few more charges and the day was ours. He halted in 200 or 300 yards, and told us to charge ahead; the enemy were before us.

The Missouri and my regiment, after crossing a deep ravine, halted for a few minutes to await your arrival. When General *Withers* rode up and ordered us forward, the enemy were near in force. After a march of 200 yards we reached a skirt of woods, and a brisk fire was opened upon us by the skirmishers of the enemy. Finding they were picking off our men . . . an advance was ordered, and we immediately crossed a deep ravine, driving their skirmishers before us. On reaching the top of a hill we were received with a destructive volley, killing and wounding about 12 of my men. Simultaneously we returned their fire and charged ahead; they fled in confusion. We killed and wounded many. We pursued for 200 or 300 yards and halted.

At this point General *Breckinridge* came up, whose noble appearance and gallant bearing inspired the men with the utmost enthusiasm. He ordered my regiment to wheel to the left and march upon the enemy. After a march of 400 or 500 yards, to where the ravine was expanded and shallow, upon turning to the right and marching to the brow of the hill we discovered the enemy in very large force, with artillery supported by infantry, his right resting on his encampment. I afterward learned that this was Prentiss' [Williams's] brigade. They poured upon us a destructive fire, which we returned with coolness, promptness, and destructive effect. . . . At this point we lost about 100 men, and would have been annihilated had not the enemy greatly overshot us. . . . After fighting for two hours the enemy fell back in good order. The regiment being entirely out of ammunition, we fell back to the camp of the enemy . . . and found a bountiful supply. [*O.R.*, X, pt. 1, pp. 621–22.]

Walk back to the parking area and continue to walk north for about 100 yards. Here you will find a small pond.

STOP 14B, BLOODY POND

The Bloody Pond, near the Peach Orchard and the Hornets' Nest, was used by wounded soldiers of both armies as they staggered or crawled into this pond to quench their thirst and wash their wounds during the battle. Although the scene of much suffering, the pond played no tactical role in the battle.

Return to your car. Driving out of the parking area, turn left (north) and drive 0.1 mile. At the edge of a large open field on the left, park next to the Twenty-eighth Illinois Infantry Marker located here. Walk across the road and down a small trail going east for 150 yards. Move past two unit markers to the third marker (Lauman's Brigade).

STOP 15, DEFENDING THE FLANK

As the Confederates pressed their attack against the Hornets' Nest and the Peach Orchard, the hard-pressed men of Hurlbut's division fell back into the woods to the north and east, re-forming to halt the attack. The confusion resulting from *Johnston's* death gave the weary Northerners a period of respite while the confused Confederate command and control system adjusted. When Gen. P. G. T. *Beauregard* learned of *Johnston's* death, he took command, leaving *Bragg* in charge of the right wing and *Ruggles* in command of the center in the area of the Hornets' Nest. Lauman's Union brigade formed along the line where you now stand, listening to the advancing Confederates crash through the woods. This was the flank unit of the only organized Union forces between the Confederates and Pittsburg Landing.

Brig. Gen. Stephen A. Hurlbut, Commander, Fourth Division, Army of the Tennessee. (U.S. Army Military History Institute)

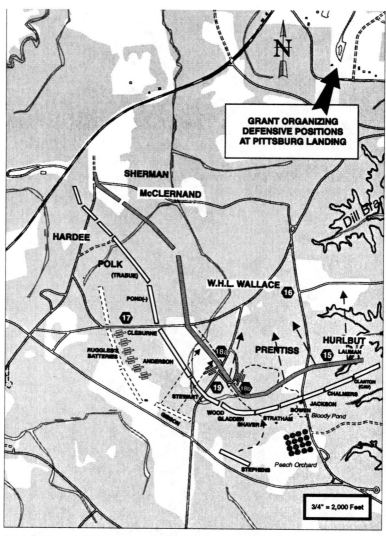

Union forces fall back and develop a strong point at the Hornets'
Nest, approximately 4:00 P.M., April 6, 1862 (Stops 15–19).

Report of Brig. Gen. James R. Chalmers, CSA, Commanding Second Brigade, Second Division, Second Corps, Army of Mississippi (continued)

After the attack [against Stuart, Stop 12], when we had gone about a quarter of a mile we again encountered the enemy in a strong position on a hill with a deep ravine in his front, and a very stubborn fight ensued, in which we lost many gallant men. . . . Here again *Gage's* battery did good service, though it was some time before it could be brought into position, owing to the rough nature of the ground and the want of roads, and I here take occasion to say that I cannot speak too highly of the energy, skill, and labor displayed by the men of this battery throughout the day in cutting their way through a thickly wooded country over ravines and hills almost impassable to ordinary wagons.

After about an hour's hard fighting the enemy again retreated, leaving many of his dead on the field. About this time the gunboats from the river began to throw their shells among us, and we passed rapidly forward in line of battle toward the center, where the battle seemed to be raging fiercely. We were soon met by an officer, stating that he belonged to General *Crittenden's* staff, and that he had been hotly engaged with the enemy and needed assistance. . . . Moving at a double-quick, over several ravines and hills, we came upon the enemy [Lauman's Brigade] and attacked him on his flank. This was the fourth fight in which my brigade had been engaged during the day, and after a severe firing of some duration, finding the enemy stubbornly resisting, I rode back for General *Jackson's* brigade, which was lying down in reserve in my rear and to my left. I did not see General *Jackson,* but finding Colonel *Wheeler,* called upon him to take up the fight, which he did with promptness and vigor. I sent a staff officer to command my brigade to lie down and rest until they received further orders. [*O.R.*, X, pt. 1, pp. 549–50.]

Report of Lieutenant Gwin, U.S. Navy, Commanding USS Tyler

The enemy attacked our lines on our left the morning of the 6th instant at 6:30 and by his overwhelming numbers forced our men to fall back in some confusion. At 9:25, finding that the rebels were still driving our left wing back, I steamed up to a point 1 mile above Pittsburg, taking a good position to support our troops should they be forced down to the banks of the river. At 10:15 the *Lexington,* Lieutenant Commanding Shirk, joined me, having come up from Crump's Landing. After a short time she returned for the purpose of supporting the command of General Wallace, which occupied that point. Not having received any instructions from the commanding general in regard to the service to be rendered by the gunboats, I awaited them patiently, although for an hour or more shot and shell were falling all around us.

Feeling that could some system of communication be established the *Tyler* could be of great advantage to our left wing, at 1:25 P.M. I sent an officer, requesting that I might be allowed to open on the woods in the direction of the batteries and advancing forces of the rebels. General Hurlbut, who commanded on our left, sent me word to do so, giving me directions how to fire, that I might do it with no damage to our troops, and expressing himself grateful for this offer of support, saying that without reinforcements he would not be able to maintain the position he then occupied for an hour. Therefore, at 2:50, I opened fire in the line directed with good effect, silencing their batteries on our left. [*Official Records of the Union and Confederate Navies in the War of the Rebellion,* series I, vol. 22 (Washington, D.C.: Government Printing Office, 1908), pp. 762–63.]

Report of Col. Charles Cruft, USA, Thirty-first Indiana Infantry, Third Brigade, Fourth Division, Army of the Tennessee

On Sunday morning . . . about 7:30 o'clock, rapid volleys of musketry from camps to the front indicated the commencement of the battle. Soon an order was received from the general commanding brigade to form the regiment for action. In ten minutes it was in brigade line on the right. In a few moments thereafter the brigade was moved in column to the front along the Hamburg road. The regiment was formed in line of battle in the position indicated by Brigadier-General Lauman.

At this time the battle was progressing actively upon the

right and left of the main line. Soon the enemy attacked our brigade in great force and with much desperation. My line met the attack with perfect coolness and with a low and steady fire. Officers and men behaved handsomely. After the expenditure of some 30 rounds [each] the enemy was repulsed. The advance was made up to within some 10 yards of my line, and the slaughter among the enemy in its front was terrible.

A second attack was shortly made with increased fury. The line stood unbroken, however, and after exhausting nearly the last cartridge again repulsed the enemy. Here a slight cessation in the attack occurred, barely long enough to procure fresh ammunition from the rear. The boxes of the men were scarcely filled before the enemy were the third time upon us. The line stood firm, and again succeeded against superior numbers. There was now a short cessation of firing, during which the cartridge-boxes of the men were again filled. A fourth assault was soon made, which was gallantly repulsed, and the enemy withdrew, leaving my regiment, with the balance of the brigade, in position. The enemy, retreating, moved off toward the left of the main line.

During the action my regiment fired an average of about 100 rounds per man. The piles of the enemy's dead which were lying along our front when he retreated attested the accuracy and steadiness of the fire. [*O.R.*, X, pt. 1, p. 235.]

Report of Brig. Gen. Jacob G. Lauman, USA, Commanding Third Brigade, Fourth Division, Army of the Tennessee

I assumed command of the Third Brigade of your [Hurlbut's] division . . . on Saturday morning, and on Sunday at 8 A.M. I received your orders to advance to the support of our troops, then engaged with the rebels. In twenty minutes the brigade was in line and moving to the front to the left of General W. H. L. Wallace's division, and to the right of Willard's battery, when we formed in line of battle [in the Peach Orchard], with an open field on the left and a heavy growth of under-brush in front of us.

We remained in this position about an hour, when our skirmishers came in and informed me that the rebels were advancing in line and would soon be upon us. I waited until I could distinctly see them advancing by the gleam of their bayonets about 100 yards distant, when I gave the order to fire, which at once checked their advance. They held their ground for some time, however, when they moved off to the right, where they had planted a battery, and under cover of which attempted to cross the open field. I immediately ordered the left wing [Seventeenth and Twenty-fifth Kentucky Regiments] to move up to the fence, and as soon as they came in short range opened fire on them, which soon caused them to fall back. Their loss here and in the front was very heavy, the ground being literally covered with their dead. To add to the horrors of the scene the woods caught fire, and the dead and dying were soon enveloped in a general conflagration.

The rebels continuing to move to the right, so as to endanger Willard's battery, I received your order to move the brigade to the left [from the Peach Orchard area], so as to check their movements in that direction. The movement was executed in fine order, and here we held our position until 4 o'clock [along the line where you are now standing], fighting against vastly superior numbers, until the batteries on the right and left of us had retired. The rebels now brought up a section of light artillery, which they brought to bear on us, and continuing their movement to the right, thereby endangering our left flank, and being without support, I was obliged to fall back, which we did in good order, reforming about a mile to the rear, which position we held until next morning. . . .

When I come to speak of the gallantry and bravery of the officers and men of my command I find great difficulty in finding language strong enough to express my feelings . . . and can only say that they fought from morning until night like veterans. Well may Indiana and Kentucky be proud of them. . . .

The aggregate strength of the brigade was 1,727. The entire loss, in killed, wounded, and missing, is . . . 468. [*O.R.*, X, pt. 1, pp. 233–34.]

Return to your car. Drive straight ahead (north) 0.4 mile to the Alabama Monument on the left. Stop and look to your left (west).

STOP 16, THE LOST OPPORTUNITY

The Confederates in this part of the field were now under the command of *Bragg*, who was intent on reducing the Union troops in the Hornets' Nest salient. He failed to grasp the opportunity to bypass the forces in the Hornet's Nest and move through the gap in the Union lines, thus outflanking the Hornets' Nest and possibly seizing Pittsburg Landing before any significant force could be organized to defend it.

Bragg pushed all his available troops "to the sound of the guns." The nearly exhausted Southerners, low on ammunition and having sustained a significant number of casualties, were harangued by an aroused *Bragg* as they moved to the attack.

Report of Brig. Gen. Jones M. Withers, CSA, Commanding Second Division, Second Corps, Army of the Mississippi

. . . The nature of the ground over which we had to pass rendered it most difficult for the artillery to keep up with the eager and rapid movements of the infantry. With such batteries, however, as *Robertson's, Girardey's,* and *Gage's* there could be no failure. . . .

. . . From this position [vicinity of Stop 15] they were also quickly driven, but soon formed a third line on a ridge running nearly parallel with the Hamburg and Pittsburg roads [where you are now standing]. General *Jackson* was ordered to move forward a short distance and rest his command in a ravine until the artillery could be brought up. This was quickly done, and it opened immediately with telling effect on the enemy, in strong force beyond an old field, concealed and protected by a worm fence and thick underbrush. After a sharp conflict they were dislodged and driven from their position, and *Chalmers* halted his command for a supply of ammunition.

These movements caused the brigades to be too widely separated, being at right angles, *Jackson's* facing north and *Chalmers'* east. *Chalmers* was therefore ordered to move his command to its position on *Jackson's* right. Satisfied by the report of the energetic and indefatigable *Clanton* that there was no enemy on our right, and being convinced by the heavy and continuous firing that they were in force on our left, the divi-

Maj. Gen. Braxton *Bragg,* Commander, Second Army Corps, Army of the
Mississippi. (U.S. Army Military History Institute)

sion was ordered to wheel on a movable pivot to the left. This movement, which was in accordance with the general plan of battle, as explained by the commanding general to the division and brigade commanders, soon developed the enemy in strong force, who stubbornly contested our advance, but were driven before the cool and steady *Jackson* and the gallant and impetuous *Chalmers*. Re-enforcements were now called for on our left, where the heavy firing was still continued; but this division being hotly engaged throughout the lines, Colonel *Rich*, of the First Missouri, whose regiment was in our rear, having become detached from General *Bowen's* brigade, was ordered to the support. He moved off immediately at double-quick, and dashed into the fight with good effect.

An order for re-enforcements was now received from General *Bragg*. As the entire line was still warmly engaged, with no support, General *Breckinridge*, who had just had a sharp conflict with and driven the enemy before him, was called on to render the desired assistance, This was done without other delay than that necessary to furnish his troops with ammunition.

The division still continued fiercely engaged until *Chalmers*, having routed the forces before him, began to sweep down on the left flank of the heavy force in front of *Jackson* at the same time that *Gladden's* brigade, now under command of Colonel *Deas* . . . began to press him on his right. Thus positioned, the enemy surrendered, and were marched out on the Hamburg road, through *Jackson's* brigade, and placed by me in charge of Colonel *Shorter*, with his regiment, the Eighteenth Alabama, and marched to Corinth. The enemy captured proved to be the command of General Prentiss.

The division was then advanced to the Pittsburg edge of the field, in which the enemy had stacked their arms, and halted for a supply of ammunition. Most of the regiments were supplied from the camps of the enemy. [*O.R.,* X, pt. 1, pp. 532–33.]

Report of Col. Joseph Wheeler, CSA, Nineteenth Alabama Infantry, Withers's Division, Second Army Corps, Army of the Mississippi

It was now about 3 o'clock in the afternoon. The regiment had been marching and fighting since 6:30 A.M., had been through three of the enemy's camps, and in three distinct engagements. The enemy being now driven from all their positions on our right, we were ordered to march to the left and center, where a heavy fire was going on. The regiment changed front forward on the tenth company, and marched rapidly by the right of companies to the front some 1½ or 2 miles in the direction indicated, coming up on the left of General *Chalmers'* brigade.

The regiment, while marching through a burning wood, encountered a heavy fire from the enemy, who were drawn up in front of and to the right of a large camp, which fire the regiment returned with effect.

I was here met by General *Chalmers,* who told me his brigade was worn-out and overpowered by superior numbers, and said the troops must move to his assistance. The regiment then moved quickly to and in advance of his left, and dislodged the enemy from a strong position they had taken in large force, screened by a ridge and house. We had advanced about 200 yards, the enemy having retreated a short distance to another hill, where they were re-enforced, and in a great measure secured from our fire.

The regiment here exhibited an example of cool, heroic courage which would do credit to soldiers of long experience in battle. Subjected as they were to a deadly fire of artillery and a cross-fire of infantry, they stood their ground with firmness and delivered their fire rapidly, but with cool deliberation and good effect. During this fire, General *Chalmers'* brigade having retired from our view, finding it necessary to move to the right, in order to support Colonel *Moore,* who had just come up with . . . the Second Texas, we were met by a new and warm fire, which was vigorously returned.

At this moment the enemy raised a white flag, which caused us to slacken our fire, but as a large force of theirs to the left of our front continued a heavy fire (probably not knowing that their commander had surrendered), I moved the regiment a few yards obliquely to the rear to secure a more favorable position. This fire was soon silenced. Our cavalry moved up and conducted the prisoners (amounting to about 3,000 men) out before us.

The regiment was then ordered to take charge of these prisoners and started with them to the rear, but was halted and formed in line, with orders to charge the enemy to the river; but after passing through the deep ravine below the lowest camps we were halted within about 400 yards of the river, and remained ready to move forward for about half an hour, when night came on and we were ordered to the rear and . . . assigned to bivouac by General *Withers*.

During all of this movement the regiment was under a heavy fire from their gunboats and other artillery. [*O.R.*, X, pt. 1, pp. 558–59.]

Trabue's movements throughout the day, leading up to the events described in the following reading, are but one illustration of the extraordinary distances, over rough ground, units fought. In the morning, *Trabue* started along the Corinth-Pittsburg Road, initially moved to the northwest, passed through McDowell Field (vicinity Stop 7), wheeled to the east, passing north of Stop 10, and participated in the final assault on the Hornets' Nest, attacking from the north. He continued to move east toward the Tennessee River, and at the end of the day was along the banks of the Tennessee.]

Report of Col. Robert P. Trabue, CSA, Fourth Kentucky Infantry, Commanding First (Kentucky) Brigade, Reserve Corps, Army of the Mississippi

I came under the enemy's fire at 9:30 A.M., having reached the verge of a long, crescent-shaped open field, which was without fencing, about one mile and a half from Pittsburg Landing. The shot and shell from the woods on the opposite side of the field fell thick and fast around us, but caused very few casualties. Gov. George W. *Johnson* and Col. Robert *Mckee*, volunteer aides, here lost their horses, when the Governor shouldered a musket and joined the company of Capt. Ben *Monroe*, Fourth Kentucky.

I here halted the command for an instant in a slight depression of the ground, and rode forward on the open field to observe what might lie before and around me and to place *Cobb's* battery in position, which I did, but it was afterward moved under orders from some one and without my knowledge.

Shortly before this, by order of General *Beauregard*, I had detached the Third Kentucky, Fourth Alabama Battalion, and *Crews'* Tennessee battalion, with *Byrne's* battery, to the right to support General *Anderson*. . . .

The examination which I made from the old field showed it to have been the scene of recent conflict, but at that time our lines there seem to have broken and no troops of ours were in sight. I discovered also to my left and front two camps of the enemy still occupied by his troops, and I saw them also in the woods across the field in front of his camps. I immediately moved by the left flank to the left and confronted him [Sherman's line]. I had scarcely taken my new position—in fact was changing the front of the left wing—when he deployed before me. I opened my fire on him when he was thus employed, and soon received his in return. The combat here was a severe one. . . . The enemy appeared to out-number us greatly.

Ignorant of the topography of the country, and not knowing his force, I was for a while reluctant to charge, and as he was in the woods, too, with some advantage of position, I fought him . . . for an hour and a quarter, killing and wounding 400 to 500 of the Forty-sixth Ohio Infantry alone, as well as many of another Ohio regiment, a Missouri regiment, and some Iowa troops, from all of whom we eventually took prisoners. . . .

At length, after having extended my line by adding my reserve to the left of it and obtaining as a support General *Stewart,* with part of his brigade, and a part of General *Anderson's* command, which I found in my rear in a wooded ravine, I gave order to fix bayonets and move forward in double-quick time at a charge, which was executed in the handsomest manner and with complete success. The enemy, . . . unable to stand this charge, ran through their camps into the woods in their rear, whither we followed them. They were, however, too badly routed to make a stand. . . . These woods intervene between the field and camps I have described and the field and camp in which General Prentiss surrendered. . . . This brigade entered the camp nearly simultaneously with General *Breckinridge* and others from the right. . . .

I then moved up and rejoined General *Breckinridge,* who, with *Statham's* and *Bowen's* brigades, was occupying the front line, being on the crest of the hill (or high land) overlooking the narrow valley of the Tennessee River, on which and near by was Pittsburg Landing.

Having been halted here for more than an hour, we endured a most terrific cannonade and shelling from the enemy's gunboats. . . . From this position, when it was nearly dark, we were ordered to the rear to encamp, which movement was effected in good order. . . . My command occupied the vacated camps of the Forty-Sixth Ohio and Sixth Iowa regiments on the Purdy road near the bridge over Owl Creek, but the tents having been mainly destroyed, my men were again exposed to rain, which fell during the night. The camps, however, were rich in subsistence. . . . After a bountiful supper they slept, despite the rain. [*O.R.*, X, pt. 1, pp. 615–17.]

Drive straight ahead for 0.2 mile. Turn left at the stop sign. Drive 0.7 mile to *Ruggles's* Batteries (on the left). Walk behind the line of guns and face the direction they are pointing (east toward the Hornets' Nest, approximately 400 yards away).

STOP 17, RUGGLES'S BATTERIES

To understand this critical part of the battle, we must go back several hours. Recall that Maj. Gen. Prentiss's Union division had been attacked (vicinity of Stop 12) at about 9:00 A.M. Under pressure from attacking Confederates, his disorganized troops fell back. Prentiss withdrew through the troops of W. H. L. Wallace's division and Lauman's brigade of Hurlbut's division to reorganize. These latter troops were formed in a line along a primitive wagon road. Prentiss rallied remnants of his command, perhaps a thousand men total, north of the wagon road. A lull ensued while hungry Southern troops helped themselves to the abundance of supplies in the overrun Union camps. Prentiss sought and received permission from Maj. Gen. Hurlbut to move his forces to support Lauman around 10:00 A.M.

At approximately 11:00 A.M., Confederate brigades under *Shaver, Stephens,* and *Gibson* began a series of frontal assaults against the defenders along the wagon road—an area that *Gibson's* Confederates labeled "a hornets' nest." General *Bragg* ordered repeated assaults, taking heavy casualties while inflicting moderate losses on the defenders. (This occurred during the actions described at Stops 13 through 16.) After *Johnston's* death, General *Beauregard* left *Bragg* to direct the Confederate right flank units and Brig. Gen. Daniel *Ruggles* responsible for the Confederate center—facing the Hornets' Nest.

Ruggles, observing the futility of the repeated infantry assaults

Brig. Gen. Daniel *Ruggles*, Commander, First Division, Second Army Corps (Bragg), Army of the Mississippi. (U.S. Army Military History Institute)

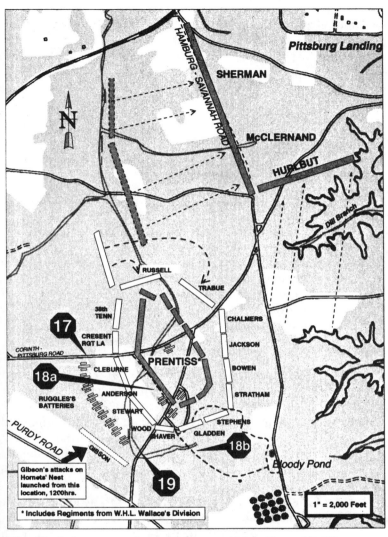

The Confederate assault on the Hornets' Nest (Stops 17–19).

against the Union position, called in artillery batteries from the surrounding area. In an hour's time he had amassed over fifty cannon in an irregular line facing the Union position. Never before in the Western Hemisphere had so many pieces of artillery been massed to attack a position. Only Napoleon, and those who later gained their experience against his armies, had used massed artillery in this manner. At about 4:00 P.M., *Ruggles's* guns opened fire, sending two to three rounds per minute from each of the cannon crashing into the Union line.

Report of Brig. Gen. Daniel Ruggles, CSA, Commanding First Division, Second Army Corps, Army of the Mississippi

The First Brigade *[Gibson's]*, united with Brigadier General *Hindman's* advance, after having driven the enemy from their camp on our right, engaged in repeated charges against the enemy's new line, now held on the margin of an open field swept by his fire [this is the field to your front].

The enemy's camps on our left being apparently cleared, I endeavored to concentrate forces on his right flank in this new position, and directed Captain *Hodgson's* battery into action there. The fire of this battery and a charge from the Second Brigade *[Anderson's]* put the enemy to flight. Even after having been driven back from this position the enemy rallied and disputed the ground with remarkable tenacity for some two or three hours against our forces in front and his right flank, where cavalry, infantry, and artillery mingled in the conflict.

As the enemy finally gave way I directed the movement of the Second Brigade toward the right along the crest of the ridge following the line of the enemy's continued resistance, and sent a section of *Ketchum's* battery into action on a road leading toward Pittsburg, in a position overlooking the broken slope below, to reply to batteries nearly in front and in the forest to the right, with which the enemy swept a large circuit around; sending also Colonel *Smith's* Louisiana Crescent regiment, Third Brigade, to support this battery, then harassed by skirmishers, and to seize the opportunity to charge the enemy's position. I then put a section of guns, commanded by First Lieut. James C. *Thrall* . . . in position on the road leading along the ridge, still farther to the right, which was soon forced to retire under the concentrated fire of the enemy's artillery.

Discovering the enemy in considerable numbers moving through the forest on the lower margin of the open field in front, I obtained *Trabue's* and *Stanford's* light batteries and . . . directed their fire on masses of the enemy then pressing forward toward our right, engaged in a fierce contest with our forces then advancing against him in that direction. I directed my staff officers at the same time to bring forward all the field guns they could collect from the left toward the right as rapidly as possible. . . .

For a brief period the enemy apparently gained ground, and when the conflict was at its height these batteries opened upon his concentrated forces, enfilading Prentiss' division on his right flank, producing immediate commotion, and soon resulted in the precipitate retreat of the enemy from the contest.

At this moment the Second Brigade and the Crescent Regiment pressed forward and cut off a considerable portion of the enemy, comprising Prentiss' division, who surrendered to the Crescent Regiment, of my command, then pressing upon its rear.

Subsequently, while advancing toward the river, I received instructions from General *Bragg* to carry forward all the troops I could find. . . . [*O.R.*, X, pt. 1, pp. 471–72.]

Report of Col. Smith P. Bankhead, CSA, First Brigade, First Division, First Corps, Army of the Mississippi

At about 2 P.M. . . . I had been compelled to fall back from a position on the extreme left of our lines, opposite a field near where Prentiss' [actually McClernand's] camp was afterward discovered to be, and under orders from Maj. Gen. L. *Polk* retired my battery about 200 yards through the woods skirting the field.

As I retired I was informed that a general attack was contemplated and then being organized by our troops on the enemy to the right of my position, and it was conjectured that the enemy had made his last stand before being driven to the banks of the river.

At this juncture my battery was ordered by a staff officer to the edge of the field near Prentiss' camp, and to a position sweeping his rear approaches, and from which I had previously retired. As I went into action Captain *Stanford* formed on my right. I found the Washington Artillery already in position on my left and firing rapidly. Captain *Robertson's* 12-pounder battery formed on the right of *Stanford,* with Captain . . . *Rutledge* on his right, and some one or two other batteries still farther to the right. . . .

The effect of this tremendous concentrated fire was very evident. The reserves, which could be plainly seen going up to Prentiss' relief, fell back in confusion under the shower of shot, shell, and canister that was poured upon them, while our infantry, encouraged by such heavy artillery support, rushed forward with a shout and carried the position.

I regret that I cannot state the name of the staff officer ordering me up or to whose staff he was attached. All I have been able to ascertain, upon consultation with battery commanders touching this remarkable concentration of artillery, is that it was not the result of accident, but under and by the direction of one controlling mind, as batteries were brought up from various portions of the field and directed to this particular position. . . . Aides to Major General *Polk* . . . state that they felt assured it was executed under the direction of Brigadier-General *Ruggles,* as they saw him at that time on our extreme left engaged in ordering up batteries for some position along the lines. [*O.R.,* X, pt. 1, pp. 475–76.]

Capt. L. D. Sandidge, CSA, Acting Inspector General, First Division, Department of Mississippi and East, to Brig. Gen. Daniel Ruggles, January 25, 1863

Being cognizant of many inquiries made by officers of the artillery who participated in the memorable battle of Shiloh . . . and particularly concerning the effect our artillery had in forcing Prentiss' division to fall back in a direction which compelled his ultimate surrender, I will . . . make a short statement of a few facts which occurred under my own observation . . . concerning the artillery fire and Prentiss' division.

Late Sunday evening, the first day of the fight, after our forces had compelled Prentiss' troops to commence a rapid retreat, I rejoined you just beyond an open space known as the enemy's parade ground . . . and found myself . . . in the wake of the retreating enemy. At this point, however, a desperate stand was made by them, and they succeeded in checking our infantry, and were apparently intending to hold the ground they then occupied till they could be reinforced.

At this juncture, about 3 P.M. as near as I can recollect, I received from you *[Ruggles]* a verbal but positive order to bring up all the artillery I could find and post it along the Woods road running between the parade ground . . . and a small cleared field in front, through the center of which passed a small brook densely crowded with large shrubbery, in which large numbers of the enemy had taken refuge, to the serious discomfort of our troops, who for the time were unable to dislodge them.

I immediately placed a section of some battery . . . — I do not recall which—in position, and was on the point of bringing more guns in position, when . . . I was directed to ride to the rear and bring up the *debris* of several disorganized infantry regiments and other officers of the staff, under your personal direction and supervision, collected all the guns of three or four batteries along the position . . . on the crest of the hills overlooking the field, and when I returned to rejoin you, after an unsuccessful attempt to forward the men . . . I found the enemy, being unable to withstand the destructive cannonade which you had directed against them, had fallen back rapidly through the field over the hills beyond, when, finding themselves cut off by portions of our division and being threatened on the flank by General *Polk,* they threw down their arms.

I have no doubt that had they been seasonably re-enforced when they checked our advancing troops they could certainly have broken our lines had you not concentrated all the artillery you could obtain at that point, which was weakest. . . . No one who observed the effects of that firing could but be agreeably surprised at its result. [*O.R.,* X, pt. 1, pp. 476–77.]

Ex-Colonel S. S. Heard, CSA to Captain Hooe, Assistant Adjutant-General, Columbus, Miss., March 18, 1863

Between 12 and 1 o'clock on Sunday we had carried all the enemy's encampments except Prentiss'. At this time, however, the enemy made a desperate stand 200 or 300 paces east of the last encampment and about north of the open space known to us as the enemy's parade ground. For two hours our success at that point appeared doubtful.

I was ordered by General *Ruggles* immediately to bring up the artillery. When I reported the artillery, the general ordered it into position 200 or 300 paces lower down the ridge, northeast of the parade ground. Our guns opened upon the enemy with great success from that position, which created great confusion in the enemy's lines. They soon gave way and were hotly pursued by our troops from that point. Other guns were brought and put into position lower down the ridge by order of General *Ruggles,* at the southwest corner of a small cleared field, where the ground north and east of the cleared land was covered with bushes and small saplings, in which the enemy had made a stand.

The general ordered the artillery to fire upon them, which they did, and very soon they returned our fire with some effect. The general now ordered the Seventeenth and Nineteenth Regiments Louisiana Volunteers, with some other infantry regiments, to march by the right flank in the direction of the Tennessee River.

In the meantime I was ordered by the general to re-enforce at that point the artillery already there. By the time we got our guns in position we heard the report of musketry, which we justly concluded was that of our troops sent in that direction. We also saw troops from north and east of the small field marching in a southerly direction, as we supposed, to re-enforce their friends.

Our guns opened fire upon them at that juncture with such unparalleled effect that in less time than twenty minutes they were in full retreat toward Prentiss' encampment, and in less than one hour Prentiss and his friends were brought to the general as prisoners. The General and staff were sitting on their horses at the north end of the small cleared field, near where several bales of hay had been set on fire by the explosion of our guns while shooting at the enemy across the field, where the general received Prentiss and other prisoners captured at the same time. . . .

These are my reasons . . . for saying that General *Ruggles* was the controlling genius on that occasion. He himself con-

Gibson's brigade charging Hurlbut's troops in the "Hornets' Nest," early in the fight for that position. Note that the vegetation is shown to be much more open than on the present battlefield. *(Battles and Leaders of the Civil War)*

ceived the plan of concentrating the artillery at those different points . . . which we all believe was the cause of Prentiss and his command surrendering at the time they did. I . . . only write from recollection, and I no doubt have omitted many things . . . that would be highly creditable to General *Ruggles'* talents, capacity, and gallantry, as displayed on the field that day. [*O.R.,* X, pt. 1, pp. 477–78.]

Return to your car. Drive back and retrace your route for 0.3 mile. Turn right on Hornets' Nest Road for an additional 0.3 mile to the Minnesota Light Artillery Monument (on the right side of the road). Park and walk to the right down the road into the Hornets' Nest.

STOP 18A, THE HORNETS' NEST

About 10:30 A.M., Prentiss moved his reconstituted force (five to six hundred of his own men plus a like number from the Twenty-third Missouri Infantry) into the area around where you are now

The "Hornets' Nest"—Prentiss's troops and Hickenlooper's Battery repulsing Hardee's troops. Note the openness depicted, as compared with the battlefield today. *(Battles and Leaders of the Civil War)*

located. As you can see, it is high ground with protecting woods and split rail fences that the defenders could use for protection. Any attack directly against this position would have to move across the open field to your front. As Prentiss put his troops into line, on his right were units from W. H. L. Wallace's division, and on his left, extending to the Peach Orchard, were the brigades of Lauman and McArthur from Hurlbut's division. To the right of Wallace, McClernand's division re-formed, and on his right stood Sherman's division. The Confederates continued to press the attack against this reconstituted line. [See map, p. 112.]

For a time the three Union division commanders in the center directed the fight in this area. When W. H. L. Wallace fell mortally wounded and Hurlbut withdrew elements of his force under heavy pressure, Prentiss found himself the senior general on the field. During the afternoon, Grant met with Prentiss and directed him to hold his position at all hazards.

In the confusion of the battle, the Confederates missed an opportunity to attack the Union forces as they were re-forming, when units were redirected away from the Hornets' Nest area to respond to calls for assistance on other parts of the battlefield. This confusion gave the Union troops invaluable time to organize their defense and reduced Confederate combat power initially available for attacking the Hornets' Nest.

Confederate attacks against the Hornets' Nest were uncoordinated, with units being sent forward piecemeal, allowing defenders to concentrate fires against the portion of the line being attacked. *Stephens's* brigade of *Cheatham's* division was the first to be repulsed. General *Bragg* then ordered Col. Randall *Gibson's* brigade to attack, without coordinating artillery support. *Gibson's* brigade assaulted across the open field, only to be thrown back as it struck the strong Union defensive line. The fiery *Bragg* ordered *Gibson* to attack again. *Gibson* reported making four attacks, suffering heavy casualties each time. During the two hours over which these attacks occurred, General *Johnston* had led the attack in the area in front of the Peach Orchard described in Stop 13.

After *Johnston's* death, *Beauregard* did nothing to stop *Bragg* from continuing to press the attacks against the Hornets' Nest. Only after *Ruggles's* massed batteries began inflicting heavy casualties on the Union defenders, coupled with the gradual progress against both flanks of the Union position by other Confederate units, did the Union position fall. Prentiss, left in command of the units in the Hornets' Nest after Wallace fell and Hurlbut withdrew, finding himself surrounded and cut off, was compelled to surrender around 5:30 P.M. The determined Union defense in the center of the line had provided sufficient time for Sherman's and McClernand's forces to withdraw and for Major General Grant to establish a formidable line in the vicinity of Pittsburg Landing.

Narrative of Col. William Preston Johnston, CSA, Son of Gen. Albert Sidney Johnston, Commanding Army of the Mississippi

General *Johnston* had pushed *Chalmers* to the right and front, sweeping down the left bank of Lick Creek, driving in pickets, until he encountered Stuart's Federal brigade on the Pittsburg and Hamburg Road. Stuart was strongly posted on a steep hill near the river, covered with thick undergrowth, and with an open field in front [Stop 12]. McArthur was to his right and rear in the woods. *Jackson* attacked McArthur, who fell back; and *Chalmers* went at Stuart's brigade. This command [Stuart's] reserved its fire until *Chalmers's* men were within forty yards, and then delivered a heavy and destructive volley; but, after a hard fight, the Federals were driven back [vicinity Stop 12].

Chalmers's right rested on the Tennessee River bottom-lands, and he fought down the bank toward Pittsburg Landing. The enemy's left was completely turned, and the Federal army was now crowded on a shorter line, a mile or more to the rear of its first position, with many of their brigades hors de combat.

The new line of battle was established before 10 o'clock. All the Confederate troops were then in the front line, except two of *Breckinridge's* brigades, *Bowen's* and *Statham's,* which were moving to the Confederate right, and soon occupied the interval to the left of *Chalmers* and *Jackson. Hardee,* with *Cleburne* and *Pond,* was pressing Sherman slowly but steadily back. *Bragg* and *Polk* met about half-past 10 o'clock, and by agreement *Polk* led his troops against McClernand, while *Bragg* directed the operations against the Federal center.

A gigantic contest now began which lasted more than five hours. In the impetuous rush forward of regiments to fill the gaps in the front line, even the brigade organization was broken; but, though there was dislocation of commands, there was little loss of effective force. The Confederate assaults were made by rapid and often unconnected charges along the line. They were repeatedly checked, and often repulsed. Sometimes counter-charges drove them back for short distances; but, whether in assault or recoil, both sides saw their brave soldiers fall in frightful numbers. The Confederates came on in motley garb, varying from the favorite gray and domestic "butternut" to the blue of certain Louisiana regiments, which paid dearly the penalty of doubtful colors. Over them waved flags and pennons as various as their uniforms. At each charge there went up a wild yell, heard above the roar of artillery; only the Kentuckians, advancing with measured step, sang in chorus their war-song: "Cheer, boys, cheer; we'll march away to battle."

On the Federal left center W. H. L. Wallace's and Hurlbut's divisions were massed, with Prentiss's fragments, in a position so impregnable and thronged within such fierce defends, that it won from the Confederates the memorable title of the "Hornets' Nest." Here, behind a dense thicket on the crest of a hill was posted a strong force of as hardy troops as ever fought almost perfectly protected by the conformation of the ground and by logs and other rude and hastily prepared defenses. To assail it an open field had to be passed, enfiladed by the fire of its batteries.

No figure of speech would be too strong to express the deadly peril of assault upon this natural fortress. For five hours brigade after brigade was led against it. *Hindman's* brigades, which earlier had swept everything before them, were reduced to fragments, and paralyzed for the remainder of the day. *A. P. Stewart's* regiments made fruitless assaults. Then *Bragg* ordered up *Gibson's* brigade . . . [which] made a gallant charge; but, like the others, recoiled from the fire it encountered. Under a cross-fire of artillery and musketry it at last fell back with very heavy loss. *Gibson* asked that artillery should be sent him; but it was not at hand, and *Bragg* sent orders to charge again. The colonels thought it hopeless; but *Gibson* led them again to the attack, and again they suffered a bloody repulse.

The brigade was four times repulsed, but maintained its ground steadily, until [Brig. Gen. W. H. L.] Wallace's position was turned, when, renewing its forward movement in conjunction with *Cheatham's* command, it helped to drive back its stout opponents. *Cheatham*, charging with *Stephens's* brigade on *Gibson's* right, across an open field, had been caught under a murderous cross-fire, but fell back in good order, and, later in the day, came in on *Breckinridge's* left in the last assault. . . . This bloody fray lasted till nearly 4 o'clock, without making any visible impression on the Federal center. But when its flanks were turned, these assaulting columns, crowding in on its front, aided in its capture. [Johnston, "Albert Sidney Johnston at Shiloh," pp. 562–63.]

Report of Brig. Gen. B. M. Prentiss, USA, Sixth Division, Army of the Tennessee

Being again assailed . . . by an overwhelming force, and not being able longer to hold the ground against the enemy, I ordered the division to fall back to the line occupied by General Hurlbut, and at 9:05 A.M. reformed to the right of General Hurlbut, and to the left of Brig. Gen. W. H. L. Wallace, who I found in command of the division assigned to Major-General Smith. At this point the Twenty-third Missouri Infantry . . . which had just disembarked from a transport and had been

ordered to report to me . . . joined me. This regiment I immediately assigned to a position on the left. My battery (Fifth
Ohio) was posted to the right on the road.

At about 10 o'clock my line was again assailed, and finding
my command greatly reduced by reason of casualties and because of the falling back of many of the men to the river, they
being panic-stricken—a majority of them having now for the
first time been exposed to fire—I communicated with General
W. H. L. Wallace, who sent to my assistance the Eighth Iowa
Infantry. . . .

After having once driven the enemy back from this position, Maj. Gen. U. S. Grant appeared upon the field. I exhibited
to him the disposition of my entire force, which disposition
received his commendations, and I received my final orders,
which were to maintain that position at all hazards. This position I did maintain until 4 o'clock P.M., when General Hurlbut,
being overpowered, was forced to retire. I was then compelled
to change front with the Twenty-third Missouri, Twenty-first
Missouri, Eighteenth Wisconsin, Eighteenth Missouri, and part
of the Twelfth Michigan, occupying a portion of the ground
vacated by General Hurlbut. I was in constant communication
with Generals Hurlbut and Wallace during the day, and both
of them were aware of the importance of holding our position
until night. When the gallant Hurlbut was forced to retire General Wallace and myself consulted, and agreed to hold our
positions at all hazards, believing that we could thus save the
army from destruction; we having been now informed for
the first time that all others had fallen back to the vicinity of
the river. A few minutes after, General W. H. L. Wallace received the wound of which he shortly afterwards died. Upon
the fall of General Wallace, his division, excepting the Eighth
Iowa . . . acting with me, and the Fourteenth Iowa, . . . Twelfth
Iowa, . . . and Fifty-eighth Illinois, . . . retired from the field.

Perceiving that I was about to be surrounded, and having
dispatched my aide . . . for re-enforcements, I determined to
assail the enemy, which had passed between me and the river,
charging upon him with my entire force. I found him advancing in mass, completely encircling my command, and nothing
was left but to harass him and retard his progress so long as
might be possible. This I did until 5:30 P.M., when, finding that
further resistance must result in the slaughter of every man in

the command, I had to yield the fight. The enemy succeeded in capturing myself and 2,200 rank and file, many of them wounded. . . . [*O.R.*, X, pt. 2, pp. 277–80.]

Report of Maj. Gen. B. F. Cheatham, CSA, Commanding Second Division, First Corps, Army of the Mississippi

About 2:30 P.M. Colonel *Maney*, with the left wing of his regiment, . . . reported to me in front of the position which the enemy had to this time held obstinately against the efforts of parts of the commands of Generals *Bragg*, *Breckinridge*, and my own. General *Breckinridge*, meantime, had moved his command forward and to my right, and was slowly but steadily pressing it through a dense wood to attack the position on its left, and with the purpose of sustaining him by vigorous cooperation against its front I directed Colonel *Maney* to immediately prepare for action, advising him, so far as time permitted, of the difficulties of the position, and instructing him as to where our different forces were located, and, at his own request, giving him the privilege of selecting his command for the purpose. The Ninth Tennessee Regiment . . . being at hand and having to this time suffered less than the others of the Second Brigade, was, with its battalion of the First Tennessee, selected to move forward with him across the field fronting the wood, while Colonel *Cummings*, Nineteenth Tennessee Regiment (properly of General *Breckinridge's* command, but which had been with Colonel *Maney* on his detached service during the morning), was placed to his right and between General *Breckinridge* and myself, with instructions to move forward with the First and Ninth Tennessee.

With these dispositions I pressed the final attack upon the position in question. Colonel *Maney* advanced his First and Ninth in excellent order across the field [to the east of the Hornets' Nest in the vicinity of the Peach Orchard], and was so fortunate as to almost reach the shelter of the woods before the enemy opened fire on him. Pressing forward to this point, he ordered his line to lie down until a general fire from the enemy's line had been delivered, and then promptly resumed his advance. The next instant I knew (from the lively cheering in his direction) that his charge had begun and the enemy routed. . . . Judging the enemy now to be in full retreat, I directed Lieutenant-Colonel *Miller*, of the First Battalion of Mississippi Cavalry . . . to move forward rapidly in the direction of the retreating column and fall upon him in his flight. This was well executed, and resulted in the capture of a number of prisoners, together with [a] . . . Michigan battery of six guns . . . which had acted vigorously in defending the position. . . .

Broken and routed, he apparently, from all directions, seemed flying toward the river and our own forces as generally closing upon him. Most of his force, with which the position had been held, fell into the hands of our army in the effort to retire.

With the balance of my command I pressed forward and joined Colonel *Maney*, who had now become my advance, and had in his pursuit captured and sent to the rear many of the routed enemy.

About this time a halt was made for the purpose of some concentration of our forces of all commands for a concerted attack upon the enemy, then understood to have concentrated on the river bank under shelter of his gunboats. . . . [*O.R.*, X, pt. 1, pp. 439–40.]

Report of Col. George Maney, CSA, First Tennessee Infantry, Commanding Second Brigade, Second Division, First Corps, Army of the Mississippi

As I approached the battle quite a number from other commands, who had dropped back seemingly exhausted by fatigue, cheered by the arrival of even this small body of fresh troops, rallied on my rear and advanced with me.

In a few moments I found and reported to Major-General *Cheatham*, at the time engaged in an effort to dislodge the enemy from a wood a little to the east of the center. My brigade, under Colonel *Stephens*, senior officer in my absence, had been warmly engaged at this position before my arrival, and the Sixth Tennessee, as I was informed, having suffered particularly severely in a gallant charge here, had been temporarily withdrawn when I came up.

General *Cheatham* directed me to immediately attack the enemy's position in this wood, giving me the privilege of selecting my command for the purpose, and advising me of its being a difficult position and of the failure of several previous efforts by our troops to carry it. Colonel *Cummings,* Nineteenth Tennessee Regiment, being now in sight, and the Ninth Tennessee at hand and comparatively fresh, were, with the First Tennessee Battalion, selected as my attacking force.

Observing the ground in advance not to favor an extended line of battle, Colonel *Douglass'* regiment was formed on the left of the First Tennessee and Major *McNairy,* aide-de-camp to Major-General *Cheatham,* was requested to move Colonel *Cummings'* regiment a short distance to the right, with instructions to advance from that position in concert with the balance of my command upon the enemy in the wood.

With the First and Ninth in line, I moved over an open field directly on the enemy in the woods, and on approaching met some of our own troops retiring before a destructive fire. My line of battle was promptly opened by the right of companies to the front, so as to allow our friends to pass to the rear, and at the same time quickening my advance I was so fortunate as to pass the field and gain the cover of the woods before the enemy's attention seemed fairly directed to me.

Here my command was ordered to lie down, and a fire was opened mainly for the purpose of ascertaining by the enemy's reply his force and exact position. This was quickly done, and immediately on his fire being delivered my advance was renewed in good order. Observing in a few moments the enemy to give indications of wavering, I on the moment ordered the First and Ninth to charge. The order was responded to with a cheer, and both regiments sprang forward with enthusiasm worthy of their cause, holding an alignment which would have done credit to veterans. Colonel *Cummings'* regiment came gallantly forward at the same time on the right.

The charge was in every way a success. The enemy could not wait to sustain the shock, but broke in disorder and fled precipitously before us. In a few moments we occupied the position which he had perhaps contested with as much obstinacy as any on that day. It proved to be a small ravine passing diagonally toward the river, fringed with a considerable growth of small timber, thus forming an excellent natural rifle pit. . . .

Deeming a constant press forward the best means of securing the advantage already gained, I made but a short halt on the position from which the enemy had been driven, and with the First and Ninth Regiments continued my advance as rap-

Print depicting the intensity of the fighting in the "Hornets' Nest." (U.S. Army Military History Institute)

idly as possible in the direction of his flight. He made no rally before my command that day, and I was halted near the river for the purpose, as I understood, of allowing some concentration of our troops for attacking the enemy at the river and near his gunboats. [*O.R.*, X, pt. 1, pp. 454–55.]

Walk back to the Minnesota Light Artillery Monument (near where your car is parked). Continue to walk across the road to the east, past the artillery pieces (Munch's Battery) and the Fourteenth and Eighth Iowa Monuments, to an area marked "For Pedestrians Only." Walk down the trail to the Twelfth Michigan Infantry Monument.

STOP 18B, THE HORNETS' NEST (continued)

Here is a much better view of the wagon road behind which parts of Prentiss's division fought throughout the day in the Hornets' Nest, until finally overwhelmed in the late afternoon and forced to surrender.

Continue to walk along the road for 100 yards to a large granite monument (Thirty-first Indiana Monument). The actions here are a continuation of the Hornets' Nest battle.

Report of Col. Charles Cruft, USA, Thirty-first Indiana Infantry, Third Brigade, Fourth Division, Army of the Tennessee

Regiment after regiment marched up from a large ravine to the left, moving in echelon in compact lines, with Confederate flags flying, in perfect order, as if on parade, and came steadily down upon our small front. An order was given for our left to advance. My regiment did so promptly. It was soon evident that the advance could not be sustained, in the absence of a reserve, against the overwhelming force of well-disciplined troops of the enemy. After my regiment had fired some ten rounds the regiment to the left was forced back. An order was now given along the entire line to fall back, and a general retreat was made about 3:30 o'clock P.M. to a ridge near the river. Here the regiment was again formed in brigade line and marched up to the support of a section of a battery of large siege guns, and occupied this position during the desperate fight which closed the day.

After the final repulse of the enemy the regiment was moved forward, with a residue of the brigade, about 3/4 of a mile, and there bivouacked for the night, at about 7:30 o'clock. [*O.R.*, X, pt. 1, pp. 235–36.]

Report of Col. Francis Quinn, USA, Twelfth Michigan Infantry, Commanding Sixth Division, Army of the Tennessee

The whole division fell back to their tents and again rallied, and although no regular line was formed, yet from behind every tree a deadly fire was poured out upon the enemy, which held them in check for about one-half hour, when, reenforcements coming to their assistance, they advanced furiously upon our camp, and we were forced to again give way. At this time we lost four pieces of artillery. The division fell back about one-half mile, very much scattered and broken. Here we were posted, being drawn up in line behind a dense clump of bushes, when General Prentiss rode up and proposed heroically for us to fight our way back to our tents, but finally gave this up and formed the line for defense where it was.

Here occurred one of the noblest and most determined resistances ever offered by an inferior number to an overwhelming foe. The remnant of the division was so posted as to command the road leading from Corinth to Pittsburg Landing, on which road were posted two pieces of artillery. Our men were ordered to lie down on the ground, which they did, nor did they have long to wait. On came the enemy, yelling and yelping, and for about ten minutes kept up a dreadful and incessant firing, with but little effect, for our men were flat on the ground, and their balls went by mostly harmless. Not so with ours, for the groans and shrieks in the bushes told the destructiveness of our fire.

Again they fell back and threw their forces more to our left, and then again came back to our point and repeated just what has been described. It was about 9 o'clock in the morning when the first charge was made upon this part of our lines. About 2 o'clock P.M., a movement being made to outflank us, the line on the left of our division fell back, forming a line at right angles with our division, which still stubbornly held its place.

Now a most determined rush was made on the Sixth Division to drive them from their place. Our men were killed at the guns; the horses were shot in the harness; but the rebels dared not venture over the bushes to take or spike the guns, for our boys were pouring into them a most destructive fire. The enemy again retired, and our boys brought the guns in by hand back of the line, and opened a way through the line of battle for them to play, which they did, adding speed to the retreating enemy. In a short time they rallied again, and made another dash at this point, but met with the same result.

Between 4 and 5 o'clock in the afternoon, as near as I can judge, two regiments, it is said, surrendered on the immediate right of our division. General Prentiss ordered me to go and rally some of our men—meaning men of the Twelfth Michigan infantry, of which regiment there were not over 40 or 50 on the ground, and very few officers. Our major had gone of his own request for this purpose early in the day, but had not returned. I immediately went, but found the fire worse in going on our right and rear than in front. Fire was also being found on our left. At this time General Prentiss must have been taken prisoner. He was a brave man, and cheered his men to duty during the whole day. Where the fight was thickest and danger the greatest there was he found, and his presence gave renewed confidence. . . .

This point was held from 9 o'clock A.M. till 4:30 P.M., amid the most dreadful carnage for a little space ever witnessed on any field of battle during this war. [*O.R.*, X, pt. 1, pp. 280–81.]

Walk to your car. Drive straight ahead for 0.1 mile. Stop and park next to the fourth marker on the left (Stephens' Brigade). Face to the rear of the car (north) toward the Hornet's Nest.

STOP 19, THE HORNETS' NEST (continued)

This is still part of the Hornets' Nest fight. Early in the attack on Prentiss's position (probably around 11:00–11:30 A.M.), troops from *Shaver's* and *Stephens's* brigades attacked one after another in this general area. Each was met by heavy rifle and artillery fire, and repulsed.

Later in the day *Anderson's* brigade came into this same area and attacked. Battered by *Ruggles's* massed batteries, the weakened Union defenders were unable to withstand the determined Confederate assaults.

Report of Brig. Gen. Patton Anderson, CSA, Commanding Second Brigade, First Division, Second Army Corps, Army of the Mississippi

The enemy's fire in front and to our left was now evidently diminishing. Not so, however, on our right [area of the Hornets' Nest]. I therefore determined to swing around on my right and endeavor to press the enemy's right center back upon his right, where General *Hardee's* invincible columns were driving him toward the river. One of his batteries lay immediately in our front, concealed by a dense undergrowth and sharp ravine. In approaching it I met Colonel *Smith*, of the Crescent Regiment, who had become detached from his brigade and now proposed to unite with mine, to which I gladly consented, and directed him to form on my left.

After consulting together for a few moments and making

some inquiry of General *Gardner,* who was passing at the moment and who had reconnoitered the ground in the vicinity of the battery, . . . I determined to move around my right a short distance, letting Colonel *Smith* go to the left, and from the positions thus gained to make a simultaneous movement upon the infantry supporting the battery, while a section of our own field pieces engaged them in front. In moving forward through the thick underbrush . . . I met a portion of a Louisiana regiment . . . returning, and its officers informed me that I could not get through that brush. I pushed forward, however, and had crossed the ravine and commenced the ascent of the opposite slope, when a galling fire from infantry and canister from howitzers swept through my ranks with deadly effect. The thicket was so dense that it was impossible for a company officer to be seen at platoon distance. . . .

A hurried reconnaissance revealed a point from which the enemy could be more advantageously assailed. Lieutenant *Davidson,* of my staff, was dispatched to General *Ruggles,* not far off, with a request that he would send up a few pieces of artillery to a position indicated, whence a vigorous fire, I felt confident, would soon silence the battery. . . . Changing my position . . . to suit the circumstances . . . I determined to make another effort to dislodge the enemy. . . .

General *Ruggles* had now placed our battery in position. Colonel *Smith,* of the Crescent Regiment, had driven the enemy's sharpshooters from the cover of a log cabin and a few cotton bales on the extreme left . . . near the road, and the enemy was being sorely pressed upon the extreme right by our columns upon that flank, and I felt the importance of pressing forward at this point. The troops, too, seemed to be inspired with the same feeling.

Our battery opened rapidly, but every shot told. To the command "Forward" the infantry responded with a shout, and in less than five minutes after our artillery commenced playing, and before the infantry had advanced within short range of the enemy's lines, we had the satisfaction of seeing his proud banner lowered and a white one hoisted in its stead. Our troops on the right had been engaging a portion of his lines, unseen by us on account of an intervening hill, and when the white flag was run up they reached it first.

The sun was now near the western horizon; the battle

around us had ceased to rage. I met General *Ruggles,* who directed me to take a road which was not far to my left and to move down it in the direction of the river. [*O.R.,* X, pt. 1, pp. 497–99.]

Report of Col. R. G. Shaver, CSA, Seventh Arkansas Infantry, Commanding First Brigade, Hindman's Division, Third Army Corps, Army of the Mississippi

It was now between 1 and 2 o'clock in the afternoon. After supplying my command with ammunition (with the exception of Col. Hawthorne [Sixth Arkansas Regiment], who . . . was detached by order of Gen. *Bragg*) I was ordered to make a movement to the right and dislodge the enemy, who were posted in considerable force in a dense undergrowth in a heavy woods to the rear and right of the encampment first captured. On the enemy's right was a battery of the presence of which (so completely was it concealed) I was not aware until it opened.

Instructions were given me as to what direction my line should take. I pressed forward, the enemy remaining close and quiet until my left was within 50 and my right about 60 yards of their lines (a dense undergrowth intervening), when a terrific and murderous fire was poured in upon me from their lines and battery. It was impossible to charge through the dense undergrowth, and I soon discovered my fire was having no effect upon the enemy, so I had nothing left me but to retire or have my men all shot down; I drew off, the enemy still holding their position. . . .

Upon reporting to *Bragg* my inability to dislodge the enemy and that my command was very much cut up, I was ordered to fall back, reform my command, and await orders. I soon received orders to advance to Pittsburg, but had only advanced a short distance when I received orders to return and encamp my command for the night. [*O.R.,* X, pt. 1, p. 574–75.]

Continue to drive straight (south) for 0.2 mile to the intersection. At the stop sign turn left on Federal Road for 0.7 mile to the next intersection. Turn left on Johnston Road for 0.8 mile. You now have three options, depending on what roads the National Park Service has open and how much time you have.

Option 1. (This option will take at least forty-five minutes to accomplish.) If the gate on Riverside Drive at the intersection with Johnston Road is closed, park your car near the gate. Get out of your car and walk east along Riverside Road for approximately fifteen minutes, until you reach a marked Indian Mound.* From this mound walk to the left (west) to a second Indian Mound (with burial marker of the Twenty-eighth Illinois Infantry on top) about 100 yards away. At the base of the second mound turn right (north) along a small path. Walk approximately 250 yards past *Gage's* Alabama Battery marker, to the edge of the Dill Branch ravine. This is the point at which to do the readings for this Stop. Note: Almost due north of *Gage's* Battery marker, across the ravine about 500 yards, is the *Chalmers's* marker, indicating the furthest advance of the attacking Confederate skirmishers on the north side of Dill Branch.

Option 2. (This will take you around thirty minutes to accomplish.) If the gate to Riverside Drive is open, turn right and drive to the parking area. Park and walk along the road to the marked Indian Mound. Follow the remaining directions from Option 1.

Option 3. (This should take you about fifteen to twenty minutes). If you do not have the time or cannot make the walk to view Dill Branch ravine from the south (Options 1 and 2), then you can drive back to the Visitor Center and park. Walk from the parking area to the right of the flagpole to four artillery pieces on a knoll (Stone's Battery). To the right of this battery, just beyond a split rail fence, is a small path leading south. Follow this path for about 350 yards. You will find a Confederate marker indicating the furthest advance of *Chalmers's* skirmishers as they attacked over Dill Branch the evening of April 6.

Shortly after 4:00 P.M. the stubborn Union defense in the Hornets' Nest became the focus of the Confederate generals, the rest

---

*These Indian mounds are part of a group of prehistoric mounds situated in the area. There are seven large mounds and dozens of smaller ones. Most were dwellings, although the large one nearest the river was a burial mound. The Smithsonian Institution did some exploration of the site in 1934, although the actual identity of the people who built the mounds has never been definitely determined. The mound sites are protected areas.

of the Union army fell back on Pittsburg Landing. Some units fought a stubborn delaying action, while others broke and ran. At no time, however, did the entire Union line crumble.

This allowed Grant and his subordinate leaders to form a new line anchored on Pittsburg Landing and extending west toward Owl Creek. The line had natural strength and was strongly reinforced by every piece of artillery the Union commanders could gather (approximately seventy pieces).

The attacking Confederates, tired, hungry, and short on ammunition, slowed their attack to cook a meal or help themselves to the bounty found in the abandoned Union camps. Others took charge of the large number of Union prisoners, moving them safely to the rear. The attitude among the Confederates was that they had won a great victory and it was time to rest.

The disorganized Confederate chain of command finally reasserted itself and tried to get the troops to make the last push against Pittsburg Landing that would seal the victory. Fresh reserves may have done just that, but all had already been committed—there were no fresh troops. (Significantly, Dill Branch is not depicted on the map used by Albert Sidney *Johnston* in planning the battle.)

Bragg sent two battle-weakened brigades, *Chalmers's* and *Jackson's*, later to be followed by *Anderson's* brigade, to push on to Pittsburg Landing. They moved up to the large ravine formed by Dill Branch, a deep, marshy, and difficult obstacle. *Gage's* Confederate artillery battery had been moved all the way from south of Stuart's initial position (Stop 12) to the edge of the ravine overlooking Dill Branch. There the Confederates could see masses of men around Pittsburg Landing in the distance and the Union artillery along the north edge of the Dill Branch ravine. To the tired Southern soldiers, almost all out of ammunition, it looked like Grant's whole army was ready to oppose them. Urged on by *Bragg*, the troops of *Chalmers* and *Jackson* crossed the ravine and attacked into the Union artillery, only to be cut to pieces. Union gunboats added to the noise and confusion, firing their guns up the ravine. The Confederates could advance no further without reinforcements. At that time one of *Beauregard's* staff officers brought *Bragg* the order to halt the attack—*Beauregard* considered the victory complete. The Confederate troops started pulling back into the gathering darkness.

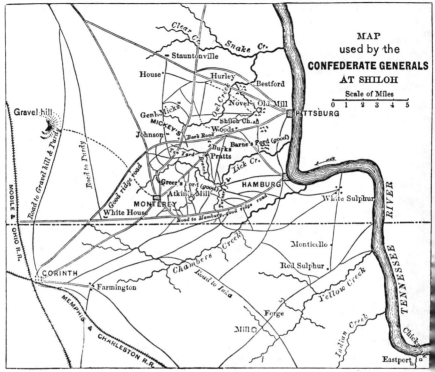

MAP
used by the
CONFEDERATE GENERALS
AT SHILOH

Scale of Miles
0 1 2 3 4 5

This is a copy of the map used by the Confederate commanders for the Shiloh battle. Note that Dill Branch is not depicted on this map. It is probable that General *Johnston* did not know his troops would have to fight across a significant ravine in order to siege Pittsburg Landing and drive the Union forces away from their river line of communications. *(The Life of General Albert Sidney Johnston)*

STOP 20, THE FINAL ASSAULT

Report of Brig. Gen. Jones M. Withers, CSA, Commanding Second Division, Second Corps, Army of the Mississippi (continued)

The order was now given by General *Bragg,* who was present on the right during the fierce fight which ended in the capture of Prentiss, to sweep everything forward. The division was moved promptly forward, although some regiments had

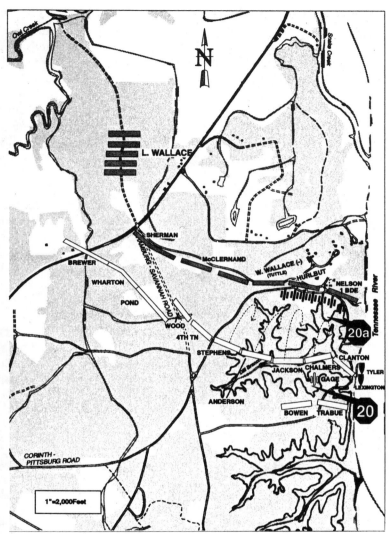

Late afternoon attacks across Dill Branch into final Union positions near Pittsburg Landing (Stop 20).

not succeeded in getting a supply of ammunition, and had just entered a deep and precipitous ravine when the enemy opened a terrific fire upon it. Staff officers were immediately dispatched to bring up all the re-enforcements to be found, and the order was given to brigade commanders to charge the batteries. These orders were being obeyed, when, to my astonishment, a large portion of the command was observed to move rapidly by the left flank from under the fire of the enemy. Orders were immediately sent to arrest the commanding officers and for the troops to be promptly placed in position for charging the batteries. Information was soon brought, however, that it was by General *Beauregard's* orders, delivered thus directly to brigade commanders, that the troops were being rapidly led from under the fire of the enemy's gunboats. Thus ended the fight on Sunday, and thus was this command disorganized, an evil sorely felt during the next day.

Receiving at this time an order from General *Bragg* to take command of all the troops on the right, and it being now near dark, the order was given to fall back about half a mile and bivouac for the night, *Chalmers'* brigade resting in rear nearest the enemy, and the remainder of the troops at the second of the camps from the one last captured. . . . Here we met General *Hardee,* with Colonel *Martin's* (Second Confederate) regiment. At 4 o'clock Monday morning the troops were put in motion to form line of battle. . . . [*O.R.,* X, pt. 1, pp. 533–34.]

Report of Brig. Gen. James R. Chalmers, CSA, Commanding Second Brigade, Second Division, Second Corps, Army of the Mississippi (continued)

It was . . . about 4 o'clock in the evening, and after distributing ammunition, we received orders from General *Bragg* to drive the enemy into the river. My brigade, together with that of Brigadier-General *Jackson,* filed to the right and formed facing the river and endeavored to press forward to the water's edge, but in attempting to mount the last ridge we were met by a fire from a whole line of batteries protected by infantry and assisted by shells from the gunboats. Our men struggled vainly to ascend the hill, which was very steep, making charge after charge without success, but continued to fight until night closed hostilities on both sides. During the engagement *Gage's*

Brig. Gen. James R. *Chalmers*, Commander, Second Brigade, Second Army Corps (Bragg), Army of the Mississippi. (U.S. Army Military History Institute)

Defending the last line. This lithograph shows *Chalmers's* Confederates attacking the Union last line on the north side of Dill Branch. While this is somewhat idealized, note the scarcity of vegetation, especially when compared with today. It is logical that many of the trees would have been cut down, because the ravine is so near the Pittsburg Landing, and the wood was used by passing steamboats. *(Battles and Leaders of the Civil War)*

battery was brought up to our assistance, but suffered so severely that it was soon compelled to retire.

This was the sixth fight in which we had been engaged during the day, and my men were too much exhausted to storm the batteries on the hill, but they were brought off in good order, formed in line of battle, and slept on the battlefield, where I remained with them. Early on the following morning I received notice that the enemy was advancing, and was ordered by General *Withers* to fall back about a half mile and form on the right of General *Jackson's* brigade, and follow him over to the left, where it was supposed the fight would be. We fell back and waited for General *Jackson* to file past to the left, intending to follow him, as directed, but before we could get away the enemy came charging rapidly upon us, and the fight of the second day commenced. . . . [*O.R.*, X, pt. 1, pp. 550–51.]

Report of Brig. Gen. John K. Jackson, CSA, Commanding Third Brigade, Withers' Division, Second Corps, Army of the Mississippi (continued)

My brigade was ordered to change direction again, face towards Pittsburg, where the enemy appeared to have made his last stand, and to advance upon him, General *Chalmers'* brigade being again on my right, and extending to the swamp of the Tennessee River. Without ammunition and with only their bayonets to rely on, steadily my men advanced under a heavy fire from light batteries, siege pieces, and gunboats. Passing through the ravine, they arrived near the crest of the opposite hill upon which the enemy's batteries were, but could not be urged further without support. Sheltering themselves against the precipitous sides of the ravine, they remained under this fire for some time.

Finding an advance without support impracticable, remaining there under fire useless, and believing any further forward movement should be made simultaneously along our whole line, I proceeded to obtain orders from General *Withers,* but before seeing him was ordered by a staff officer to retire. This order was announced to me as coming from General *Beauregard,* and was promptly communicated to my command.

In the darkness of the night which had fallen upon us my regiments became separated from each other, Colonel *Farris,* with the Seventeenth Alabama, falling back to the line occupied by us in the morning, Colonel *Moore,* with the Second Texas, and Colonel *Wheeler,* with the Nineteenth Alabama, taking a different position, and the battery, with which I remained, falling back to Shiloh Church. Colonel *Shorter,* with the Eighteenth Alabama, had taken the prisoners to Corinth. Thus closed Sunday, April 6, upon my brigade. [*O.R.,* X, pt. 1, p. 555.]

Report of Lieutenant Gwin, U.S. Navy, Commanding USS Tyler (continued)

At 3:50 ceased firing and dropped down opposite the landing at Pittsburg; sent Mr. Peters, gunner, on shore to communicate with General Grant for further instructions. His response

The Union gunboats *Lexington* (above) and *Tyler* (below) came into action as Grant's army withdrew behind Dill Branch, inflicting casualties on *Chalmers's* tired brigade and forcing *Gage's* Battery to withdraw. Later the gunboats launched eight-inch shells into the Confederate positions every ten minutes throughout the night—demoralizing the tired Southern troops. (*The Photographic History of the Civil War*)

Gunboats *Tyler* and *Lexington* firing into the Dill Branch area in the late afternoon of the first day of the Shiloh battle. (U.S. Army Military History Institute)

was to use my own judgment in the matter. At 4 P.M. the *Lexington*, Lieutenant Commanding Shirk, having arrived from Crump's Landing, the *Tyler*, in company with the *Lexington*, took position three-fourths of a mile above Pittsburg and opened heavy fire in direction of the rebel batteries on their right, the missiles of which were falling all around us. We silenced them in thirty minutes. At 5:35, the rebels having succeeded in gaining a position on the left of our line, an eighth of a mile above the landing at Pittsburg and a half a mile from the river, both vessels opened a heavy and well-directed fire on them, and in a short time, in conjunction with our artillery on shore, succeeded in silencing their artillery, driving them back in confusion.

At 6 P.M. the *Tyler* opened deliberate fire in the direction of the rebel right wing, throwing 5-second and 10-second shell. At 6:25 ceased firing. [*Official Records of the Union and Confederate Navies*, series I, vol. 22, p. 763.]

Get in your car. Drive back to Johnston Road. Turn right onto Johnston Road and drive 0.2 mile. Turn right at the stop sign and drive 1.0 mile to the Visitor Center. Park. Walk back past the cemetery toward the river to a point where you can overlook Pittsburg Landing.

This is the area that was teeming with frightened Union soldiers from units that had broken and run. Grant had landed his command ship here, and he waited for the reports from his subordinate commanders in the rain that started about midnight. All the while fresh troops from Maj. Gen. Don Carlos Buell's Army of the Ohio ferried across the Tennessee and moved into position above Pittsburg Landing.

STOP 21, PITTSBURG LANDING

Report of Maj. Gen. Don Carlos Buell, USA, Commanding Army of the Ohio

I . . . arrived at Savannah on the evening of the 5th. General Nelson, with his division, which formed the advance, arrived the same day. The other divisions marched with intervals of about 6 miles.

On the morning of the 6th the firing of cannon and musketry was heard in the direction of this place [Pittsburg Landing]. Apprehending that a serious engagement had commenced, I went to General Grant's headquarters to get information as to the best means of reaching the battle-field with the division that had arrived. At the same time orders were dispatched to the divisions in rear to leave their trains and push forward by forced marches. I learned that General Grant had just started, leaving orders for General Nelson to march to the river opposite Pittsburg Landing to be ferried across. On examination of the road up the river I discovered it to be impracticable for artillery, and General Nelson was directed to leave his [guns] to be carried forward by steamers.

The impression existed at Savannah that the firing was only an affair of outposts, the same thing having occurred for the two or three previous days; but as it continued I determined

Pittsburg Landing a few days after the battle. The steamer on the right is the *Tycoon*, a Sanitary Commission boat. The next boat is the *Tigress*, Grant's headquarters boat. The *Tyler* is seen on the opposite side of the river. (U.S. Army Military History Institute)

to go at once to the scene of action, and accordingly started with my chief of staff, Colonel Fry, on a steamer, which I had ordered to get under steam. As we proceeded up the river groups of soldiers were seen upon the west bank, and it soon became evident that they were stragglers from the army that was engaged. The groups increased in size and frequency, until, as we approached the Landing, they amounted to whole companies, and almost regiments, and at the Landing the banks swarmed with a confused mass of men of various regiments. The number could not have been less than 4,000 or 5,000, and later in the day it became much greater.

Finding General Grant at the Landing I requested him to send steamers to Savannah to bring up General Crittenden's division, which had arrived during the morning, and then went ashore with him.

The throng of disorganized and demoralized troops increased continually by fresh fugitives from the battle, which steadily grew nearer the Landing, and with these were mingled

Maj. Gen. Don Carlos Buell, Commander, Army of the Ohio. *(The Great Civil War)*

great numbers of teams, all striving to get as near as possible to the river. With few exceptions all efforts to form the troops and move them forward to the fight utterly failed.

In the mean time the enemy had made such progress against our troops that his artillery and musketry began to play into the vital spot of the position, and some persons were killed

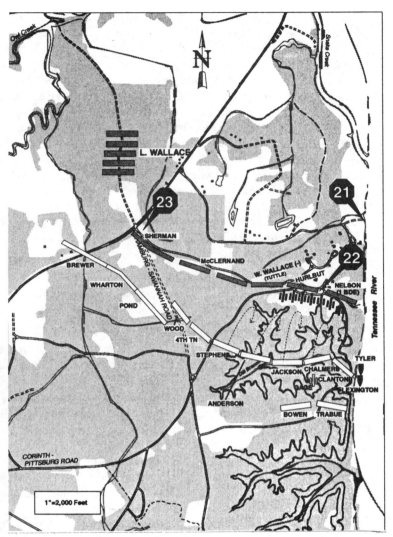

Union dispositions at the end of the day, April 6, 1862 (Stop 21).

on the bank at the very Landing. General Nelson arrived with Colonel Ammen's brigade at this opportune moment. It was immediately posted to meet the attack at that point, and, with a battery of artillery which happened to be on the ground and was brought into action, opened fire on the enemy and repulsed him. The action of the gunboats also contributed very much to that result. The attack at that point was not renewed night having come on, and the firing ceased on both sides.

In the mean time the remainder of General Nelson's division crossed, and General Crittenden's arrived from Savannah by steamers. After examining the ground as well as was possible at night in front of the line on which General Grant's troops had formed and as far to the right as General Sherman's division, I directed Nelson's and Crittenden's divisions to form in front of that line, and move forward as soon as it was light in the morning. [*O.R.*, X, pt. 1, pp. 291–92.]

Report of Brig. Gen. William Nelson, USA, Commanding Fourth Division, Army of the Ohio

The Fourth Division of the Army of the Ohio . . . left Savannah at 1:30 P.M. on Sunday, April 6, and marched by land to the point opposite Pittsburg Landing. The anxiety of the soldiers to take part in the battle . . . on the left bank of the river enabled me to achieve the distance, notwithstanding the dreadful state of the road over a lately overflowed bottom, in four hours. At 5 [P.M.] the head of my column marched up the bank at Pittsburg Landing and took up its position in the road under the fire of the rebel artillery, so close had they approached the Landing. I found a semi-circle of artillery, totally unsupported by infantry, whose fire was the only check to the audacious approach of the enemy.

The Sixth Ohio and Thirty-sixth Indiana Regiments had scarcely deployed, when the left of the artillery was completely turned by the enemy and the gunners fled from their pieces. The gallantry of the Thirty-sixth, supported by the Sixth Ohio, under the able conduct of Colonel Ammen, commanding Tenth Brigade, drove back the enemy and restored the line of battle. This was at 6:30 P.M., and soon after the enemy withdrew, owing, I suppose, to the darkness. I found cowering under the river bank when I crossed from 7,000 to 10,000 men, frantic with fright and utterly demoralized, who received my gallant division with cries, "We are whipped; cut to pieces." They were insensible to shame or sarcasm—for I tried both on them—and, indignant at such poltroonery, I asked permission to open fire upon the knaves.

By 9 P.M. the infantry of my division were all across the river. . . . Colonel Ammen's brigade . . . on the left. On the right of them Bruce's brigade was posted . . . [and] on the right of Bruce's brigade the brigade of Colonel Hazen was posted. . . . Heavy pickets were immediately thrown well forward and every precaution taken to prevent surprise during the night. These dispositions were made by the direction and under the inspection of General Buell, who gave me orders to move forward and attack the enemy at the earliest dawn.

The night passed away without serious alarm. . . . Lieutenant Gwin, of the Navy, commanding the gunboats in the river, sent to me and asked how he could be of service. I requested that he would throw an 8-inch shell into the camp of the enemy every ten minutes during the night, and thus prevent their sleeping, which he did very scientifically, and, according to the report of the prisoners, to their infinite annoyance.

At 4 A.M. I roused up the men quietly by riding along the line, and when the line of battle was dressed and the skirmishers well out and the reserves in position, I sent an aide to notify the general that I was ready to commence the action; whereupon the Fourth Division of the Army of the Ohio, in perfect order, as if on drill, moved toward the enemy. At 5:20 I found them, and the action commenced with vigor. My division drove them with ease, and I followed them up rapidly. . . . [O.R., X, pt. 1, pp. 323–24.]

Report of Col. J. Ammen, USA, Tenth Brigade, Fourth Division, Army of the Ohio

April 6, at 1 o'clock P.M., the Tenth Brigade marched from Savannah for the battle-field. Arriving at the river opposite Pittsburg Landing the brigade was passed over on steamboats with the greatest practicable expedition, and on reaching the shore thousands of human beings, who had fled from their colors and assembled here, obstructed the road and caused considerable delay.

Reaching the top of the bank with the Thirty-sixth Indiana, General Grant directed me to send that regiment to support a battery less than a quarter of a mile from the Landing. The Thirty-sixth marched promptly, and had been placed in position but a few minutes when the enemy attacked the battery and was repulsed. The enemy continued to assail the battery until the close of the day with a large force, but were repulsed by the Thirty-sixth with great coolness and gallantry. The Twenty-fourth and Sixth Ohio crossed the river as speedily as possible, and on arriving at the top of the bank the Twenty-fourth was ordered by General Grant to repair to a point one-half mile to the right, on a part of the line of battle threatened by the enemy. The Sixth Ohio was held in reserve.

During the night I received orders to assemble my brigade and form into line of battle on the extreme left. Strong parties of skirmishers were sent forward to examine the ground and ascertain the position of the enemy, if possible. Afterward the line of battle was formed about 300 yards in front of the battery. . . . The men in line were permitted to rest on their arms until the break of day.

April 7, in obedience to orders from General Nelson "to march forward in pursuit of the enemy and attack him," the Tenth Brigade was put in motion at daylight. The march was made slowly and with caution, the skirmishers examining the ground with great care and to my entire satisfaction. The regiments in line of battle . . . advanced in good order, considering the nature of the ground. After marching about 2 miles the enemy was attacked in force. [O.R., X, pt. 1, pp. 327–28.]

Report of Surgeon Robert Murray, USA, Medical Director, Army of the Ohio

On the morning of the 6th I was at Savannah, and being ordered to remain at that place, I occupied myself in procuring all the hospital accommodation possible in that small village and in directing the preparation of bunks and other conveniences for wounded. In the afternoon the wounded were brought down in large numbers, and I then superintended their removal to hospitals, and did all in my power to provide for their comfort.

On Sunday evening, the divisions being under orders to

come up as rapidly as possible, I ordered the medical officers, as it was impossible to take their medical and hospital supplies—the teams and ambulances being in the rear and the roads blocked up with trains—to take their instruments and hospital knapsacks and such dressings and stimulants as could be carried on horseback, and to go on with their regiments. I left Savannah by the first boat on Monday and arrived at Pittsburg Landing at about 10 A.M.

I found the principal depot for wounded established at the small log building now used as a field post-office. They were coming in very rapidly, and very inadequate arrangements had been made for their reception. I found Brigade Surgeon Goldsmith endeavoring to make provision for them, and at his suggestion immediately saw General Grant and obtained his order for a number of tents to be pitched about the log house.

I then rode to the front and reported to you. The great number of wounded which I saw being transported to the main depot, and the almost insurmountable difficulties which I foresaw would exist in providing for them, convinced me that my presence was needed there more than at any other point on the field. After spending an hour in riding a little to the rear of our lines, and seeing as far as possible that there were surgeons in position to attend immediately to the most urgent cases, I returned to the hill above the Landing, and used every exertion to provide for the wounded there. I ordered Brigade Surgeons Gross, Goldsmith, Johnson and Gay to take charge of the different depots which were established in tents on the hills above the Landing, directing such regimental and contract surgeons as I could find to aid them.

Many of the wounded were taken on board boats at the Landing and some of our surgeons were ordered on board to attend them. On Tuesday I had such boats as I could obtain possession of fitted up with such bed-sacks as were on hand and with straw and hay for the wounded to lie upon, and filled to their utmost capacity, and at once dispatched to convey the worst cases to the hospitals on the Ohio River at Evansville, New Albany, Louisville, and Cincinnati.

In removing the wounded we were aided by boats fitted up by sanitary commissions and soldiers' relief societies and sent to the battle-field to convey wounded to the hospitals. Some of these, especially those under the direction of the

United States Sanitary Commission, were of great service. They were ready to receive all sick and wounded, without regard to States or even to politics, taking the wounded Confederates as willingly as our own. Others, especially those who came under the orders of Governors of States, were of little assistance and caused much irregularity. Messages were sent to the regiments that a boat was at the Landing ready to take to their homes all wounded and sick from certain States. The men would crowd in numbers to the Landing, a few wounded, but mostly the sick and homesick. After the men had been enticed to the river and were lying in the mud in front of the boats it was determined in one instance by the Governor to take only the wounded, and his boat went off with a few wounded, leaving many very sick men to get back to their camps as best they could.

By the end of the week after the battle all our wounded had been sent off, with but few exceptions of men who had been taken to the camps of regiments in General Grant's army during the battle. These have since been found and provided for.

The division medical directors were very efficient in the discharge of their duties, and they report most favorably of the energy and zeal displayed by the medical officers under them in the care of the wounded under most trying circumstances— of want of medical and hospital stores, and even tents. Owing to the fact that a large majority of the wounded brought in on Monday and Tuesday were from General Grant's army, . . . it was impossible to attend particularly to those from our own divisions. Many Confederate wounded also fell into our hands, and I am happy to say that our officers and men attended with equal assiduity to all. Indeed, our soldiers were more ready to wait on the wounded of the enemy than our own. I regret to say that they showed incredible apathy and repugnance to nursing or attending to the wants of their wounded comrades, but in the case of the Confederates this seemed in some measure overcome by a feeling of curiosity and a wish to be near them and converse with them.

We were poorly supplied with dressings and comforts for the wounded and with ambulances for their transportation and it was several days after the battle before all could be brought in. Our principal difficulty, however, in providing for the wounded was in the utter impossibility to obtain prope details of men to nurse them and to cook and attend generally to their wants, and in the impossibility of getting a sufficient number of tents pitched, or in the confusion which prevailed during and after the battle to get hay or straw as bedding for the wounded or to have it transported to the tents. The only details we could obtain were from the disorganized mob which lined the hills near the Landing, and who were utterly inert and inefficient.

From the sad experience of this battle and the recollections of the sufferings of thousands of poor wounded soldiers crowded into tents on the wet ground, their wants partially attended to by an unwilling and forced detail of panic-stricken deserters from the battlefield, I am confirmed in the belief of the absolute necessity for a class of hospital attendants, enlisted as such, whose duties are distinct and exclusive as nurses and attendants for the sick, and also of a corps of medical purveyors, to act not only in supplying medicines, but as quartermasters for the medical department. [*O.R.*, X, pt. 1, pp. 297–99.]

Now walk back to the vicinity of the Visitor Center, past the flagpole to the rail fence and artillery position (Stone's Battery).

STOP 22, GRANT IN CONTROL

This area is part of the Union final line. Grant had all available artillery positioned along a line running from the river along the high ground toward McClernand's and Sherman's positions. Throughout the night, Buell's troops moved from the landing and took up the eastern part of the Union line, getting ready for the counterattack that Grant had ordered to begin the next morning.

Narrative of Maj. Gen. U. S. Grant, USA, Commanding Army of the Tennessee

The situation at the close of Sunday was as follows: along the top of the bluff just south of the log-house which stood at Pittsburg Landing, Colonel J. D. Webster of my staff had arranged twenty or more pieces of artillery facing south or up the river. This line of artillery was on the crest of a hill overlooking a deep ravine [Dill Branch, vicinity Stop 22] opening

Heavy siege guns on Grant's last line. These twenty-four-pound guns had not yet moved from their positions overlooking Dill Branch when this photo was taken. This artillery was the base along which Buell's Army of the Ohio formed as they moved to Pittsburg Landing in the late afternoon and evening of the first day. (U.S. Army Military History Institute)

into the Tennessee. Hurlbut with his division intact was on the right of this artillery, extending west and possibly a little north.

McClernand came next in the general line, looking more to the west. His division was complete in its organization and ready for any duty. Sherman came next, his right extending to Snake Creek. His command, like the other two, was complete in its organization and ready, like its chief, for any service it might be called upon to render. All three divisions were . . . more or less shattered and depleted in numbers from the terrible battle of the day.

The division of W. H. L. Wallace, as much from the disorder arising from changes of division and brigade commanders, under heavy fire, as from any other cause, had lost its organization and did not occupy a place in the line as a division. Prentiss' command was gone as a division, many of its members having been killed, wounded or captured; but it had rendered valiant services before its final dispersal, and had contributed a good share to the defense of Shiloh.

The right of my line rested near the bank of Snake Creek, a short distance above the bridge which had been built by the troops for the purpose of connecting Crump's Landing and Pittsburg Landing. Sherman had posted some troops in a log-house and out-buildings which overlooked both the bridge over which Wallace was expected and the creek above that point. In this last position Sherman was frequently attacked before night, but held the point until he voluntarily abandoned it to advance in order to make room for Lew Wallace, who came up after dark.

There was . . . a deep ravine in front of our left. The Tennessee River was very high and there was water to a considerable depth in the ravine. Here the enemy [had] made a last desperate effort to turn our flank, but was repelled. The gun-boats *Tyler* and *Lexington* . . . with the artillery under Webster, aided the army and effectually checked their further progress. Before any of Buell's troops had reached the west bank of the Tennessee, firing had almost entirely ceased; anything like an attempt on the part of the enemy to advance had absolutely ceased. . . . The attack had spent its force. . . .

So confident was I before firing had ceased on the 6th that the next day would bring victory to our arms if we could only take the initiative, that I visited each division commander in person before any reinforcements had reached the field. I directed them to throw out heavy lines of skirmishers in the morning as soon as they could see, and push them forward until they found the enemy, following with their entire divisions in supporting distance, and to engage the enemy as soon as found. To Sherman I told the story of the assault at Fort Donelson, and said that the same tactics would win at Shiloh. Victory was assured when Wallace arrived, even if there had been no other support.

I was glad, however, to see the reinforcements of Buell and credit them with doing all there was for them to do. During the night . . . the remainder of Nelson's division, Buell's army, crossed the river and were ready to advance in the morning, forming the left wing. Two other divisions, Crittenden's and McCook's, came up the river from Savannah in the transports and were on the west bank early on the 7th. Buell commanded them in person. My command was thus nearly doubled in numbers and efficiency.

During the night rain fell in torrents and our troops were exposed to the storm without shelter. I made my headquarters under a tree a few hundred yards back from the river bank. My ankle was so much swollen from the fall of my horse the Friday night preceding, and the bruise was so painful, that I could get no rest. The drenching rain would have precluded the possibility of sleep without this additional cause.

Some time after midnight, growing restive under the storm and the continuous pain, I moved back to the log-house under the bank. This had been taken as a hospital, and all night wounded men were being brought in, their wounds dressed, a leg or an arm amputated as the case might require, and everything being done to save life or alleviate suffering. The sight was more unendurable than encountering the enemy's fire, and I returned to my tree in the rain. [Grant, *Memoirs,* I: 345–50.]

Report of Lieutenant Gwin, U.S. Navy, Commanding USS Tyler *(continued)*

At 9 P.M. the *Tyler* again opened fire by direction of General Nelson (who greatly distinguished himself in yesterday's engagement), throwing 5-second, 10-second, and 15-second shell, and an occasional shrapnel from the howitzer, at intervals of ten minutes in direction of the rebel right wing until 1 A.M., when the *Lexington* relieved us and continued the fire at intervals of fifteen minutes until 5 A.M. . . . [*Official Records of the Union and Confederate Navies,* series I, vol. 22, p. 763.]

THE SECOND DAY

Narrative of Maj. Gen. U. S. Grant, USA, Commanding Army of the Tennessee

The advance on the morning of the 7th developed the enemy in the camps occupied by our troops before the battle began, more than a mile back from the most advanced position of the Confederates on the day before. It is known now that they had not yet learned of the arrival of Buell's command. Possibly they fell back so far to get the shelter of our tents during the rain, and also to get away from the shells that were dropped upon them by the gunboats every fifteen minutes during the night.

The position of the Union troops on the morning of the 7th was as follows: General Lew Wallace on the right; Sherman on his left; then McClernand and then Hurlbut. Nelson, of Buell's army, was on our extreme left, next to the river. Crittenden was next in line after Nelson and on his right; McCook followed and formed the extreme right of Buell's command. My old command thus formed the right wing, while the troops directly under Buell constituted the left wing of the army. These relative positions were retained during the entire day, or until the enemy was driven from the field.

In a very short time the battle became general all along the line. [Grant, *Memoirs*, I: 349–50.]

Report of Maj. Gen. Don Carlos Buell, USA, Commanding Army of the Ohio (continued)

Soon after 5 o'clock in the morning of the 7th, General Nelson's and General Crittenden's divisions, the only ones yet arrived on the ground, moved promptly forward to meet the enemy. Nelson's division, marching in line of battle, soon came upon his [the enemy's] pickets, drove them in, and at about 6 o'clock received the fire of his artillery. The division was here halted and Mendenhall's battery brought into action to reply, while Crittenden's division was being put into position on the right of Nelson's. Bartlett's battery was posted in the center of Crittenden's division in a commanding position, opposite which the enemy was discovered to be formed in force.

By this time McCook's division arrived on the ground, and was immediately formed on the right of Crittenden's. Skirmishers were thrown to the front and a strong body of them to guard our left flank, which, though somewhat protected by rough ground, it was supposed the enemy might attempt to turn, and, in fact, did, but was handsomely repulsed with great loss. Each brigade furnished its own reserve, and in addition Boyle's brigade, from Crittenden's division, though it formed at first in the line, was kept somewhat back when the line advanced, to be used as occasion might require. I found on the ground parts of two regiments—perhaps 1,000 men—and subsequently a similar fragment came up of General Grant's force. The first I directed to act with General McCook's attack and the second was similarly employed on the left. . . . I have no direct knowledge of the disposition of the remainder of General Grant's forces. . . .

The force under my command occupied a line of about 1 1/2 miles. In front of Nelson's division was an open field [field south of the Peach Orchard, vicinity Stop 14A], partially screened toward his right by a skirt of woods, which extended beyond the enemy's line, with a thick undergrowth [Hornets' Nest thicket] in front of the left brigade of Crittenden's division; then an open field in front of Crittenden's right and McCook's left, and in front of McCook's right woods again, with a dense undergrowth. The ground, nearly level in front of Nelson, formed a hollow in front of Crittenden, and fell into a small creek or ravine, which empties into Owl Creek, in front of McCook.

What I afterward learned was the Hamburg road (which crosses Lick Creek a mile from its mouth) passed perpendicularly through the line of battle near Nelson's left. On a line slightly oblique to ours, and beyond the open fields, the enemy was formed, with a battery in front of Nelson's left, a battery commanding the woods in front of Crittenden's left and flanking the fields in front of Nelson, a battery commanding the same woods and the field in front of Crittenden's right and McCook's left, and a battery in front of McCook's right. . . .

Very soon after our line advanced, with strong bodies of skirmishers in front, the action became general and continued with severity during the greater part of the day and until the enemy was driven from the field. . . .

The loss of the forces under my command is 263 killed, 1,816 wounded, 88 missing; total 2,167 [later revised to 2,103]. [*O.R.*, X, pt. 1, pp. 293–95.]

Return to your car and follow the signs toward Route 22. From the stop sign at the Visitor Center drive 1.0 mile. Stop 100 yards from the stop sign at Route 22, near the rail fence opposite the marker for Buckland's Brigade. Walk across the road to the marker for Buckland's Brigade.

STOP 23A, BUCKLAND'S BRIGADE

This is part of the area of Sherman's final line, occupied late in the evening of April 6. Sherman's troops had fought their way back from the vicinity of Shiloh Church along both sides of what is now Route 22, and into position along the line you can now see. He could pull back no further because he had to protect the Hamburg-Savannah Road, along which Gen. Lew Wallace was marching to reinforce the Union army. (If you look past the stop sign at Route 22 to a gate across the road, you can see the route over which Wallace marched.)

Through the long rainy night, the wounded of both sides suffered as they lay where they had fallen. The Confederates had pulled back for the most part to the camps the Union troops had occupied before the battle, with only a thin line of skirmishers in front. Grant ordered his commanders to counterattack at dawn.

Report of Col. Ralph P. Buckland, USA, Commanding Fourth Brigade, Fifth Division, Army of the Tennessee

[On April 6] we formed line again on the Purdy road, but the fleeing mass from the left broke through our lines, and many of our men caught the infection and fled with the crowd. Colonel Cockerill became separated from Colonel Sullivan and myself, and was afterwards engaged with part of his command at McClernand's camp. Colonel Sullivan and myself kept together and made every effort to rally our men, but with very poor success. They had become scattered in all directions. We were borne considerably to the left, but finally succeeded in forming a line and had a short engagement with the enemy, who made his appearance soon after our line was formed. The enemy fell back and we proceeded to the road. . . . At this point I was joined by Colonel Cockerill, and we there formed line of battle, and slept on our arms Sunday night. Colonel Sullivan, being out of ammunition, marched to the Landing for a supply, and while there was ordered to support a battery at that point.

The next morning he joined me, and we rallied all the men we could, and advanced, under your directions, to McClernand's camp. At that point we were again brought into action at a critical time and under heavy fire. . . . In this action we advanced our line upon the enemy a considerable distance, and my brigade kept up their fire until their ammunition was expended, when we fell back, replenished, and again advanced, but were not afterwards engaged, the enemy being in full retreat. We encamped on Monday night in the camp we left on Sunday morning. [O.R., X, pt. 1, pp. 267–68.]

Report of Col. Joseph R. Cockerill, USA, Seventieth Ohio Infantry, Fourth Brigade, Fifth Division, Army of the Tennessee

Early on the morning of the 7th a severe cannonade was opened by General Wallace's battery on our right, and we were ordered to advance, which we did in good order, the Forty-eighth on the right, Seventieth in the center, and Seventy-second on the left. We, under your orders and that of General Sherman, after advancing about one-half mile, were moved to the right and ascended a hill and passed by the flank under a severe fire, where we were ordered to halt and remained for about two hours, while the batteries on both sides were in full play.

About 12 m. [noon] we were ordered to advance, and the Seventy-second, Forty-eighth, and Seventieth (in this order) advanced to the southeast about three-quarters of a mile into McClernand's camp (precisely the position occupied by the

Seventieth the day before), where we deployed into line under the immediate orders and presence of General Sherman (superintended by yourself), where we opened fire with good effect upon the enemy, one-half of the Seventieth Regiment firing to the right and the other to the left oblique. The enemy fell back under this fire, and we advanced to the edge of the woods at the head of the camp near a pond [Water Oaks Pond].

Our ammunition at this point failed, and part of General McCook's division coming up opened upon the enemy in fine style. The whole brigade retired to receive a fresh supply of ammunition, which as soon as we received we again advanced over the same ground and towards our encampment; but the enemy was rapidly retiring, and we entered our original camp about 5 o'clock P.M. Our camp had been torn down by the enemy, and we lay upon our arms during the night exposed to a severe rain-storm, the enemy having hastily retreated and with great loss.

Our camp was plundered of nearly everything—officers' uniforms, camp equipments, blankets, knapsacks, haversacks, clothing, etc. Our men, when called out on Sunday morning, supposed it was only to support the pickets, who had been in constant alarm for the two preceding days, and we never made any provision whatever for any retreat. [O.R., X, pt. 1, p. 271.]

Walk straight ahead (south) for 100 yards up the small hill with cedar trees. Move to the second-day marker for Smith's Brigade.

STOP 23B, GRANT'S COUNTERATTACK

During the night Grant had ordered all his commanders to begin the counterattack at first light. By now the Union troops had been resupplied and were in relatively good order, with clear lines of command and control. The Confederate troops had spent a wretched night in the rain and cold. Many were hungry and had not yet been resupplied with ammunition. Col. Nathan Bedford *Forrest*, the Tennessee cavalry leader, had sent reconnaissance parties out during the night and told the Confederate leadership that the Union had been reinforced. He reported to *Hardee*, but was unable to find *Beauregard*. *Hardee* took no action. The Confederates were spread out across the battlefield, with no continuous defensive lines. When the attacking Union troops hit the forward Southern positions, the Confederates quickly fell back.

Report of Brig. Gen. William T. Sherman, USA, Commanding Fifth Division, Army of the Tennessee

About 4 P.M. [on Sunday] it was evident that Hurlbut's line had been driven back to the river, and knowing that General Wallace was coming from Crump's Landing with re-enforcements, General McClernand and I, on consultation, selected a new line of defense, with its right covering the bridge by which General Wallace had to approach. We fell back as well as we could, gathering, in addition to our own, such scattered forces as we could find, and formed a new line. During this change the enemy's cavalry charged us, but was handsomely repulsed by an Illinois regiment. . . . The Fifth Ohio Battery, which had come up, rendered good service in holding the enemy in check for some time; and Major Taylor also came up with a new battery, and got into position just in time to get a good flanking fire upon the enemy's columns as he pressed on General McClernand's right, checking his advance, when General McClernand's division made a fine charge on the enemy, and drove him back into the ravines to our front and right.

I had a clear field about 200 yards wide in my immediate front, and contented myself with keeping the enemy's infantry at that distance during the rest of the day.

In this position we rested for the night. My command had become decidedly of a mixed character. Buckland's brigade was the only one with me that retained its organization. Colonel Hildebrand was personally there, but his brigade was not. Colonel McDowell had been severely injured by a fall from his horse and had gone to the river, and the three regiments of his brigade were not in line. The Thirteenth Missouri . . . had reported to me on the field and fought well, retaining its regimental organization, and it formed a part of my line during Sunday night and all of Monday. Other fragments of regiments and companies had also fallen into my division, and acted with it during the remainder of the battle. General Grant and Buell visited me in our bivouac that evening, and from them I learned the situation of affairs on the other parts of the field. General Wallace arrived from Crump's Landing shortly after dark, and formed his line to my right and rear. It rained hard during the night, but our men were in good spirits and lay on their arms, being satisfied with such bread and meat as could be gathered from the neighboring camps, and determined to redeem on Monday the losses of Sunday.

At daylight on Monday I received General Grant's orders to advance and recapture our original camps. I dispatched several members of my staff to bring up all the men they could find, and especially the brigade of Colonel Stuart, which had been separated from the division all the day before. . . .

At the appointed time the division, or rather what remained of it, with the Thirteenth Missouri and other fragments, marched forward and reoccupied the ground on the extreme right of General McClernand's camp, where we attracted the fire of a battery located near Colonel McDowell's former headquarters. Here I remained, patiently waiting for the sound of General Buell's advance upon the main Corinth road.

About 10 A.M. the heavy firing in that direction and its steady approach satisfied me, and General Wallace being on our right flank with his well-conducted division, I led at the head of my column to General McClernand's right, formed line of battle facing south, with Buckland's brigade directly across the ridge and Stuart's brigade on its right in the wood, and thus advanced slowly and steadily, under a heavy fire of musketry and artillery. Taylor had just got to me from the rear, where he had gone for ammunition, and brought up three guns, which I ordered into position, to advance by hand, firing. . . . These guns . . . did most excellent service. Under cover of their fire we advanced till we reached the point where the Corinth road crosses the line of McClernand's camps, and here I saw for the first time the well-ordered and compact columns of General Buell's Kentucky forces, whose soldierly movements at once gave confidence to our newer and less-disciplined forces. Here I saw Willich's regiment advance upon a point of water-oaks and thicket, behind which I knew the enemy was in great strength, and enter it in beautiful style. Then arose the severest musketry fire I ever heard, which lasted some twenty minutes, when this splendid regiment had to fall back. This green point of timber is about 500 yards east of Shiloh Meeting house, and it was evident that here was to be the struggle . . . [Water Oaks Pond—next stop]. [*O.R.*, X, pt. 1, pp. 250–51.]

Report of Maj. Gen. Lewis Wallace, USA, Commanding Third Division, Army of the Tennessee

Shortly after daybreak Captain Thompson opened fire on a rebel battery posted on a bluff opposite my First Brigade, and across a deep and prolonged hollow, threaded by a creek [Tilghmans Branch, to your front] and densely wooded on both sides. From its position and that of its infantry support lining the whole length of the bluff, it was apparent that crossing the hollow would be at heavy loss, unless the battery was first driven off. Thurber was accordingly posted to assist Thompson by a cross-fire and at the same time sweep the hiding place of the rebels on the brow of the hill. This had the desired effect. After a few shells from Thurber the enemy fell back. . . . During this affair General Grant came up and gave me my direction of attack, which was formed at a right angle with the river, with which at that time my line ran almost parallel.

The battery and its supports having been driven from the opposite bluff, my command was pushed forward, the brigades in echelon—the First in front and the whole preceded by skirmishers. The hollow was crossed and the hill gained almost without opposition. As General Sherman's division, next on my left, had not made its appearance to support my advance, a halt was ordered for it to come up. I was then at the edge of an oblong field that extended in a direction parallel with the river. On its right was a narrow strip of woods, and beyond that lay another clear field, square and very large. Back of both fields, to the north, was a range of bluffs overlooking the swampy low grounds of Snake Creek, heavily timbered, broken by ravines, and extending in a course diagonal with that of my movement.

An examination satisfied me that the low grounds afforded absolute protection to my right flank, being impassable for a column of attack. The enemy's left had rested upon the bluff, and, as it had been driven back, that flank was now exposed. I resolved to attempt to return it. For that purpose it became necessary for me to change front by a left half-wheel of the whole division.

While this movement was in progress, across a road through the woods at the southern end of the field we were resting by, I discovered a heavy column of rebels going rapidly to re-enforce their left, which was still retiring, covered by skirmishers, with whom mine were engaged. Thompson's battery was ordered up, and shelled the passing column with excellent effect; but, while he was so engaged he was opened on by a full battery, planted in the field just beyond the strip of wood on the right. He promptly turned his guns at the new enemy. A fine artillery duel ensued. . . . His ammunition giving out in the midst of it, I ordered him to retire and Lieutenant Thurber to take his place. Thurber obeyed with such alacrity that there was scarcely an intermission in the fire, which continued so long and with such warmth as to provoke an attempt on the part of the rebels to change position. Discovering the intention, the First Brigade was brought across the field to occupy the strip of woods in front of Thurber. The [Confederate] cavalry made the first dash at the battery, but the skirmishers of the Eighth Missouri poured an unexpected fire into them, and they retired pell-mell. Next the infantry attempted a charge. The First Brigade easily repelled them. All this time my whole division was under a furious cannonade, but being well masked behind the bluff, or resting in the hollows of the wood, the regiments suffered but little.

A handsome line of battle now moved forward on my left to engage the enemy. I supposed it to be Sherman's troops, but was afterwards otherwise informed. Simultaneously mine were ordered to advance, the First Brigade leading. Emerging from the woods, it entered the second field . . . speedily followed by the Second Brigade, when both marched in face of the enemy, aligned as regularly as if on parade. Having changed front . . . my movement was now diagonal to the direction originally started on, though the order was still in echelon, with the center regiment of each brigade dropped behind its place in line as a reserve. . . . The position of the enemy was now directly in front at the edge of the woods fronting, and on the right of the open field my command was so gallantly crossing. The ground to be passed . . . dipped gradually to the center of the field, which is there intersected by a small run.

Clearing an abrupt bank beyond the branch, the surface ascends to the edge of the wood held by the enemy, and is without obstruction. . . . Over the branch, up the bank, across the rising ground, moved the steady First Brigade; on its right, with equal alacrity, marched the Second—the whole in view, their banners gaily decking the scene. The skirmishers, in action all the way, cleared the rise and grouped themselves behind the ground-swells within 75 yards of the rebel line.

As the regiments approached . . . suddenly a sheet of musketry blazed from the woods and a battery opened upon them. About the same instant the regiments supporting me on my left fell hastily back. To save my flank I was compelled to order a halt. In a short time, however, the retiring regiments rallied and repulsed the enemy, and recovered their lost ground. My skirmishers meanwhile clung to their hillocks sharpshooting at the battery.

Again the brigades advanced, their bayonets fixed for a charge; but, pressed on their flank and so threatened in front the rebels moved their guns and fell back from the edge of the woods. . . . Many soldiers . . . perished or were wounded in the same field. It was now noon, and the idea of flanking them further had to be given up. . . .

About 4 o'clock the enemy to my front broke into rout and ran through the camps occupied by General Sherman on Sunday morning. Their own camp had been established about 2 miles beyond. There, without halting, they filled their wagons full of arms (Springfield muskets and Enfield rifles) ingloriously thrown away by some of our troops the day before, and hurried on. After following them until nearly nightfall I brought my division back to Owl Creek and bivouacked it. [*O.R.,* X, pt. 1, pp. 170–73.]

Return to your car. Carefully turn around and drive back toward the Visitors Center for 0.8 mile. Turn right onto Confederate Drive, also called the Corinth-Pittsburg Road, before reaching the Visitors Center. Drive 1.9 miles. Stop when you see Water Oaks Pond on the right and Bouton's Battery on the left. Water Oaks Pond is located in a large open field. Pull off onto the shoulder and park.

The Union counterattack. This scene depicts Rosseau's Brigade of McCook's Second Division, Army of the Ohio, recapturing artillery that was lost on the first day of the battle. (U.S. Army Military History Institute)

STOP 24, UNION COUNTERATTACK

The Union attack was successful everywhere. The Union had overwhelming numbers across the battlefield. Wherever some Confederate troops fought well and held up the Union advance, others would give way, forcing withdrawal or isolation and probable surrender. The intensity and lethality of the fighting on the second day matched that of the previous day's. But with the advantage gained from the added combat power of Buell's Army, Grant's forces clearly had the advantage. The Confederates slowly fought their way back toward the south and Corinth—where they had started from on April 3.

Water Oaks Pond

Report of Maj. Gen. John McClernand, USA, Commanding First Division, Army of the Tennessee

Left unsupported and alone [on the 6th] the Twentieth and Seventeenth Illinois, together with other portions of my

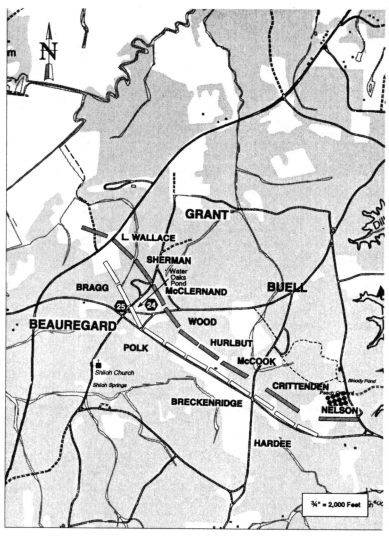

Dispositions of counterattacking Union forces midday, April 7, 1862
(Stops 24 and 25).

division not borne back by the retreating multitude, retired in good order . . . and reformed under my direction, the right resting near the former line and the left at an acute angle with it. A more extended line, comprising portions of regiments, brigades, and divisions, was soon after formed on this nucleus by the efforts of General Sherman, myself, and other officers. Here, in the eighth position occupied by my division during the day, we rested in line of battle upon our arms, uncovered and exposed to a drenching rain during the night. Yet night, inclement as it was, and the arrival of re-enforcements, which came, were prayed for as the assurance of better fortune the next day.

Having been directed . . . to assume command of all detached and fragmentary corps in the vicinity of my line, your order of the morning of the 7th for a forward movement found the Forty-sixth Illinois on my right and portions of Generals Hurlbut's and Buell's troops on my left. The Fifty-third Ohio was formed as a reserve, the Twenty-ninth Illinois having been ordered still farther to the left and near the landing, for the purpose of driving and keeping back fugitives.

Moving forward obliquely to the left I passed unobstructedly over the scene of my last engagement and reached the scene of the cavalry charge. Here I ordered a halt, and adjusted my line in a wood, extending to the left and skirting a field in front. Meanwhile McAllister's battery was brought near the corner of the field, and replied to a battery posted beyond the camp of my First Brigade. After this fire had been continued for a few minutes I pushed on to my old camp and readjusted my line just behind it. The Twenty-eighth Illinois . . . here joined me, and was formed on my left obliquely to the rear.

McAllister's battery was again brought up to the center of my line, and again replied to the battery in front and to another to its left. A few minutes after I discovered troops to my right, near Owl Creek, which I was informed were General L. Wallace's. One or more batteries, supposed to belong to his command, were advanced in the field in front and near the right of my camp, and also opened fire upon the battery in front of my line.

Thus clearing the woods in front in that direction, preceded by skirmishers, my line advanced through my camp obliquely to the south-west, thus retaking it. At the same time

Generals Sherman and Wallace were seen advancing in the same direction. Approaching a hasty and rude breastwork of logs formed by the enemy during Sunday night, his skirmishers opened an irregular fire, which caused the Fifty-third Ohio to retire in disorder, breaking my line. My right staggered for a moment, recovered itself, and . . . opened an oblique fire which immediately dispersed the enemy in that direction, leaving us in possession of my recaptured camp.

At the same time information was brought that the enemy were advancing in strong force to turn the left of my line. To prevent this I ordered my command to move by the left flank, which, being promptly done, confronted the opposing forces.

Here one of the severest conflicts ensued that occurred during the two days. We drove the enemy back and pursued him with great vigor to the edge of a field, a half mile east and to the left of my headquarters, where reserves came to his support. Our position at this moment was most critical and repulse seemed inevitable, but fortunately the Louisville Legion, forming part of General Rousseau's brigade, came up at my request and supported me. Extending and strengthening my line, this gallant body poured into the enemy's ranks one of the most terrible fires I ever witnessed. Thus breaking its center, it fell back in disorder, and henceforth he was beaten at all points until our successful pursuit was staid. . . .

Crossing the field . . . portions of my own and other divisions again encountered the enemy, who had rallied and offered obstinate resistance. Some of our men temporarily retired, while others persisted until the enemy was again driven back. [*O.R.*, X, pt. 1, pp. 119–20.]

Report of Col. William H. Gibson, USA, Commanding Sixth Brigade, Second Division, Army of the Ohio

We reached Pittsburg Landing about 11 o'clock [on the 7th], and at once hastened forward to the scene of conflict in the center, where a portion of the Second Division [McCook's] was then engaged.

Colonel Willich, with the Thirty-second Indiana, being the first to debark and to reach the field, was detached from the brigade and placed in position by General McCook in person. Nothing further was heard from him by me during the day, but his list of casualties shows that he was hotly engaged, and the testimony of distinguished officers who witnessed the conduct of his command justifies me in saying that officers and men gave proof of skill and courage. . . .

Obedient to orders, the balance of the brigade was deployed in line of battle in rear of the Fourth Brigade, under General Rousseau, then closely engaged. His ammunition being exhausted, the Sixth Brigade was ordered to advance, which . . . was executed promptly and in perfect order. The enemy's infantry, concealed by tents, behind trees, and in dense undergrowth, opened a terrific fire on our whole line simultaneously. With one battery he opened on the left of the Fifteenth Ohio, holding the right; with another he annoyed the left of the 49th Ohio, holding the left, and with a third he poured a torrent of grape upon the Thirty-ninth Indiana, holding the center. The fire of the enemy's infantry was promptly responded to along our entire line. Our volleys were delivered with rapidity, regularity, and effect. The enemy's lines were shaken, and we steadily pressed forward, driving him before us at least 80 rods.

I here discovered that, under cover of a ravine, the enemy was turning my left, and I at once ordered the Forty-ninth Ohio to change line of battle to the rear on the first company, which movement was executed with perfect order under a heavy fire. Lieut. William C. Turner was dispatched to General McCook to inform him of the danger to my left, but the fire of the Forty-ninth Ohio from its new position soon drove the enemy back, and the regiment moved forward into line.

The enemy now, with increased force, made a second demonstration on my left, and the Forty-ninth Ohio again changed line to the rear, and quickly arrested his advance.

Captain Bouton, with two guns of his Chicago battery, reached the ground at this juncture, and after silencing the enemy's battery, which had been annoying my left, moved quickly to the left of the Fifteenth Ohio and opened on the batteries which had up to that time harassed that regiment and the Thirty-ninth Indiana. The enemy's guns were quickly silenced. . . .

The Forty-ninth Ohio having again moved forward into line, and my left being supported by troops ordered forward for that purpose by General McCook, I again ordered an advance, and our entire line pushed forward in gallant style, driving the enemy before us a full half mile, and taking possession of the camp from which a portion of General Sherman's division had been driven the day before, including the General's headquarters.

The enemy now abandoned the contest and retreated under the protection of his cavalry, leaving us in possession of that portion of the field and two of his hospitals crowded with his wounded. [*O.R.,* X, pt. 1, pp. 315–16.]

Report of Col. August Willich, USA, Commanding Thirty-second Indiana Infantry, Sixth Brigade, Second Division, Army of the Ohio

The regiment arrived at 10 A.M. at Pittsburg Landing and marched up the hill, where it received orders from General Grant to start immediately for the field of action. The regiment marched as fast as possible, and having received no special direction, took its course to the heaviest firing. Having arrived at the line of battle, General McCook ordered the regiment to form the reserve of the center of his division, and in case the enemy should throw our lines, to advance and charge bayonet. The regiment took its position about 200 yards in the rear of the second line of battle.

About this time, neither party advancing nor retreating, I asked General McCook for permission to pass with the regiment to the front and make a bayonet charge, which was granted. The regiment formed into double column to the center, marched up about 200 yards toward the enemy, when he turned and retreated, without stopping to receive the charge; after which the regiment was deployed into line of battle, to give him the benefit of all our rifles.

The whole division then advanced for some time. The Thirty-second formed into the double column to the center again, and two companies deployed as skirmishers, until General *Beauregard* in person brought up his reserve [from vicinity of Shiloh Church] against our forward movement, when, by bad management in our squeezed-up position, our skirmishers received fire from regiments behind, right and left, putting them in immense danger, which caused them to retreat in a hasty manner, when they should have retreated slowly and firing, and bringing disorder in the whole regiment for a few moments, forcing the commander to order a retreat into a ravine, where it was formed again in double column to the center, and immediately marched up to charge the enemy once more, supported by only one regiment on its left wing.

After having advanced for some time in this formation the regiment was deployed in line of battle, made a charge with the bayonet, and succeeded, after short and heavy firing, to check the enemy's advance till re-enforcements came up, which, supported by batteries, fell on both flanks of the enemy, when the whole of our force advanced again and threw the enemy back finally. . . . Then the regiment advanced on the line of the enemy's retreat for over a mile, where the complete exhaustion of the men obliged me to give them some rest. . . .

It was a very unhappy accident for the regiment that the ambulances had been left behind at Savannah and that I was ordered so rapidly to the scene of action that my surgeon could not follow, which obliged me to weaken my command considerably by having the wounded carried to the hospitals by their comrades. [*O.R.*, X, pt. 1, pp. 317–18.]

Drive straight ahead for 0.1 mile to the intersection. On the right side is a small sign for Beauregard's Headquarters. Pull off on the shoulder near this sign.

STOP 25, BEAUREGARD'S HEADQUARTERS

At his headquarters *Beauregard* received reports from all over the field describing the relentless Union pressure. Nowhere was there a continuous line upon which to rally. *Beauregard* directed his chief of staff, Colonel *Jordan,* to form a rear guard out of some of the broken commands in the area. *Jordan* took approximately two thousand men and twelve guns to a defensive position south of Shiloh Church. Under the protection offered by this rear guard, the remainder of the Confederate forces obeyed their commander's orders and withdrew to the south, followed by the rear guard. A determined federal pursuit could have inflicted severe damage, but many of the Union troops were as exhausted as the Confederates, although Buell's and Lew Wallace's troops had only participated in the counterattack and were relatively fresh. With

Gen. P. G. T. Beauregard, CSA, Second-in-command and later Commander, Army of the Mississippi. (U.S. Army Military History Institute)

Lithograph showing General Beauregard at Shiloh Chapel sending his
aides to the corps commanders with orders to begin the retreat. The tents
are part of Sherman's camp, which was reoccupied by him Monday evening. This was in the afternoon of the second day of the battle, approximately 2:00 P.M. *(Battles and Leaders of the Civil War)*

nightfall came heavy rains, turning all roads into quagmires. The Battle of Shiloh had ended.

Report of General P. G. T. Beauregard, CSA, Commanding Army of the Mississippi

It was after 6 P.M. [on April 6] . . . when the enemy's last position was carried, and his forces finally broke and sought refuge behind a commanding eminence covering the Pittsburg Landing, not more than half a mile distant, and under the guns of the gunboats, which opened on our eager columns a fierce and annoying fire with shot and shell of the heaviest description.

Darkness was close at hand; officers and men were exhausted by a combat of over twelve hours without food, and jaded by the march of the preceding day through mud and water. It was, therefore, impossible to collect the rich and opportune spoils of war scattered broadcast on the field left in our possession, and impracticable to make any effective dispositions for their removal to the rear.

I accordingly established my headquarters at the church of Shiloh, in the enemy's encampments, with Major-General *Bragg,* and directed our troops to sleep on their arms in such positions in advance and rear as corps commanders should determine, hoping, from news received by a special dispatch, that delays had been encountered by General Buell in his march from Columbia, and that his main force, therefore, could not reach the field of battle in time to save General Grant's shattered fugitive forces from capture or destruction on the following day.

During the night the rain fell in torrents, adding to the discomforts and harassed condition of the men. The enemy, moreover, had broken their rest by a discharge at measured intervals of heavy shells thrown from the gunboats; therefore on the following morning the troops under my command were not in condition to cope with an equal force of fresh troops, armed and equipped like our adversary, in the immediate possession of his depots and sheltered by such an auxiliary as the enemy's gunboats.

About 6 o'clock on the morning of April 7, however, a hot fire of musketry and artillery, opened from the enemy's quarter on our advanced line, assured me of the junction of his forces, and soon the battle raged with a fury which satisfied me I was attacked by a largely superior force. But from the outset our troops, notwithstanding their fatigue and losses from the . . . day before, exhibited the most cheering, veteran-like steadiness. On the right and center the enemy was repulsed in every attempt he made with his heavy columns in that quarter of the field. On the left, however, and nearest to the point of arrival of his re-enforcements, he drove forward line after line of his fresh troops, which were met with a resolution and courage of which our country may be proudly hopeful. Again and again our troops were brought to the charge, invariably to win the position in issue; invariably to drive back their foe. But hour by hour, thus opposed to an enemy constantly re-enforced, our ranks were perceptibly thinned under the unceasing, withering fire of the enemy, and by 12 m. [noon] eighteen hours of hard fighting had sensibly exhausted a large number. My last reserves had necessarily been disposed of, and the enemy was evidently receiving fresh re-enforcements after each repulse.

Accordingly about 1 P.M. I determined to withdraw from so unequal a conflict, securing such of the results of the victory of the day before as was then practicable. Officers of my staff were immediately dispatched with the necessary orders to make the best dispositions for a deliberate, orderly withdrawal from the field, and to collect and post a reserve to meet the enemy, should he attempt to push after us. . . .

About 2 P.M. the lines in advance, which had repulsed the enemy in their last fierce assault on our left and center, received the orders to retire. This was done with uncommon steadiness and the enemy made no attempt to follow.

The line of troops established to cover this movement had been disposed on a favorable ridge commanding the ground of Shiloh Church. From this position our artillery played upon the woods beyond for a while, but upon no visible enemy and without reply. Soon satisfied that no serious pursuit would be attempted this last line was withdrawn, and never did troops leave a battle-field in better order; even the stragglers fell into the ranks and marched off with those who had stood more steadily by their colors.

A second strong position was taken up about a mile in rear,

where the approach of the enemy was awaited for nearly an hour, but no effort to follow was made, and only a small detachment of horsemen could be seen at a distance from this last position, warily observing our movements.

Arranging through my staff officers for the completion of the movements thus begun, Brigadier-General *Breckinridge* was left with his command as a rear guard to hold the ground we had occupied the night preceding the first battle, just in front of the intersection of the Pittsburg and Hamburg roads [Bark Road], about 4 miles from the former place, while the rest of the army passed to the rear in excellent order.

On the following day General *Breckinridge* fell back about 3 miles to Mickey's, which position we continued to hold, with our cavalry thrown considerably forward in immediate proximity to the battle-field. Unfortunately, toward night of the 7th . . . it began to rain heavily. This continued throughout the night; the roads became almost impassable in many places, and much hardship and suffering now ensued before all the regiments reached their encampments; but, despite the heavy casualties of the two eventful days . . . this army is more confident of ultimate success than before its encounter with the enemy. . . . Not only did the obstinate conflict for twelve hours on Sunday leave the Confederate Army masters of the battle-field and our adversary beaten, but we left that field on the next day only after eight hours' incessant battle with a superior army of fresh troops, whom we had repulsed in every attack on our lines—so repulsed and crippled, indeed, as to leave it unable to take the field for the campaign for which it was collected and equipped at such enormous expense and with such profusion of all the appliances of war.

These successful results were not achieved, however, . . . without severe loss—a loss not to be measured by the number of the slain or wounded, but by the high social and personal worth of so large a number of those who were killed or disabled, including the commander of the forces, whose high qualities will be greatly missed in the momentous campaign impending.

I deeply regret to record also the death of the Hon. *George W. Johnson,* provisional Governor of Kentucky, who went into action with the Kentucky troops and continually inspired them by his words and example. Having his horse shot under him on Sunday, he entered the ranks of a Kentucky regiment on Monday, and fell mortally wounded toward the close of the day. . . .

Another gallant and able soldier . . . was lost to the service of the country when Brigadier-General *Gladden,* commanding the First Brigade, *Withers'* division, Second Army Corps, died from a severe wound received on the 6th . . . after having been conspicuous to his whole corps and the army for courage and capacity.

Major-General *Cheatham,* commanding First Division, First Corps, was slightly wounded and had three horses shot under him.

Brigadier-General *Clark,* commanding Second Division of the First Corps, received a severe wound also on the first day. . . .

Brigadier-General *Hindman,* engaged in the outset of the battle, was conspicuous for a cool courage, efficiently employed in leading his men ever in the thickest of the fray, until his horse was shot under him and he was . . . severely injured by the fall. . . .

I turn to [a duty] . . . in the highest degree unpleasant. . . . Some officers, non-commissioned officers, and men abandoned their colors early on the first day to pillage the captured encampments; others retired shamefully from the field on both days while the thunder of cannon and the roar and rattle of musketry told them that their brothers were being slaughtered by the fresh legions of the enemy. I have ordered the names of the most conspicuous on this roll of laggards and cowards to be published in orders. . . .

Our loss on the two days, in killed outright, was 1,728; wounded, 8,012, and missing, 959, making an aggregate of casualties, 10,699. This sad list tells in simple language of the stout fight made by our countrymen in front of the rude log chapel of Shiloh, especially when it is known that on Monday, from exhaustion and other causes, not 20,000 men on our side could be brought into action. [*O.R.,* X, pt. 1, pp. 387–91.]

Report of Brig. Gen. William T. Sherman, USA, Commanding Fifth Division, Army of the Tennessee (continued)

The enemy had one battery close by Shiloh and anothe. near the Hamburg road, both pouring grape and caniste: upon any column of troops that advanced toward the greer point of water-oaks. Willich's regiment had been repulsed, bu a whole brigade [Rousseau's] of McCook's division advancec beautifully, deployed, and entered this dreaded woods. I or dered my Second Brigade [Stuart's] . . . to form on its right and my Fourth [Buckland's] . . . on its right, all to advanc(abreast with . . . Rousseau's brigade of McCook's division. gave personal direction to the 24-pounder guns, whose well directed fire first silenced the enemy's guns to the left, anc afterwards at the Shiloh Meeting-house. Rousseau's brigad(moved in splendid order steadily to the front, sweeping every thing before it, and at 4 P.M. we stood upon the ground of ou. original front line and the enemy was in full retreat.

I directed my several brigades to resume at once thei: original camps. Several times during the battle cartridges gav(out, but General Grant had thoughtfully kept a supply comin; from the rear. When I appealed to regiments to stand fast although out of cartridges, I did so because to retire a regimen for any cause has a bad effect on others. I commend the Forti eth Illinois and Thirteenth Missouri for thus holding thei: ground under a heavy fire, although their cartridge boxe: were empty.

I am ordered by General Grant to give personal credi: where it is due and censure where I think it merited. I concedc that General McCook's splendid division from Kentucky drov(back the enemy along the Corinth road, which was the grea central line of this battle. There *Beauregard* commanded in per son, supported by *Bragg's, Johnston's,* and *Breckinridge's* division I think *Johnston* was killed by exposing himself in front of hi: troops at the time of their attack on Buckland's brigade or Sunday morning, although in this I may be mistaken.

My division was made up of regiments perfectly new nearly all having received their muskets for the first time a Paducah. None of them had ever been under fire or behelc heavy columns of an enemy bearing down on them as they dic on us last Sunday. They knew nothing of the value of combination and organization. When individual fears seized them the first impulse was to get away. To expect of them the coolness and steadiness of older troops would be wrong. My Third Brigade did break much too soon, and I am not yet advised where they were during Sunday afternoon and Monday morning. Colonel Hildebrand, its commander, was as cool as any man I ever saw, and no one could have made stronger efforts to hold men to their places than he did. He kept his own regiment, with individual exceptions, in hand an hour after Appler's [Fifty-third Ohio] and Mungen's [Fifty-seventh Ohio] regiments had left their proper field of action. Colonel Buckland managed his brigade well. I commend him to your notice as a cool, judicious, intelligent gentleman, needing only confidence and experience to make a good commander. His subordinates, Colonels Sullivan [Forth-eighth Ohio] and Cockerill [Seventieth Ohio], behaved with great gallantry, the former receiving a severe wound on Sunday, and yet commanding and holding his regiment well in hand all day, and on Monday, till his right arm was broken by a shot. Colonel Cockerill held a larger portion of his men than any colonel in my division, and was with me from first to last. Col. J. A. McDowell, commanding the First Brigade, held his ground on Sunday till I ordered him to fall back, which he did in line of battle, and when ordered he conducted the attack on the enemy's left in good style. In falling back to the next position he was thrown from his horse and injured, and his brigade was not in position on Monday morning. . . .

My Second Brigade, Colonel Stuart, was detached nearly 2 miles from my headquarters. He had to fight his own battle on Sunday, as the enemy interposed between him and General Prentiss early in the day. Colonel Stuart was wounded severely, and yet reported for duty on Monday morning, but was compelled to leave during the day, when the command devolved on Col. T. Kilby Smith . . . who was always in the thickest of the fight and led the brigade handsomely. . . .

Of my personal staff I can only speak with praise and thanks. I think they smelt as much gunpowder and heard as many cannon-balls and bullets as must satisfy their ambition. . . . Major Sanger's intelligence, quick perception, and rapid execution were of very great value to me, especially in bringing into line the batteries that co-operated so efficiently in our movements. . . . To Surgeon Hartshorn and Dr. L'Hommedieu, hundreds of wounded men are indebted for kind and excellent treatment received on the field of battle and in the various temporary hospitals created along the line of our operations. They worked day and night, and did not rest till all the wounded of our own troops, as well as of the enemy, were in safe and comfortable shelter.

To Major Taylor, chief of artillery, I feel under deep obligations for his good sense and judgment in managing the batteries, on which so much depended. [*O.R.*, X, pt. 1, pp. 251–54.]

Report of Lieutenant Gwin, U.S. Navy, Commanding, USS **Tyler**

. . . When our land forces having attacked the enemy, forcing them gradually back, it made it dangerous for the gunboats to fire. At 7, I received a communication from General Grant (enclosed is a copy) which prevented the gunboats from taking an active part throughout the rest of the day. Lieutenant Commanding Shirk deserves the greatest praise for the efficient manner in which the battery of the *Lexington* was served.

At 5:35 P.M. the enemy were forced to retreat in haste, having contested every inch of the ground with great stubbornness during the entire day.

The officers and men of this vessel displayed their usual gallantry and enthusiasm during the entire day and night.

Your old wooden boats, I feel confident, rendered invaluable service on the 6th instant to the land forces.

Gunner Herman Peters deserves great credit for the prompt and courageous manner in which he traversed our lines, conveying communications from this vessel to the commanding generals. [*Official Records of the Union and Confederate Navies*, series I, vol. 22, p. 763.]

AFTER THE BATTLE

Narrative of Maj. Gen. U. S. Grant, USA, Commanding Army of the Tennessee

After the rain of the night before and the frequent and heavy rains for some days previous, the roads were almost impassable. The enemy carrying his artillery and supply trains over them in his retreat made them still worse for troops following. I wanted to pursue, but had not the heart to order the men who had fought desperately for two days, lying in the mud and rain whenever not fighting, and I did not feel disposed to positively order Buell, or any part of his command, to pursue. Although the senior in rank at the time I had been so only a few weeks. Buell . . . had been for some time past, a department commander, while I commanded only a district. I did not meet Buell in person until too late to get troops ready and pursue with effect; but had I seen him at the moment of the last charge I should have at least requested him to follow.

I rode forward several miles the day after the battle, and found that the enemy had dropped much, if not all, of their provisions, some ammunition and the extra wheels of their caissons, lightening their loads to enable them to get off their guns. About five miles out we found their field hospital abandoned. An immediate pursuit must have resulted in the capture of a considerable number of prisoners and probably some guns.

Shiloh was the severest battle fought at the west during the war, and but few in the East equalled it for hard, determined fighting. I saw an open field, in our possession on the second day, over which the Confederates had made repeated charges the day before, so covered with dead that it would have been possible to walk across the clearing, in any direction, stepping on dead bodies, without a foot touching the ground. On our side National and Confederate troops were mingled together in about equal proportions; but on the remainder of the field nearly all were Confederates. On one part, which had evidently not been ploughed for several years, probably because the land was poor, bushes had grown up, some to the height of eight or ten feet. There was not one of these left standing unpierced by bullets. The smaller ones were all cut down.

Contrary to all my experience up to that time . . . we were on the defensive. We were without intrenchments or defensive advantages of any sort, and more than half the army engaged the first day was without experience or even drill as soldiers. The officers with them, except the division commanders and possibly two or three of the brigade commanders, were equally inexperienced in war. The result was a Union victory that gave the men who achieved it great confidence in themselves ever after.

The enemy fought bravely, but they had started out to defeat and destroy an army and capture a position. They failed in both, with very heavy loss in killed and wounded, and must have gone back discouraged and convinced that the "Yankee" was not an enemy to be despised.

After the battle I gave verbal instruction to division commanders to let the regiments send out parties to bury their own dead, and to detail parties, under commissioned officers from each division, to bury the Confederate dead in their respective fronts and to report the numbers so buried. . . .

The criticism has often been made that the Union troops should have been intrenched at Shiloh. Up to that time the pick and spade had been but little resorted to at the West. . . . Besides this, the troops with me, officers and men, needed discipline and drill more than they did experience with the pick, shovel, and axe. Reinforcements were arriving almost daily, composed of troops that had been hastily thrown together into companies and regiments—fragments of incomplete organizations, the men and officers strangers to each other. Under all these circumstances I concluded that drill and discipline were worth more to our men than fortifications. . . .

The endeavor of the enemy on the first day was simply to hurl their men against ours—first at one point, then at another, sometimes at several points at once. This they did with daring and energy, until at night the rebel troops were worn out. Our effort during the same time was to be prepared to resist assaults wherever made.

The object of the Confederates on the second day was to get away with as much as their army and material as possible. Ours then was to drive them from our front, and to capture or destroy as great a part as possible of their men and material. We were successful in driving them back, but not so successful in captures as if further pursuit could have been made. As it was, we captured or recaptured on the second day about as much artillery as we lost on the first; and, leaving out the one great capture of Prentiss, we took more prisoners on Monday than the enemy gained from us on Sunday. . . .

The navy gave a hearty support to the army at Shiloh. . . . The nature of the ground was such, however, that on this occasion it could do nothing in aid of the troops until sundown on the first day. The country was broken and heavily timbered, cutting off all view of the battle from the river, so that friends would be as much in danger from fire from the gunboats as the foe. But about sundown, when the National troops were back in their last position, the right of the enemy was near the river and exposed to the fire of the two gun-boats, which was delivered with vigor and effect. After nightfall, when firing had entirely ceased on land, the commander of the fleet informed himself, approximately, of the position of our troops, and suggested the idea of dropping a shell within the lines of the enemy every fifteen minutes during the night. This was done with effect, as is proved by the Confederate reports.

Up to the battle of Shiloh I . . . believed that the rebellion . . . would collapse suddenly and soon, if a decisive victory could be gained over any of its armies. . . . But when Confederate armies were collected which not only attempted to hold a line . . . from Memphis to Chattanooga, Knoxville, and on to the Atlantic, but assumed the offensive and made such a gallant effort to regain what had been lost, then . . . I gave up all idea of saving the Union except by complete conquest. . . . [Grant *Memoirs,* I: 354–58, 365–68, and passim.]

This concludes the staff ride. From this position, turn around and retrace your route to the Visitor Center. From here you may depart the Battlefield Park or peruse the displays found in the Visitor Center.

APPENDICES

I. The Campaign and Battle of Shiloh, April 1862. Army War ollege Course in Military Art, 1909–10. A lecture by Maj. Eben wift, General Staff, February 4, 1910.

II. Correspondence between Maj. Gen. Lewis Wallace, Gen. I. W. Halleck, Maj. Gen. Jas. B. McPherson, Lieut. Col. John A. awlins, Maj. Gen. U. S. Grant, Col. J. C. Kelton, and the Honorable . M. Stanton relating to the failure of Maj. Gen. Lewis Wallace to articipate in the first day's fighting at Pittsburg Landing.

III. Order of Battle, United States Army. Organization of the nion Armies of the Tennessee and Ohio, and of the Confederate rmy of the Mississippi.

IV. Recapitulation of casualties.

APPENDIX I. "THE CAMPAIGN AND BATTLE OF SHILOH, APRIL 1862"

FEBRUARY 1, 1862

The Federal troops were posted along the Ohio from Bird's Point to Louisville. The Confederates from Columbus, by Forts Henry and Donelson, to Bowling Green and Munfordsville.

The Confederates were commanded by Albert Sydney *Johnston*. The Federals were under two commands, Halleck at Cairo and Buell at Louisville.

The idea of piercing the Confederate defensive line by the Cumberland and Tennessee Rivers seems to belong to Buell.

FEBRUARY 6–16

Grant captured Fort Henry on the 6th and Fort Donelson on the 16th, assisted by the fleet under Commodore Foote.

The effect was remarkable. *Polk* evacuated Columbus and *Johnston* fell back through Nashville and finally to Corinth through northern Alabama. Thus all of Kentucky and most of Tennessee fell into the hands of the Federals.

Still more decisive results might have followed if Grant had moved to the east, joined with Buell, and attacked *Johnston*, or if he had moved to the west against *Polk*, but the divided commands were probably largely responsible.

The Confederate formed a new line of defense on the Memphis and Charleston Railroad without molestation by Grant. Halleck then decided to break the Confederate line once more, this time in the vicinity of Florence. Grant was ordered to send General Sherman up the river in boats and C. F. Smith to Savannah. Meanwhile Buell had been transferred to Halleck's command.

MARCH 16

Sherman found the country flooded by the spring rains and
stopped at Pittsburg Landing which was the only good landing
place above water. It was a shipping point for Corinth, 22 miles to
the southwest, where large forces of Confederates were known
to be concentrating. Halleck ordered Buell to Savannah from
Nashville.

MARCH 19

Two divisions were camped at Shiloh (Pittsburg Landing).
Buell's advanced troops reached Duck River.

Beauregard came as adviser and assistant to *Johnston*. *Bragg's*
corps joined from Mobile. Van Dorn was ordered up from Arkansas.

APRIL 1

Grant remained at Savannah with headquarters. He had one
division under Lewis Wallace at Crumps Landing and four divisions under Sherman, W. H. L. Wallace, Prentiss, Hurlbut and
McClernand on the Shiloh plateau, between Lick Creek and Owl
Creek, at the west of the Landing.

On the other hand, the Confederate Army was scattered from
Burnsville to Bethel [, Tennessee].

APRIL 3

The Confederate commander learned of the advance of Buell
and that he would be at Savannah in a few days, so he planned to
attack Grant before he could be reinforced. At 1 A.M. the order
was issued for the concentration of the army at Mickey's, 14 miles
from Corinth and 8 miles from the Landing, on the next day, so
as to attack on the morning of the 5th.

As the order was very long, some 1500 words, it could not be
issued before the movement began, so it was explained verbally to
the 3 corps commanders who were in Corinth. The army was to
concentrate on Mickey's. Two corps less 1 division were to march
by the Bark Road with an interval of a half hour of time, but a
third corps was to be interpolated between the two corps. After

reaching Mickey's the command would be corked up, with only one outlet in the direction of the enemy.

APRIL 5

The Confederate concentration was delayed. The 14 miles between Corinth and Mickey's were not covered. *Hardee's* corps left Corinth at 3 P.M., April 3 by Ridge Road; at 7:30 A.M., April 4 his corps had passed through Mickey's.

Bragg's corps did not get through Mickey's till 4:30 P.M. on the afternoon of April 5.

Polk's corps was under arms from 3 A.M. till 2 P.M. on the 5th April on the Ridge Road waiting for *Bragg's* column to pass.

Breckinridge marched from Burnsville to the loop in 2 days with unobstructed roads.

As a result the time for attack was postponed. During the day the army was formed in 3 lines about 1½ miles from the Federal camps, on a front of 2000 yards.

At noon the leading division [Nelson's] of Buell's army reached Savannah.

APRIL 6: BATTLE OF SHILOH
The Position

The Federal army was scattered about in isolated camps. A superior enemy was known to be twenty-two miles away. There was no defensive line, no point of assembly, no proper outpost, no one to give orders in the absence of the regular commander, whose headquarters were nine miles away. The greenest troops were in the most exposed position. Sherman had three brigades on the right and one on the left, with an interval of several miles.

The Field

The field of battle was triangular in shape, consisting of between three and four thousand acres of plateau, about 80 feet above the river. The surface was broken by many deep ravines and on the south, running east and west, was a heavily wooded ridge which rose one hundred and fifty feet above the plateau. The ground was mostly covered with forest, and sometimes very thick underbrush. Not more than one-sixth was cultivated. A field of fire of six hundred yards was hard to find.

Two creeks which rise near Monterey and flow into the Tennessee, one above the other below the Landing, enclose the field of battle. At the time of which we speak they could only be crossed at a few places where bridges were maintained. In one respect, therefore, the position was excellent, as it had its flanks resting on impassible obstacles. The distance from one flank to the other was about five miles in an air line. These creeks flowed through wide, low, marshy bottoms. Within the limits of the field were several smaller creeks. They were: Shiloh Branch, Tilghman Branch and Dill Branch.

From the Landing to Corinth the road runs southwest between the two creeks. It divides about a mile from the Landing and the two come together again about five miles out. Cutting these almost at right angles are the river road, from Hamburg above to Crump's Landing below on the river, and the Purdy-Hamburg road. Along the high ridge at the south the Bark road runs east and west.

Near the junction of the Corinth and the Purdy roads was the Shiloh meeting house, which gave one of the names to the battle.

Maps

The maps used by both sides were so inaccurate that it is hard to understand how military movements could have been based on them. On the Federal side the commander of a division six miles away was not able to reinforce the army because he lost the road. Likewise the road from Grant's Headquarters to the army was unknown, which was the principal reason why another division did not reach the field till dark.

The Troops

The war had been going on for a year. Each side employed its best officers who were aided by all the resources of the country and the support of the people. Of the two the Confederate army was the best organized and the better led. In the most important positions there were thirteen graduates of the military academy, having from forty-four to fourteen years' service, of high reputation and experience in war. Among regimental commanders and staff officers were seventeen men who had served in the regular army.

In the federal army Grant and Sherman alone among the higher commanders had served in the regular army, and both had been out of the service for some years. Sherman had not served in the Mexican War. There were not more than seven officers in all who had been in the regular army.

Three divisions of Grant's army had fought at Forts Donelson and Henry and a few regiments were at Belmont. Among the others the average amount of service was about six months.

Grant had about 40,000 men including 3000 cavalry and 123 guns. The Confederate army was slightly larger.

Organization

The Confederate army was commanded by a general with another general as second in command, or chief of staff. It was organized into four [three] corps and a reserve corps, commanded by major-generals. Two corps were divided into two divisions each, commanded by major-generals and brigadiers. The other corps were not organized into divisions. These were sixteen brigades, all of which except five were commanded by brigadiers; and five were commanded by colonels. The staffs were fairly complete.

The Federal army was commanded by a major-general with a colonel as chief of staff. There were no army corps, but instead there were six divisions commanded by two major generals and four brigadiers. There were eighteen brigades, all but two of which were commanded by colonels. The staffs, as a rule, were not complete. Only one staff had a quartermaster and a commissary. The cavalry and artillery of both armies were scattered about among divisions and brigades. There was no chief of artillery and the chief of cavalry was at Halleck's headquarters far to the rear.

Outpost and Reconnaissance

The Confederate army approached unobserved by the Federals and bivouacked in several lines of battle on a front of about 2000 yards, between one and two miles in front of the Federal camps. They stood at about 22 men to a yard of front.

A single battalion constituted the main outpost of the Confederate army. It was about four hundred yards in advance.

The Federals had done some reconnaissance. General Sherman had shown his customary activity and had, a few days before [April 3], sent a force as far as Monterey. Two days before the battle his scouting party had encountered troops of the three arms but he did not give it serious consideration. With such a force, wild and alarming rumors are likely to be prevalent and the General thought it necessary to tone up his command by belittling the question of danger. It rained on the day before the battle, and General Sherman's cavalry regiment, which he would have sent out that day, happened to be moving its camp. The balance of the 3000 cavalry seems to have been doing nothing. Not a patrol left the camp, although the enemy had been very active for a week. It was scattered about in the manner habitual at that day. Prentiss sent out a patrol of infantry under a colonel on the day before the battle, but it returned after traveling as reported, five miles, without discovering the enemy which was close in front.

Many stories are told of Confederate cavalry all day watching the camps from various points in the outskirts of the camp. It is remarkable that there was not a deserter or traitor in that army to betray its position.

For the Federal army the claim has been made that one company from each regiment was placed one and a half miles out on picket and that vedettes were still further one mile, but the Confederate line of battle was within these distances.

In Prentiss' Division there was an old soldier by the name of Major Powell who went out on the Corinth road with three companies before daylight of the 6th. He ran into Major *Hardcastle* who was posted as outpost for the Confederate army, 400 yards in its front. This started the battle. Powell was killed and his story has never been told. I have always had an idea that he himself conceived the idea which he executed and that he should be considered as one of the heroes of Shiloh. This engagement of the outposts took place about 5 A.M. and lasted till about 6:30, when Powell was driven back by the advancing Confederate army.

The Battle

At 7:30 A.M. Prentiss had supported his scouting party and by 7:30 his entire force was formed in advance of his camps. Sherman's brigades formed at their camps.

Johnston had given the order to attack at daybreak. The first line consisted of *Hardee's* corps and *Gladden's* brigade of *Wither's* division of *Bragg's* corps. There were probably ten or twelve thousand men in this line. *Cleburne* moved towards Sherman's camp, *Wood* and *Shaver* attacked Prentiss at about 9:30 A.M.

At 8:00 A.M. *Gladden* and *Chalmers* got in position in front of Prentiss, *Cleburne* in front of Sherman.

At 9:30 A.M. Prentiss was attacked and driven through his camps. *Cleburne* attacked and his division [brigade] became dispersed. *Anderson* and Johnston *[Johnson]* came up in his rear and renewed the attack.

The second line under *Bragg* at 800 yards, somewhat stronger than the first was thus getting engaged. They took their places in the front line, but as the second was used to extend the line to the right and left and to fill gaps in the center, the integrity of the commands of *Bragg* and *Hardee* was destroyed at once. The same soon happened with divisions and went down to smaller commands. The higher generals then took command of any troops in sight and by common consent assigned themselves to certain parts of the field.

Sherman's advanced troops had been driven back at the same time as Prentiss. McClernand's brigades had formed but had not advanced.

At 9:00 A.M. we simply show the arrival of *Russell's* brigade, without other changes.

At 10:30 A.M. Sherman was being driven to the rear, along with McClernand's 3d brigade. Prentiss rallied about 500 men on a sunken road in rear of the Duncan field, was joined by a regiment from the Landing and by Tuttle's brigade of W. H. L. Wallace's division. Hurlbut had brought up two brigades and formed on Prentiss' left. Far on the left, Stuart was being driven from his camps. In rear of Sherman, McClernand had formed his remaining brigades; a brigade of Hurlbut's had taken position in support. Hurlbut's and Wallace's remaining troops were moving to the front. It was five hours since the firing began. The cannonade brought Grant from Savannah, nine miles away, but the troops in rear had not gotten up. Prentiss had been driven a mile and had practically lost his division. Sherman's division was about to go to pieces.

On the Confederate side *Chalmers* and *Jackson*, after the capture of Prentiss' camp, were moved to the extreme right by *Johnston's* order. *Statham* and *Bowen*, with the last reserves, were coming up to fill the gap. *Gibson* was coming up to give his four separate attacks on the Hornet's Nest. Stevens *[Stephens]* and *Stewart* had attacked in the center and *Pond* far on the left had made his advance. *Trabue* was alone in rear of the center and left.

At 11:00 A.M. the Confederate reserves were all engaged. The line of battle was four miles long, from Lick Creek to the Purdy bridge. Both flanks of the Federals were turned and the Confederates were hammering at the center, throwing brigade after brigade and regiment after regiment in unsupported, isolated attacks.

At 12:00 o'clock the flanks of the Federal army were in full retreat, but the Confederates were making no impression on the center.

At 4:00 P.M. the Federal right was bent far to the rear. The Confederate commander in chief, while personally directing *Bowen's* brigade, was killed, Sherman's entire division had disappeared. McClernand opposed a feeble resistance to a small force of Confederates but his line dissolved and broke to the rear.

The line did not have the continuity shown on the map. Thousands of stragglers were wandering about. Various commanders were holding small fractions of their troops at the front, and the Confederates were closing around the remains of Prentiss', Hurlbut's and Wallace's forces, which had remained together.

At 5:00 P.M. Hurlbut had been driven off. Prentiss was surrounded. Wallace was killed. About 2000 were captured. The line of battle, which at 1:00 o'clock extended four miles, is now represented by a small circle around the Hornet's Nest; Grant's fighting force is shown by the 2000 prisoners taken there. The two regiments furthest to the right and left of the attack, here joined and each captured the remnant of a regiment. Both sides were exhausted and probably little more could be done on either side.

At 6:00 P.M. Meanwhile from the Landing back to the river road a desperate effort was being made to rally a sufficient force to oppose another advance of the Confederates. A number of heavy guns were placed in position and a fragment of about 5000 [actually 18,000–20,000] men was put in line.

It made a formidable line, and would have made a strong defense. General *Bragg*, who, upon the death of *Johnston*, seems to have been the leading element of the Southern side, now made strenuous efforts to organize another attack. A half dozen remnants of brigades were gotten up, in which I wish to call attention to those of *Chalmers* and *Jackson* of *Withers's* division, which had made many attacks on that day, still ready for another. If you consider how some divisions were broken to pieces by one attack you will appreciate this. A feeble attack was made and orders were received from *Beauregard* which had been sent several hours earlier to retire for the night.

The Confederate Attack

Each subordinate commander acted as if he were fighting the battle on his own account. All rushed to the front as if afraid the battle would end before they had a chance to take a part.

The Confederate formation shows the mistake of using extended lines instead of deep formations for attack. The long lines moving forward spread out to the right and left. Gaps in the forward line were filled by portions of the lines coming up from the rear. Corps, divisions and brigades were soon mixed in hopeless confusion. Attacks were made and lost before supporting troops came up. No one knew from whom to take orders. One regiment received orders from three different corps commanders within a short time. As a result many aimless and conflicting orders were issued which unnecessarily exhausted and discouraged the troops. The highest commanders, including the adjutant general, went into the fight and devoted themselves to urging the troops forward without any plan or system. By 11 A.M., there was not a reserve on the field. Instead of feeding the fight with their own troops the corps commanders finally sought various parts of the field and took command without regard to the order of the battle. *Bragg* may be found at the center, at the right and then at the left. The commander-in-chief was killed at the front doing the work of a brigadier. *Beauregard* remained near Shiloh Church, without a reserve, and unable to exercise any influence on the battle.

The front of attack, which was at first less than 2000 yards in length, in three hours extended from the Tennessee River on the east to Owl Creek on the west, nearly four miles. *Bragg's* corps was right, left and center, at the same time. The attack was turning both flanks and breaking the center, all at once. The Federals, instead of being driven down the river as *Johnston's* intention was, were driven to the Landing where their gunboats and supplies were.

The Federal Defense

Prentiss and Sherman occupied the most advanced camps. The former held on for a short time though not attacked by a very superior force; the latter held on till 10 A.M. and repulsed numerous attacks. But Prentiss rallied a few hundred men and halted on a sunken road where they defeated many attacks and probably contributed greatly to saving the army; while Sherman's troops after the stand in the camps did little more on that day.

One division was camped about a mile from Shiloh Church and two divisions were near the Landing and at 7:30 A.M. they had information of the danger at the front. Prentiss was driven a mile before he was supported. Sherman, after holding his camps for two hours and more, was driven out of them before he received support, except by the regiments of McClernand's Division which were in the first line themselves.

These things could be explained by the absence of a commander-in-chief, or of some one to give orders for him, but General Grant says that he arrived on the field about 8 A.M. while Rawlins and McPherson were there before him.

Exhaustion

At the close of the first day's battle both sides had fought to a standstill. The victorious troops had been demoralized by reckless attacks which were never supported and thousands of them immediately gave up the battle to pillage the camps. At 5 P.M. Grant probably had not more than 5000 in line ready to resist a further advance and they were badly shaken up as was seen by the action of McClernand's troops breaking to the rear after defeating *Pond's* weak attack. The balance of the fine army were killed, wounded, prisoners, but mostly stragglers. The same was true of the Confederate army, which had no greater force in line at the close of the day.

The depletion of the commands on both sides was enormous. Regiments were reduced to squads [companies], and brigades to battalions [regiments] in many cases, while a number of large commands practically disappeared from the field.

Lack of Confidence

As a result of the confusion, looseness of tactical bonds, and unfamiliarity with military service, it seemed that mutual distrust of everybody prevailed. Even while performing the most gallant work a cry of retreat was often raised and sufficient to start the troops to the rear. No man knew who gave the order, each man blamed his neighbor. The report was easily started and quickly believed that the troops on both flanks had retired and that the enemy was getting in rear. The reports quite uniformly state that the author did not retreat until forced to do so by the withdrawal of troops on the right and left. The reports of the officers on the right and left also make the identical remark, and so on. This lack of confidence is peculiar to raw troops. Later in the war these things never occurred. The best divisions in 1864 would not move an inch to the rear without orders.

Leadership

Among Confederate commanders, General Jones M. *Withers* seems to have held a greater proportion of his command in hand than any other and fought six actions. General Sherman on the other side was able to pursue the enemy on the day after the battle with a brigade that was broken to pieces on the first day. Generals Prentiss and W. H. L. Wallace held the Hornets' Nest until surrounded by the effective strength of the entire Confederate army except a part of *Pond's* brigade and lost only 2200 prisoners. The character of the action is well shown here by the fact that the right and left of the Confederate army each captured prisoners at the Hornets' Nest.

Losses

It is probable that the heaviest losses occurred in retreat. Tuttle's brigade which held its position in the Hornets' Nest for five hours against repeated assaults and the fire of sixty guns lost not so many as a number of single regiments which yielded their positions.

The loss of each army was in the neighborhood of 10,000 men, or from 20 to 25 per cent of the men engaged which made it one of the bloodiest battles. About half of the regimental and higher commanders were killed, wounded and missing. The Sixth Mississippi lost 300 in killed and wounded out of 425. *Cleburne's* brigade lost in killed and wounded 1000 out of 2700 and other losses reduced it to 800 men in the evening.

Conclusion

The first day at Shiloh shows better than any other in our history the kind of work performed by a new army before it has had experience and discipline. As the result of a year of preparation it is a most instructive lesson.* [Maj Eben Swift, General Staff, "The Campaign and Battle of Shiloh, April, 1862," lecture presented to the U.S. Army War College, February 8, 1910, found in U.S. Army Military History Institute.]

---

*The original lecture notes continued at this point with what are talking points concerning the Lew Wallace–Grant controversy (see Appendix II). These talking points have been omitted by the editors.

II. THE WALLACE-GRANT
CONTROVERSY

Maj. Gen. Lew Wallace to Maj. Gen. H. W. Halleck,
March 14, 1863

I have heard of prejudices against me at your headquarters, relative to my failure to participate in the first day's battle at Pittsburg Landing. I have also heard that you yourself entertain them. For very obvious purposes, therefore, I respectfully submit to you the following explanation of that affair:

On Sunday morning (April 6, 1862) my division, consisting of eleven regiments of infantry, one battalion of cavalry, and two batteries, was posted on the road from Crump's Landing to Purdy; the First Brigade at the Landing; the Second Brigade 2½ miles out, and the Third Brigade at Adamsville, 5 miles.

Very early that morning I became satisfied that a battle was in progress at Pittsburg Landing, and at once prepared my command for moving instantly upon receipt of an order from General Grant, and as the general was then at Savannah, 4 miles below, my expectation was that he would give me marching orders as he passed up the river to the scene of action. Accordingly my Second and Third Brigades sent their baggage to Crump's Landing, where it could be guarded by a single detachment. The First and Third Brigades joined the Second at its encampment.

About 9 o'clock General Grant passed up the river. Instead of an order to march, he merely left me a direction *to hold myself in readiness for orders.*

At exactly 11:30 A.M. a quartermaster by the name of Baxter brought me an order in *writing unsigned* by *anybody.* It directed me to leave a detachment to guard the public property at Crump's Landing, then march my division and form junction with the right of the army; after junction I was to form line of battle at a right angle with the river. This order, Captain Baxter told me, was from General Grant; that it had been given him verbally, but that in coming down the river he had reduced it to writing, leaving it unsigned. As I had resolved to march toward the cannonading at 12 o'clock without orders, if by that time none came, and as I had so informed Col. (now General) John M. Thayer, commanding my Second Brigade, I made no point upon the informality of the order brought by Baxter, but was glad to receive it in any shape.

Half an hour was given the men to eat dinner. Then I started the column at exactly 12 o'clock to execute General Grant's order. After leaving two regiments and one gun at Crump's Landing the column consisted of nine regiments of infantry and the cavalry and artillery stated; and as the regiments averaged 500 effectives, the whole command did not exceed 5,000 men of all arms.

The route was well known to my cavalry, since, in anticipation of a necessity for my retiring upon the main army, it had, by my order, *corduroyed* the road to the very point of junction.

Why, then, did I not make the junction sooner? There are two reasons why:

1st. Because of the lateness of the hour I received the orders to march—11:30 A.M.

2d. Arrived with my column within a short distance of the point of junction, I was overtaken by an aide of General Grant's, sent by him to tell me that our army had been beaten back from the position it held in the morning, and was then fighting a desperate and losing battle close about Pittsburg Landing. General Grant sent no additional order, and that brought me by Baxter *made* no provision for such a contingency. I was therefore left to my own judgment. Certainly General Grant did not intend I should continue my march and unsupported form line of battle on the ground his whole army had been beaten from; certainly he did not intend that with 5,000 men I should thrust myself into a position where, without possibility of help from the main army—which according to the account was then unable to help itself—I would, in [all] likelihood, be cut to pieces by the enemy's reserves and detachments. The point of junction to which I was proceeding was at least 2¼ miles from Pittsburg Landing. Could I have successfully cut my way through the enemy, fighting superior forces over that space, in what condition would my regiments have been to give the general the assistance he so much required?

In this dilemma I resolved, as the most prudent course, to carry out *the spirit of General Grant's order, and join the right of his army as it then rested.* That could only be done by carrying my column to the lower or river road from Crump's to Pittsburg Landing, by following which I could cross Snake Creek by a good bridge at the very point of junction. A counter-march was therefore ordered, which, in the absence of any cross-road, was necessarily continued to within half a mile of the camp I had started from. On the diagram, in red ink [dotted lines], my whole march is distinctly traced. A little after sunset I made the required junction.

At no time during that afternoon's march was my column halted longer than to allow it to be closed up; the column was brought in in perfect order and without a straggler; the length of its march in the time (from 12 m. to a little after sunset) was nearly 15 miles; certainly there could have been no idling on the way.

Next morning, on the extreme right in the order of battle, my division had the honor of opening the fight; at the close of the day it was the farthest advanced of any along the line.

For your better understanding of my explanation it is accompanied with a diagram showing the situation of my division on the morning of the first day's battle and its route to the battle-field after the order to march was received.

I submit this as an official explanation, solely to vindicate my conduct from unjust aspersions.

Respectfully submitted to Major-General Grant for his remarks. By order of Major-General Halleck [General in Chief]:

J. C. KELTON
Assistant Adjutant-General
[*O.R.*, X, pt. 1, pp. 174–76.]

Maj. Gen. Jas. B. McPherson to Lieut. Col. John A. Rawlins, Assistant Adjutant-General, March 26, 1863

I have the honor to submit the following in relation to the position of the troops and the battle of Shiloh:

When the troops first disembarked at Pittsburg Landing the Tennessee River was very high, the water backing up in all the streams, covering the bottoms in the vicinity of the river from 2 to 6 feet, rendering Lick and Snake Creeks impassable.

Four divisions of the army were encamped on the field of Shiloh in the relative positions indicated in the sketch, and one division

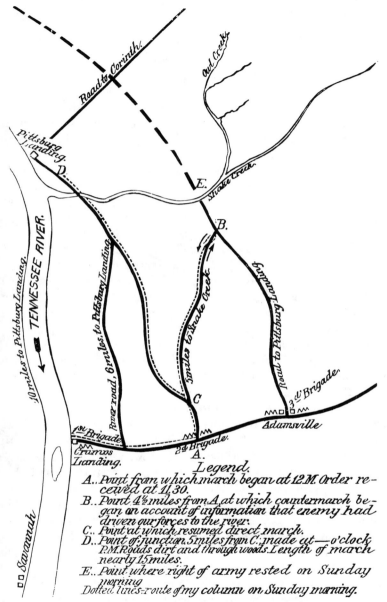

Wallace's diagram of his route of march to the battlefield at Shiloh.
(*The War of the Rebellion: A Compilation of the Official Records of the Union and Confederate Armies*)

(Maj. Gen. Lewis Wallace's) at Crump's Landing, about 6 miles below.

My attention was frequently called to the crossing of Snake Creek, on the direct road from Pittsburg Landing to Crump's, as it was considered very important that a line of land communication between the two portions of the army should be kept open.

As soon as the water subsided sufficiently the bridge across the creek was reconstructed, and a company of cavalry sent through to communicate with General Wallace's command. This was on Thursday, previous to the battle.

Sunday morning, the first day of the battle, I was with Brig. Gen. W. H. L. Wallace, who, in consequence of the severe illness of General C. F. Smith, commanded this division. It was well known the enemy was approaching our lines, and there had been more or less skirmishing for three days preceding the battle.

The consequence was our breakfasts were ordered at an early hour and our horses saddled, to be ready in case of an attack. Sunday morning, shortly before 7 o'clock, word came to the Landing that the battle had commenced. I immediately started, in company with General W. H. L. Wallace and staff; found his division in line ready to move out. At this time, not later than 7:30 A.M., General McClernand had moved a portion of his division up to support General Sherman's left. General Hurlbut had moved to the support of General Prentiss, and General W. H. L. Wallace's division was moved up to support the center and right. I was actively engaged on the field, and did not see General Grant until some time after his arrival, when I met him on the field, with Brig. Gen. W. H. L. Wallace. He informed me that when he came up from Savannah, at 7:30, he had notified Maj. Gen. Lewis Wallace, at Crump's Landing, to hold his command in readiness to march at a moment's notice, and that immediately on his arrival at Pittsburg Landing, finding that the attack was in earnest and not a feint, he had sent Captain Baxter, assistant quartermaster, with orders to him to move up immediately by the River road and take a position on our right. Shortly after this Captain Baxter returned, certainly not later than 10:30, and said that he had delivered the order.

At about 12m. [noon] General Wallace not having arrived, General Grant became very anxious, as the tide of battle was setting against us, and shortly after dispatched Captain Rowley, one of his aides, to hasten up General Wallace. The battle still continued without cessation, our troops being forced back gradually at all points,

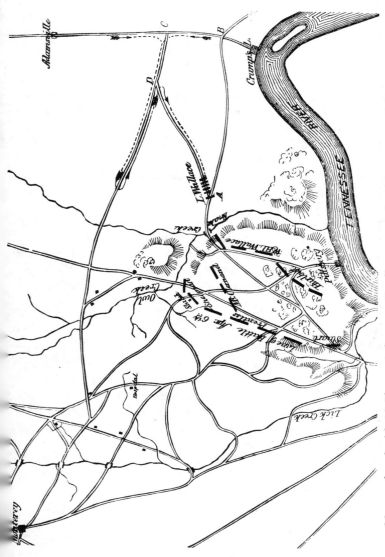

Map enclosed with McPherson's letter to Rawlins, supporting his account of the movement of Wallace's division. (*The War of the Rebellion: A Compilation of the Official Records of the Union and Confederate Armies*)

though fighting most heroically. Two hours rolled around and no news from General Wallace, when at 2:30 P.M. General Grant directed me to go in search of him, report to him how matters stood, and hasten him forward, if possible. I asked Captain (now Lieutenant-Colonel) Rawlins to accompany me, and taking two orderlies, we started at a rapid pace on the River road, expecting to meet the command at every step; pushed on to the junction of the Purdy and Crump's Landing road; saw some soldiers, who could give us no information where General Wallace was; galloped down toward the Landing a short distance and met a surgeon, who said he had started some time before with his command for Pittsburg Landing on a road branching off between Adamsville and the River road; pushed on in this direction, and at the point D met his Second Brigade returning, the rear of the First Brigade having just filed off on the road DA. We pushed on to the head of the column and found General Wallace, when I delivered my instructions, and told him for "God's sake to move forward rapidly."

I understood him to say that his guide had led him wrong, and I was most decidedly of the impression that he had mistaken the road, for his command had already marched a great deal farther than was necessary to reach the battle-field.

I told him, however, to hurry on and we might yet be there in time. I thought we could get there; sun three-quarters of an hour high. We did not, however, reach the ground until after dark.

After I had reached the head of the column I must say it seemed to me that the march was not as rapid as the urgency of the case required. Perhaps this arose in a great measure from my impatience and anxiety to get this force on the field before dark, as I knew very well unless we arrived before sunset we could be of no use in that day's battle and would not be able to retrieve the fortunes of the day. [*O.R.*, X, pt. 1, pp. 180–82.]

Lieut. Col. Jno. A. Rawlins, USA, Assistant Adjutant-General to Grant, April 1, 1863

I have the honor to submit the following statement of your orders to Maj. Gen. Lewis Wallace, . . . and the manner in which he obeyed them, together with facts and circumstances transpiring that day and the one immediately preceding, deemed necessary to a clear understanding of them: In pursuance of the following order—

GENERAL ORDERS, NO. 30, HEADQUARTERS DISTRICT OF
WEST TENNESSEE, *Savannah, March 31, 1862*

Headquarters of the District of West Tennessee is hereby
changed to Pittsburg Landing. An office will be continued at
Savannah, where all official communications may be sent by
troops having easier access with that point than Pittsburg
Landing.

By command of Major-General Grant:

JNO. A. RAWLINS, *Assistant Adjutant-General*

I was in charge of the office at Savannah, Tenn., with instructions to make out the necessary orders, and send forward to Pittsburg Landing all troops arriving from below. Up to the 5th day of
April, 1862, . . . you had run up every morning to Pittsburg Landing and returned at night on the steamer *Tigress,* used for your
headquarters boat, and on which boat steam was continually kept
up. Orders were issued for everything to be moved to Pittsburg
Landing on Sunday, the 6th day of April, 1862, and arrangements
were being made accordingly.

April 5, 1862, a dispatch was received from Maj. Gen. D. C.
Buell, Commanding Army of the Ohio, stating that he would be
in Savannah, Tenn., with one and perhaps two divisions of his army
the next day, and requesting to meet you there.

General Nelson's division of the Army of the Ohio reached
Savannah on the afternoon of the 5th of April, but General Buell
himself did not arrive; and . . . you determined to ride out the
next morning to meet him. . . .

While at breakfast, private Edward N. Trembly . . . reported
artillery firing in the direction of Pittsburg Landing. Breakfast was
left unfinished, and, accompanied by your staff officers, you went
immediately on board the steamer *Tigress.* . . . The horses . . . were
sent at once on the boat and orders given . . . to start for Pittsburg
Landing, delaying only long enough for you to write an order to
General Nelson to move his division by the road from Savannah
to the river opposite Pittsburg Landing, and a note to Maj. Gen.
D. C. Buell, informing him of the supposed condition of affairs at
or in the vicinity of Pittsburg Landing.

In passing Crump's Landing . . . where was stationed the division commanded by Maj. Gen. Lewis Wallace, the *Tigress* ran close
alongside the boat on which Major-General Wallace had his head-

quarters, and addressing him in person, you directed him to hold his division in readiness to move on receipt of orders, which he might expect when you ascertained the condition of affairs . . . but in the mean time to send out and ascertain if there was any enemy on the Purdy road, apprehending, as you did, that the real attack might be intended against his position. His reply was that he was then in readiness, and had already taken the precautionary steps you directed as to the Purdy road. This was not far from 7 or 7:30 o'clock A.M.

From thence you continued direct to Pittsburg Landing, which place you reached about 8 o'clock A.M., and, with your staff, started immediately to the front. About half a mile from the river you met Brig. Gen. W. H. L. Wallace, who commanded Maj. Gen. C. F. Smith's Second Division of the Army of the Tennessee. From him you ascertained the particulars of the attack and how matters stood up to that time. You then directed me to return to the river and send Capt. A. S. Baxter, . . . on the steamer *Tigress,* without delay, to Crump's Landing, with orders to Maj. Gen. Lewis Wallace to bring forward his division by the River road to Pittsburg Landing to a point immediately in rear of the camp of Maj. Gen. C. F. Smith's division, and there form his column at right angles with the river on the right of our lines and await further orders. . . .

I proceeded to the river, and found Captain Baxter at the Landing near where the *Tigress* lay, and communicated to him your orders. . . . [He] requested me to give him a written memorandum . . . and I went on board the steamer . . . where a pen and ink could be procured, and at my dictation he wrote substantially as follows:

> Major-General Wallace: You will move forward your division from Crump's Landing, leaving a sufficient force to protect the public property at that place, to Pittsburg Landing, on the road nearest to and parallel with the river, and form in line at right angles with the river, immediately in rear of the camp of Maj. Gen. C. F. Smith's division on our right, and there await further orders.

Captain Baxter took this memorandum and started on the steamer *Tigress* to convey your orders to Maj. Gen. Lewis Wallace. This was not later than 9 o'clock A.M. Captain Baxter returned and reported before 12 o'clock m. his delivery of your orders . . . bringing at the same time from General Wallace . . . the report of

Col. Morgan L. *Smith*, that there was no enemy in the direction of Purdy; the result of his reconnaissance that morning.

About an hour after Captain Baxter had gone down . . . to General Wallace an officer of the Second Illinois Cavalry, who was well acquainted with the road leading to Crump's Landing, was sent by you with a verbal message to Major-General Wallace to hurry forward with all possible dispatch. This officer returned between 12 o'clock m. and 1 o'clock P.M., and reported that when he delivered your message General Wallace inquired if he had not written orders. He replied in the negative, and General Wallace said he would only obey written orders . . . and that his division was then all ready to move. He should have been by this time on the field. His presence then would have turned the tide of battle. . . .

You then immediately dispatched Capt. William R. Rowley, of your staff, with orders to him. You then rode back to the house . . . designated for headquarters to learn what word, if any, had been received from General Nelson. . . . You there met Maj. Gen. D. C. Buell, who had arrived at Savannah, and taken a steamer and come up to see you, and learn how the battle was progressing. . . . Among his first inquiries was, "What preparations have you made for retreating." To which you replied, "I have not yet despaired of whipping them, general"; and went on to state to him your momentary expectation of the arrival of General Wallace. . . . You then directed Lieut. Col. J. B. McPherson, chief of engineers, and myself to go and meet him . . . and conduct him to a certain position on the field you had pointed out to Lieutenant-Colonel McPherson, as we passed around the lines, in support of General Prentiss' division. We started, and before reaching the crest of the hill on the road between the river and Snake Creek, and over which General Wallace would be required to pass, the enemy's artillery was sweeping across it. We hurried on, anxiously expecting each moment to meet General Wallace.

We reached Snake Creek Bridge and crossed it—the foot of the hill beyond, but no General Wallace. We . . . continued on until we reached the road leading from Crump's Landing to Purdy. We there turned to the right and went toward the river until we met a surgeon of one of the regiments of General Wallace's division, who informed us General Wallace had taken the left-hand road leading from the camp of one of his brigades . . . between a quarter and half mile from the intersection of the main Pittsburg and Crump's Landing road with the Purdy road and towards Purdy, and about

4 1/2 miles from Pittsburg Landing by the direct road. . . . [W]e proceeded on the road General Wallace was said to have taken. . . . About one-half mile from the camp we met Colonel Thayer's brigade of General Wallace's division, and Colonel Thayer informed us that the rear of Col. Morgan L. *Smith's* brigade had filed off on a cross road leading into the main Pittsburg Landing road, and that General Wallace was with the head of the column. Taking this cross road we came up with him about 3:30 o'clock P.M. General Wallace said his guide had misled him, and that he had marched about 10 miles. Capt. W. R. Rowley, of your staff, . . . was with him, and informed us that he had overtaken him about 5 miles from his camp and not on the road he was expected to take; that when he (Captain Rowley) informed him he was wrong, he sent forward and halted his cavalry . . . and counter-marched his command to within a half mile of where he had started in the forenoon. I here stated to General Wallace the report of the officer sent to him in the morning of his refusing to obey or receive any but written orders, which he denounced as wholly untrue, and manifested in his talk a great desire to get into the fight. Colonel McPherson, Captain Rowley, and myself represented to him how matters stood when we left. I urged upon him, with all the earnestness I possessed, the importance of his presence on the field; that General Nelson was expected, but might have difficulty in crossing the river. He said there was no danger; he would yet reach there in good season, and with his fresh division would soon end the fight in a victory for us.

General Wallace at this point expressed doubt as to our being on the road leading into the main Pittsburg and Crump's Landing road. Colonel McPherson went to a house near by, and . . . ascertained that we were on the right road. After halting the head of his column for a considerable length of time, to enable it to close up and rest, he gave the order to march, and continued coolly and leisurely forward until we reached the main Pittsburg Landing road. Here Colonel McPherson suggested that to disencumber and facilitate the march, the artillery, which was immediately in the rear of the advance brigade, fall to the rear of the column, which suggestion was concurred in by General Wallace, and the artillery moved out of the road while the column filed by. This was an excuse for considerable delay—I should say for full half an hour—during which time he was dismounted and sitting down. From thence he continued his march until we reached the low bottom-lands through which runs Snake Creek, where we met some citizens, who informed us that the bridge across Snake Creek was in possession of the enemy. He then halted his column and sent forward his cavalry to ascertain if it was true.

Colonel McPherson and Captain Rowley went forward with the cavalry. I remained with General Wallace. In a few minutes a messenger came back from the cavalry with a message that the bridge was safe. General Wallace still remained stationary, waiting for his column to close up and his troops to rest. About this time the artillery firing at Pittsburg Landing became terrific, and we who had been there knew that it was our heavy guns, and that the enemy had attained a nearness to the river that filled our minds, situated as we were, with terrible apprehension for the fate of the brave army that had been fighting against such fearful odds and without intermission from early morning.

It seemed as though the enemy was immediately between where we were and the river, which seeming gained credence from the fact that as we passed out his artillery was sweeping the road in that direction.

General Wallace here asked, if such was the position of the opposing forces, what had best be done. Colonel McPherson said, "Fight our way through until communication can be had with General Grant"; to which General Wallace replied, "That is my purpose." Colonel McPherson and Captain Rowley again rode forward. General Wallace still gave no orders to move, but manifested the utmost coolness and indifference. I asked him if it would not be well to send forward a brigade to hold the bridge, lest the enemy should destroy it, and thus prevent his joining you. He replied that it was a "capital idea," and accordingly ordered Col. Morgan L. Smith, with his brigade, to move forward until the rear of his column rested on the farther side of Snake Creek Bridge and there halt until he received further orders from you or himself.

Colonel *Smith* moved forward as ordered, and General Wallace, dismounting from his horse, seated himself on a log. I then rode forward until I came up with Colonel McPherson, to whom I communicated the order given by General Wallace to Colonel Smith, and submitted to him the propriety of giving the order, as from you to Colonel *Smith*, to push forward with his brigade. But he hesitated to take such a step. It was now near night; the firing ceased; the sun sank to rest, and darkness had spread her mantle over friend and foe, when a cavalryman brought the report that there was no enemy between General Wallace and the river; upon the hearing of which the orders were given to move forward. Without opposition he reached the field of battle and received orders from you in person after night and about a mile from the steamboat landing at Pittsburg Landing.

The excuse that his guides misled him should avail nothing in extenuation of his want of knowledge of the road, for he had taken up his position at Crump's Landing on the 13th of March immediately preceding in the face of an enemy, and should have been perfectly familiar with all the roads leading to and from his camps.

Colonel McPherson and I came up to him about 3:30 o'clock P.M. He was then not to exceed 4 or 4½ miles from the scene of action; the roads were in fine condition; he was marching light; his men were in buoyant spirits, within hearing of the musketry, and eager to get forward. He did not make a mile and a half an hour, although urged and appealed to push forward. Had he moved with the rapidity his command were able and anxious to have moved after we overtook him, he would have reached you in time to have engaged the enemy before the close of Sunday's fight. . . . [*O.R.*, X, pt. 1, pp. 183–88.]

Maj. Gen. U. S. Grant to Col. J. C. Kelton, Assistant Adjutant-General, April 13, 1863

I have the honor to acknowledge the receipt of a copy of a communication of Maj. Gen. Lewis Wallace to Major-General Halleck, of date March 14, 1863, relative to his failure to participate in the first day's fight at Pittsburg Landing, and submitted to me for my remarks.

Instead of making a detailed report myself in answer to said communication I called upon Maj. Gen. J. B. McPherson, Lieut. Col. John A. Rawlins, and Maj. W. R. Rowley, all of whom were members of my staff at that time and were cognizant of the facts, for their statements in reference to the same, and these I herewith respectfully transmit.

All these reports are substantially as I remember the facts. I vouch for their almost entire accuracy; and from these several statements, separate and independent of each other, too, a more correct judgment can be derived than from a single report.

Had General Wallace been relieved from duty in the morning, and the same orders communicated to Brig. Gen. Morgan L. *Smith* (who would have been his successor), I do not doubt but the division would have been on the field of battle and in the engagement before 10 o'clock of that eventful 6th of April. There is no estimating the difference this might have made in our casualties. [*O.R.,* X, pt. 1, p. 178.]

Maj. Gen. Lew Wallace to Hon. E. M. Stanton, Secretary of War, July 18, 1863

Sir, some months ago I discovered that Maj. Gen. U. S. Grant in forwarding to your Department my official report of the battle of Pittsburg Landing, accompanied it with the following indorsement:

HEADQUARTERS ARMY OF THE TENNESSEE,
PITTSBURG LANDING, APRIL 25, 1862

I directed this division at 8 o'clock A.M. to be held in readiness to move at a moment's warning in any direction it might be ordered. Certainly not later than 11 o'clock A.M. the order reached General Wallace to march by a flank movement to Pittsburg Landing. Waiting until I thought he should be here, I sent one of my staff to hurry him, and afterwards sent Colonel McPherson and my assistant adjutant-general.

This report in some other particulars I do not fully indorse.

Respectfully forwarded to headquarters of the department.

U. S. GRANT, *Major General*

It will be observed that the indorsement contains several serious imputations against me, and in some particulars amounts to a denial of my official report.

1st. It says that at 11 o'clock A.M. I received an order to march by a flank movement to Pittsburg Landing. In my report, on the other hand, it is distinctly asserted that the order received by me came to hand at 11:30 A.M., and directed me to march to the right of the army and form junction there; a point nearly, if not quite, 3½ miles from Pittsburg Landing.

If General Grant's statement is true, then, in marching to a point so distant from Pittsburg Landing, I was guilty of disobedience of orders, for which, in the disastrous turn of the battle at the time, there can be but slender apology. If his statement is true, then I am also guilty of making a false report in a very material matter.

2d. The indorsement says that "waiting until he should be here, I sent one of my staff officers to hurry him, and afterwards sent Colonel McPherson and my assistant adjutant-general." The imputations contained in the sentence quoted are of the gravest character. If they are true, I am unfit to hold a commission of any kind in the United States Army. The imputations can be easily shaped into charges of cowardice and treachery, and I regret to say such charges have been made and are yet existing against me in consequence of the time it took me to reach the battle-field from my position at Crump's Landing.

3d. General Grant, in his indorsement, further says that there are some other particulars in my official report which he cannot fully indorse. This amounts to saying that I have made a false report.

I have waited with all patience for the arrival of a period when the state of the war would permit me to ask a court of inquiry without detriment to the service. That time, in my judgment, has now come, and I therefore respectfully ask that such a court may be ordered, and that the scope of its investigation may cover my whole conduct in connection with the battle of Pittsburg Landing. That this investigation may be full and complete, I also request that Judge-Advocate General Holt may be specially charged with the duty of prosecution. [*O.R.*, X, pt. 1, pp. 188–89.]

III. ORDER OF BATTLE
UNITED STATES ARMY AND
CONFEDERATE STATES ARMY

Organization of the Union forces at the battle of Pittsburg Landing, or Shiloh, Tennessee, April 6–7, 1862. [*O.R.*, X, pt. 1, pp. 100–107.]

THE ARMY OF THE TENNESSEE*
Maj. Gen. U. S. Grant

FIRST DIVISION
Maj. Gen. John A. McClernand

First Brigade	Second Brigade	Third Brigade
Col. A. M. Hare	Col. C. C. Marsh	Col. Julius Raith
(Col. M. M. Crocker)	11th Illinois	(Lieut. Col. E. P. Wood)
8th Illinois	20th Illinois	17th Illinois
18th Illinois	45th Illinois	29th Illinois
11th Iowa	48th Illinois	43d Illinois
13th Iowa		49th Illinois
2d Illinois Light Artillery,		Carmichael's Illinois
Battery D		Cavalry

Not Brigaded
Stewart's Illinois Cavalry
1st Illinois Light Artillery, Battery D
2d Illinois Light Artillery, Battery E
14th Ohio Battery

SECOND DIVISION
Brig. Gen. W. H. L. Wallace
(Col. James M. Tuttle)

First Brigade	Second Brigade	Third Brigade
Col. James M. Tuttle	Brig. Gen. John	Col. T. W. Sweeny
2d Iowa	McArthur	(Col. S. D. Baldwin)
7th Iowa	(Col. Thomas Morton)	8th Iowa
12th Iowa	9th Illinois	7th Illinois
14th Iowa	12th Illinois	50th Illinois
	81st Ohio	52d Illinois
	13th Missouri	57th Illinois
	Birge's Sharpshooters	58th Illinois
	(14th Missouri)	

---

*Official designation at the time of the battle was Army of the District of West Tennessee. Later changed to, and listed in *Official Records* as, Army of the Tennessee.

Army of the Tennessee, Second Division, *continued*

Not Brigaded
2d U.S. Cavalry, Company C
2d Illinois Cavalry, Companies A
   and B
4th U.S. Cavalry, Company I
1st Illinois Light Artillery, Battery A
1st Missouri Light Artillery,
   Batteries D, H, and K

THIRD DIVISION
Maj. Gen. Lewis Wallace

First Brigade	Second Brigade	Third Brigade
Col. Morgan L. Smith	Col. John M. Thayer	Col. Charles Whittlesey
8th Missouri	1st Nebraska	20th Ohio
11th Indiana	23d Indiana	56th Ohio
24th Indiana	58th Ohio	76th Ohio
	68th Ohio	78th Ohio

Not Brigaded
1st Missouri Light Artillery, Battery I
9th Indiana Battery
5th Ohio Cavalry, Third Battalion
11th Illinois Cavalry, Third Battalion

FOURTH DIVISION
Brig. Gen. S. A. Hurlbut

First Brigade	Second Brigade	Third Brigade
Col. N. G. Williams	Col. James C. Veatch	Brig. Gen. J. G. Lauman
(Col. Isaac C. Pugh)	25th Indiana	31st Indiana
3d Iowa	14th Illinois	44th Indiana
28th Illinois	15th Illinois	17th Kentucky
32d Illinois	46th Illinois	25th Kentucky
41st Illinois		

Not Brigaded
5th Ohio Cavalry, First and Second
   Battalions
13th Ohio Battery
Missouri Light Artillery, Mann's
   Battery
2d Michigan Battery

FIFTH DIVISION
Brig. Gen. W. T. Sherman

First Brigade	Second Brigade	Third Brigade
Col. J. A. McDowell	Col. David Stuart	Col. J. Hildebrand
6th Iowa	(Col. T. K. Smith)	53d Ohio
46th Ohio	55th Illinois	57th Ohio
40th Illinois	54th Ohio	77th Ohio
6th Indiana Battery	71st Ohio	

Fourth Brigade
Col. R. P. Buckland
  48th Ohio
  70th Ohio
  72d Ohio

Not Brigaded
  4th Illinois Cavalry, First
    and Second Battalions
  1st Illinois Light
    Artillery, Batteries
    B and E

SIXTH DIVISION
Brig. Gen. B. M. Prentiss

First Brigade
Col. Everett Peabody
  21st Missouri
  25th Missouri
  16th Wisconsin
  12th Michigan

Second Brigade
Col. Madison Miller
  18th Missouri
  61st Illinois
  16th Iowa

Unassigned Troops
  15th Michigan
  14th Wisconsin
  8th Ohio Battery
  1st Illinois Light
Artillery,
    Batteries H and I
  2d Illinois Light
Artillery,
    Batteries B and F

Not Brigaded
  11th Illinois Cavalry
    (8 companies)
  5th Ohio Battery
  1st Minnesota Battery
  18th Wisconsin
  23d Missouri
  15th Iowa

ARMY OF THE OHIO
Maj. Gen. Don Carlos Buell

SECOND DIVISION
Brig. Gen. A. McD. McCook
5th U.S. Artillery, Battery H

Fourth Brigade
Brig. Gen. L. H. Rousseau
  15th U.S. Infantry,
    1st Battalion
  16th U.S. Infantry,
    1st Battalion
  19th U.S. Infantry,
    1st Battalion
  1st Ohio
  6th Indiana
  5th Kentucky

Fifth Brigade
Col. E. N. Kirk
  77th Pennsylvania
  29th Indiana
  30th Indiana
  34th Illinois

Sixth Brigade
Col. W. H. Gibson
  15th Ohio
  49th Ohio
  32d Indiana
  39th Indiana

FOURTH DIVISION
Brig. Gen. William Nelson
2d Indiana Cavalry

Tenth Brigade
Col. Jacob Ammen
  6th Ohio
  24th Ohio
  36th Indiana

Nineteenth Brigade
Col. William B. Hazen
  6th Kentucky
  9th Indiana
  41st Ohio

Twenty-second Brigade
Col. S. D. Bruce
  1st Kentucky
  2d Kentucky
  20th Kentucky

Army of the Ohio, *continued*

FIFTH DIVISION
Brig. Gen. T. L. Crittenden

Eleventh Brigade	Fourteenth Brigade	Not Brigaded
Brig. Gen. J. T. Boyle	Col. W. S. Smith	3d Kentucky Cavalry
19th Ohio	13th Ohio	1st Ohio Light Artillery,
59th Ohio	11th Kentucky	Battery G
9th Kentucky	26th Kentucky	4th U.S. Artillery,
13th Kentucky		Batteries H and M

SIXTH DIVISION
Brig. Gen. T. J. Wood

Twentieth Brigade	Twenty-first Brigade
Brig. Gen. J. A. Garfield	Col. G. D. Wagner
64th Ohio	15th Indiana
65th Ohio	40th Indiana
13th Michigan	57th Indiana
51st Indiana	24th Kentucky

Organization of the Confederate forces at the battle of Pittsburg Landing, or Shiloh, Tennessee, April 6–7, 1862. [*O.R.*, X, pt. 1, pp. 382–84.]

THE ARMY OF THE MISSISSIPPI
Gen. Albert Sidney Johnston
Gen. P. G. T. Beauregard

FIRST CORPS
Maj. Gen. Leonidas Polk
First Mississippi Cavalry
Brewer's Battalion
Cox's Cavalry
Jenkins's Cavalry
Lindsay's Cavalry
Robins' Cavalry
Tomlison's Cavalry

FIRST DIVISION
Brig. Gen. Charles Clark

First Brigade	Second Brigade
Col. R. M. Russell	Brig. Gen. A. P. Stewart
11th Louisiana	13th Arkansas
12th Tennessee	4th Tennessee
13th Tennessee	5th Tennessee
22d Tennessee	33d Tennessee
Bankhead's Battery	Stanford's Battery

SECOND DIVISION
Brig. Gen. B. F. Cheatham

First Brigade
Brig. Gen. B. R. Johnson
  Mississippi Battalion
  (Blythe's)
  2d Tennessee
  15th Tennessee
  154th Tennessee (senior)
  Polk's Battery

Second Brigade
Col. W. H. Stephens
  7th Kentucky
  1st Tennessee
  6th Tennessee
  9th Tennessee
  Smith's Battery

SECOND CORPS
Maj. Gen. Braxton Bragg

FIRST DIVISION
Brig. Gen. Daniel Ruggles

First Brigade
Col. R. L. Gibson
  1st Arkansas
  4th Louisiana
  13th Louisiana
  19th Louisana
  Bains's Battery

Second Brigade
Brig. Gen. Patton
  Anderson
  1st Florida (battalion)
  17th Louisiana
  20th Louisiana
  9th Texas
  Confederate Guards
  Response
  Battalion
  Hodgson's Battery

Third Brigade
Col. Preston Pond Jr.
  16th Louisiana
  18th Louisiana
  Cresent (Louisiana)
  Regiment
  38th Tennessee
  Orleans Guard Battalion
  Ketchum's Battery

SECOND DIVISION
Brig. Gen. Jones M. Withers

First Brigade
Brig. Gen. A. H. Gladden
  21st Alabama
  22d Alabama
  25th Alabama
  26th Alabama
  1st Louisiana
  Robertson's Battery

Second Brigade
Brig. Gen. J. R.
  Chalmers
  5th Mississippi
  7th Mississippi
  9th Mississippi
  10th Mississippi
  51st Tennessee
  52d Tennessee
  Gage's Battery

Third Brigade
Brig. Gen. J. K. Jackson
  17th Alabama
  18th Alabama
  19th Alabama
  Alabama Battalion*
  Arkansas Battalion*
  2d Texas
  Girardey's Battery

*These units did not participate in the battle.

Army of the Mississippi, *continued*

THIRD CORPS
Maj. Gen. W. J. Hardee

First Brigade
Brig. Gen. T. C. Hindman
  2d Arkansas
  5th Arkansas
  6th Arkansas
  7th Arkansas
  3d Confederate
  Miller's Battery
  Swett's Battery

Second Brigade
Brig. Gen. P. R.
  Cleburne
  15th Arkansas
  6th Mississippi
  5th [35th] Tennessee
  23d Tennessee
  24th Tennessee
  Shoup's Artillery
    Battalion
    Calvert's Battery
    Trigg's Battery
    Hubbard's Battery
  Watson Battery

Third Brigade
Brig. Gen. S. A. M. Wood
  7th Alabama
  16th Alabama
  8th Arkansas
  9th Arkansas Battalion
  3d Mississippi Battalion
  27th Tennessee
  44th Tennessee
  55th Tennessee
  Harper's Battery

RESERVE CORPS
Brig. Gen. J. C. Breckinridge

First Brigade
Col. R. P. Trabue
  4th Alabama Battalion
  31st Alabama
  3d Kentucky
  4th Kentucky
  5th Kentucky
  6th Kentucky
  Tennessee Battalion (Crew's)
  Byrne's Battery
  Cobb's Battery

Second Brigade
Brig. Gen. J. S. Bowen
  9th Arkansas
  10th Arkansas
  2d Confederate
  1st Missouri
  Hudson's Battery

Third Brigade
Col. W. S. Statham
  15th Mississippi
  22d Mississippi
  19th Tennessee
  20th Tennessee
  28th Tennessee
  45th Tennessee
  Rutledge's Battery

Wharton's Texas Ranger, Forrest's Regiment Tennessee Cavalry, Wirt Adam's Mississippi Cavalry Regiment, Clanton's regiment [cavalry], and McClung's Battery, not accounted for above, are mentioned in reports.

IV. RECAPITULATION OF CASUALTIES

Estimates of numbers engaged in the two days of fighting at and around Pittsburg Landing on April 6 and 7 vary, and statistics on killed, wounded, captured, and missing are incomplete. Participants attempted to fill gaps as they wrote their official reports, and historians have tried to refine the data. The tabulation that follows is drawn from *O.R.*, vol. X, pt. I, pp. 101–8, 395–96, and from Thomas L. Livermore, *Numbers and Losses in the Civil War in America, 1861–1865* (New York: Houghton, Mifflin, 1901), pp. 79–80.

	Killed	Wounded	Captured or Missing	Aggregate
UNION ARMIES				
The Army of the Tennessee				
Total Engaged 42,682				
First Division	285	1,372	85	1,742
Second Division	270	1,173	1,306	2,749
Third Division	41	251	4	296
Fourth Division	317	1,441	111	1,869
Fifth Division	325	1,277	299	1,901
Sixth Division	236	928	1,008	2,172
Unassigned	39	159	17	215
Total	1,513	6,601	2,830	10,944
The Army of the Ohio				
Total Engaged 20,000				
Second Division	88	823	7	918
Fourth Division	93	603	20	716
Fifth Division	60	377	28	465
Sixth Division		4		4
Total	241	1,807	55	2,103
Grand Total Armies of the Tennessee and Ohio	1,754	8,408	2,885	13,047
CONFEDERATE ARMY				
Total Engaged 40,335				
Polk's Corps	385	1,953	19	2,357
Bragg's Corps	553	2,441	634	3,628
Hardee's Corps	404	1,936	141	2,481
Reserve Corps (Breckinridge)	386	1,682	165	2,233
Total	1,728	8,012	959	10,699

BIBLIOGRAPHY

Bearss, Edwin C. *Historical Base Map, Shiloh Military Park and Cemetery.* Denver: National Park Service, United States Department of the Interior, 1973.

Dillahunty, Albert. *Shiloh National Military Park, Tennessee.* National Park Service Handbook Series, no. 10. Washington, D.C.: Government Printing Office, 1955.

Grant, U. S. *Personal Memoirs of U. S. Grant.* 2 vols. New York: Charles Webster and Co., 1885.

Griess, Thomas E., series ed. *The American Civil War.* Wayne, N.J.: Avery Publishing Group [1987].

Harper's Weekly. Saturday, May 3, 1862.

Hobart, Edwin L. *The Truth about Shiloh.* N.p., n.d. [Found in USAMHI Library; donated November 20, 1909, by Mr. Hobart to the War Department.]

Johnson, Robert, and Clarence Buel, eds. *Battles and Leaders of the Civil War.* Grant-Lee edition, 4 vols. New York: The Century Company, [1884–88].

Johnston, William Preston. *The Life of General Albert Sidney Johnston.* New York: D. Appleton and Company, 1878.

Leslie, Frank. *The American Soldier in the Civil War.* New York: Brian, Taylor, and Co. [1895].

Miller, Francis T., ed. *The Photographic History of the Civil War.* 10 vols. New York: The Review of Reviews Co., 1911.

Moat, Louis Shepheard, ed. *Frank Leslie's Illustrated Famous Leaders and Battle Scenes of the Civil War.* New York: Mrs. Frank Leslie [1896].

Nevin, David. *The Road to Shiloh: Early Battles in the West.* Alexandria, Va.: Time-Life Books [1983].

"Shiloh National Military Park, Tennessee." Aurora, Colo.: Trailhead Graphics, 1995.

Stanley, Henry M. *The Autobiography of Sir Henry Morton Stanley.* Boston: Houghton Mifflin, 1909.

Steele, Matthew Forney. *American Campaigns.* 2 vols. Harrisburg, Pa.: The Military Service Publishing Co. [1949].

Thompson, Atwell, and D. W. Reed. "Map of the Shiloh Battlefield 6–7 April 1862." Publication location unknown: Shiloh National Military Park Commission, 1900.

Tomes, Robert. *The Great Civil War.* 3 vols. New York: Virtue and Yorston [1865].

The War of the Rebellion: A Compilation of the Official Records of the Union and Confederate Armies. 70 vols., 128 parts. Washington, D.C.: Government Printing Office, 1880–1901.

Official Records of the Union and Confederate Navies in the War of the Rebellion. 31 vols. Washington, D.C.: Government Printing Office, 1894–1927.

INDEX